THE NAVAL HISTORY OF THE
WORLD WAR

The Naval History of the World War

THE UNITED STATES IN THE WAR
1917–1918

BY

THOMAS G. FROTHINGHAM

With Maps and Diagrams

BOOKS FOR LIBRARIES PRESS
FREEPORT, NEW YORK

First Published 1924-1926
Reprinted 1971

INTERNATIONAL STANDARD BOOK NUMBER:
0-8369-5940-X

LIBRARY OF CONGRESS CATALOG CARD NUMBER:
70-165633

PRINTED IN THE UNITED STATES OF AMERICA

THIS WORK HAS BEEN COMPILED FROM DATA
PROVIDED BY THE
HISTORICAL SECTION, UNITED STATES NAVY

Military Historical Society of Massachusetts

ACKNOWLEDGMENT

In this book, as in the two preceding books of this work, the author has received the invaluable help of Captain Dudley W. Knox, U. S. N., Chief of the Historical Section, United States Navy, in conjunction with whom this Naval History of the World War has been written. He has also had the benefit of the continued advice of Lord Sydenham. The comments of this leading British authority have been of great assistance in shaping the text. After the lamented death of Admiral Twining, Rear Admiral William Veazie Pratt, President of the Naval War College, coöperated in the text of the present volume, and this has given the author the help, not only of Admiral Pratt's keen ability, but also of his intimate knowledge of the situation through his services as Assistant and Acting Chief in the Office of Naval Operations in the World War. The constructive comments and suggestions of all three are here gratefully acknowledged.

CONTENTS

LIST OF MAPS

Note as to the Maps. As in the two preceding books of this work, every effort has been made to avoid the usual bulky and cumbersome charts, and to reduce these maps to the simplest forms.

THE NAVAL HISTORY OF THE
WORLD WAR

CHAPTER I

THE SITUATION AT THE BEGINNING OF 1917

(See Map at page 22)

IT has been shown in the preceding volume of this work, by the statements of the Germans themselves, that, at the beginning of 1917, the German Government had finally decided to attempt to gain victory in the World War by means of unrestricted U-boat warfare. The steps have been traced by which this idea progressed, until at last the prestige of the Battle of Jutland gave to the German naval leaders the power to dominate the whole military and naval situation in Germany. It has also been explained that the preservation of the German Battle Fleet in this naval action gave them the physical ability to carry out this U-boat campaign. Consequently, the German naval and military leaders were united in their adoption of this extreme measure, and the date of the beginning of the U-boat campaign had been set for February 1, 1917. As in 1914, the German leaders were supremely confident of the result. But again, as in 1914, the German calculations had been founded upon German formulas alone, and had not taken into account other great forces that would be aroused against them.[1]

It was a strange stroke of fate for the Central Powers that this provocative means of warfare, which had been originally conceived in an unfavorable situation, was

[1] "The blockade must succeed within a limited number of weeks, within which America cannot effectively participate in the operations."—Bethmann-Hollweg, 1917.

3

eventually to be carried out in a most favorable situation, when there were other means of victory actually in the grasp of the Central Powers. As a matter of fact, the last months of 1916 had seen the end of the fighting strength of Russia. This powerful enemy was already on the verge of collapse and revolution when the Central Powers began the fateful naval campaign, which was destined to bring into the World War a stronger enemy, to take the place of Russia and turn German victory into German defeat.[1]

Most fortunately for the Entente Allies, at this stage, the impending collapse of Russia had not been foreseen by either side. Not only had the Central Powers failed to grasp their opportunity,[2] but the Entente Allies had escaped the demoralizing effect of the knowledge of this great loss of strength. On the part of the Entente Allies, at the beginning of 1917, it is evident that, instead of any discouragement, there was a new optimism in France and Great Britain. In France the exultation was so great over the repulse of the Germans at Verdun, that the French were demanding a military offensive for 1917. In Great Britain the Asquith Ministry had fallen in December, 1916, and a War Cabinet had been constituted under the leadership of Lloyd George.

For the first time the Entente Allies had a plan for concerted military operations, "unanimously agreed upon by a conference of military representatives of the

[1] "Had we been able in Germany to foresee the Russian Revolution, we should perhaps not have needed to regard the submarine campaign of 1917 as a last resort. But in January, 1917, there was no visible sign of the Revolution." — "The War of Lost Opportunities." Hoffmann.

[2] "No intelligence had come through to us which revealed any striking indications of the disintegration of the Russian army." — Hindenburg, "Out of My Life."

Allied Powers held at French Headquarters in November, 1916. This plan comprised a series of offensives on all fronts, so timed as to assist each other by depriving the enemy of the power of weakening any one of his fronts in order to reinforce another." [1]

The following, from a speech of Lloyd George, reflected vividly this mistaken optimism, and the utter lack of appreciation of the true situation among the leaders of the Entente Allies: "The Russian Army was better equipped in guns, in machine guns, and in munitions than it had ever been during the whole period of the war. For the first time in the whole course of the war the Russian gunners had plenty of ammunition — this year the Russian Army began and was ready with the best equipment any Russian army ever had, and naturally our expectation was that, with a well-equipped and powerful Russian army pressing in the east, a well-equipped British and French army pressing in the west, and a well-equipped Italian army pressing in Italy, we should have been able to bring such a pressure to bear upon the Prussian Army as to inflict a decisive defeat."

Nothing could have been farther away from a description of the actual position at the beginning of 1917. Instead of this favorable state of affairs in the East, the situation was so bad in Russia that the Russian Revolution broke out in March, 1917. On March 15 Czar Nicholas was forced to abdicate. From this time there were only fitful efforts on the part of the Russians, and their armies rapidly degenerated into a mob. Soon there was only a semblance of any Russian military threat against the Central Powers. Yet this phantom of the former strength of the Russian armies still influ-

[1] Sir Douglas Haig's Despatches.

enced the course of the World War, because the German General Staff failed to see that there was no substance to this shadow, and continued to maintain strong Austro-German armies on the Russian front, which prevented the Central Powers from using these troops in other theatres of warfare.

A study of the map will show the great military results that had been won in the East by the Central Powers at the end of 1916, as Rumania had also been overrun, after entering the war when it was too late for the Russian armies to coöperate. In fact, almost the only favorable element for the Entente Allies in the East was the situation of Greece,[1] and this had been brought about by the presence of the strong Allied Army at Salonica, which had been established and maintained by Sea Power.

At this time, the influence of Sea Power had grown to be unmistakable, and it had become the outstanding factor in the World War. The Central Powers were on the point of making their great effort to win the war on the sea. For the Entente Allies Sea Power had won results that were compensations for the disastrous military failures and defeats of 1915 and 1916. Aside from the incalculable benefits the Entente Allies were receiving through their command of the seas, it was Sea Power alone that was pressing upon Germany. As has been explained, at last the right means were being taken to enforce the blockade. Consequently, Germany was beginning to feel the pinch, and by this time the strain of the war was telling upon the German people.

These new deprivations and hardships were arousing

[1] Provisional Government of Greece declared war against Germany and Bulgaria November 28, 1916.

impatience in Germany, as, even after the series of victories of 1915 and 1916, not only were the expected rewards of victory withheld, but also the conditions of living were growing irksome throughout the country. The German leaders saw the beginnings of discontent, and the various moves of the German Government for peace, in the latter part of 1916, were for effect at home as well as abroad. But it must not be thought that these proposals for peace were signs of actual military weakening on the part of Germany, as was too hastily assumed among the Entente Allies at the time. On the contrary, as the year 1918 afterwards proved, Germany was still capable of a tremendous military effort. Therefore, the German attempt to win the World War on the sea must not be considered as a last desperate resort, but as a carefully calculated effort to win by means which were thought to be infallible. The German leaders had decided that they could win by these means — and the result of this decision was upon their own heads.

CHAPTER II

THE ENTRANCE OF THE UNITED STATES

THE German Government adhered to its illegal program, and on February 1, 1917, the German U-boats began to destroy ships, casting aside all international law on the seas. This U-boat campaign had been carefully planned, and in contrast to their former attempts, the Germans in 1917 had naval forces sufficient to carry out their undertaking. It became at once evident that the submarine, thus operated without regard for the safety of passengers and crews, was the most formidable destroyer of commerce in the world's history.

The methods which had hitherto been used against the U-boats by the Allied navies, and which had been too hastily assumed sufficient to check their ravages, were found totally inadequate. Sinkings were recorded in the first weeks of the campaign which threatened a great decrease of the world's tonnage of shipping,[1] and there is no question of the fact that the attack of this new weapon was a grave danger to the sea power of the Entente Allies. Yet, before giving any account of the operations of this new phase of the naval history of the World War, it is necessary to impress upon the reader's mind the other all-important fact, that this successful use of the U-boat, in defiance of the laws of humanity, at once became a boomerang for the German Government. It recoiled upon Germany by bringing into the war the

[1] "The immediate effect of the new campaign was to double the rate of losses which had been incurred during 1916, and these losses rose rapidly to a climax in March and April." — Report of War Cabinet, 1917.

one force that would mean defeat for the Central Powers.

When it was found that the German Government intended to persist in this unlawful undertaking, the United States broke off relations with the German Government, and war between the United States and Germany became inevitable. The cynical conduct of the German Government was a direct challenge; and there was no course other than to hand the German Ambassador his passports — to have no more dealings with a Government that had broken its pledges when it felt strong enough to do so.

On February 3, 1917, the President of the United States addressed both houses of Congress, and announced that diplomacy had failed, and that relations with Germany had been severed. In his address President Wilson made the sharp distinction between the people of Germany and its autocratic Government, which was destined to influence the whole remaining course of the war: "We are sincere friends of the German people and earnestly desire to remain at peace with the Government which speaks for them. God grant we may not be challenged by acts of wilful injustice on the part of the Government of Germany."

These acts of injustice were not long delayed. The German Ambassador, after receiving his papers, had asked his Government to delay action until he had made a plea for peace to the Emperor, but the Imperial Government refused to change its policy and persisted in carrying forward its campaign of unrestricted U-boat warfare. On March 12 orders were given to arm American merchantmen against the submarines.

On March 1 the United States Government had revealed the contents of an intercepted letter written by Zimmermann, the German Foreign Secretary, to the German Minister in Mexico.

It was dated at Berlin, January 19, 1917: "On the first of February we intend to begin submarine warfare unrestricted. In spite of this, it is our intention to keep neutral the United States of America. If this attempt is not successful, we propose an alliance on the following basis with Mexico: that we shall make war together and together make peace. We shall give general financial support and it is understood that Mexico is to reconquer the lost territory in New Mexico, Texas and Arizona."

"You are instructed to inform the President of Mexico of the above in great confidence as soon as it is certain that there will be an outbreak of war with the United States and suggest that the President of Mexico, on his own initiative, should communicate with Japan suggesting adherence at once to this plan; at the same time, offer to mediate between Germany and Japan."

"Please call to the attention of the President of Mexico that the employment of ruthless submarine warfare now promises to compel England to make peace in a few months. Zimmermann."

Aside from all other matters, this outrageous letter was in itself a cause of war. It is hard to see how anything could have been written that would show more clearly the utter hostility of the German Government towards the United States. In all sections of the country there was no longer any possibility of doubt as to the character of the German rulers and their intentions in regard to the United States.[1] Additional provocation

[1] "According to the views of our ambassador (Von Hintze) — Zimmermann's well-known telegram rendered Wilson decisive assistance in the realization of his wish to take his stand against us." — Tirpitz, "My Memoirs."

soon followed from the conduct of the German submarine campaign, and on April 6 Congress passed the resolution of war with Germany. The President signed the Declaration of war on the same day.

After long patience the United States had been driven into a declaration of war by repeated hostile acts of Germany. These acts were not only Germany's ruthless conduct upon the seas, but Germany's proved attempts to incite Mexico and Japan to war with the United States, to disrupt the country and take away its territory. If ever a nation was justified in entering a war, the United States was justified and in the right, and we should believe that this right prevailed.

Our nation was made strong by the fact that there was no trace of selfish aims in our participation in the World War. In all other respects our position was above question. The conditions that had brought on the war were not in any way made by us. We had not committed any hostile act. On the contrary, in our relations with Germany, we had exhausted all the resources of peaceful diplomacy. Our President had stated our objects so plainly that they could not be mistaken, and, in spite of all accusations, even our enemies were forced to believe that the United States fought for a principle and not for gain.[1]

So evident was this that the United States became a moral force in the war, and this had a disturbing influence upon the nations allied with Germany. Especially in Austria-Hungary it was noticeable that the entrance of the United States against the Central Powers had a

---

[1] In a tirade against propaganda Ludendorff himself unconsciously paid a high tribute to the spirit of America: "For American soldiers the war became as it were a crusade against us." — "Ludendorff's Own Story."

widespread effect against the German Government. Even in Germany, where every attempt was made to brand the United States with hypocrisy, the German people could not help seeing that our nation was fighting for a cause, and that our nation believed this cause to be just.

The most wise distinction made by our President between the German Government and the German people became an issue in Germany itself, and the cause of a rift in the hitherto united nation. This was slight at first, but unquestionably had come into existence. It was no mere coincidence that the German Emperor, in the month of our declaration of war, made tentative proposals of popular legislative government for the Germans. The German leaders had read the signs of the times. The vague dissatisfaction of the German people had been given a tangible basis, and, in spite of all attempts to divert attention, the beginning of a cleavage was there. From the time of the entrance of the United States the German Government was being scrutinized and held accountable by the German people.

This was the strong moral force exerted upon the war by the United States, apart from all our physical force, and this was a disturbing and disintegrating influence that was always working within the Central Powers throughout the rest of the World War. It is true that this moral force would not have prevailed, if it had not been backed up by physical force. If the German Government had won its war, the German people would have stood by it. But, if the German Government did not win, the German people would repudiate it. Consequently, this moral force must be counted as a very real and potent factor, in conjunction with the unexpected strength of the United States, for bringing about the defeat and disintegration of the carefully built German structure. As Ludendorff bitterly expressed it, "By working on our democratic sentiments the enemy propaganda succeeded in bringing our Government into discredit in Germany."

It cannot be stated too strongly that the physical force exerted by the United States upon the World War was an utter surprise to the German leaders — a thing outside all their calculations. As has been explained, these calculations of the German leaders had been founded entirely upon their own German formulas. Their methods of creating armies involved years of training and, from their point of view, our nation was incapable of organizing an army in time to have any effect on the course of the war.[1]

The German leaders had appreciated our great resources in material and wealth, and they had been reluctant to involve the United States in the war — to have all this at the command of the Entente Allies. But they never counted the United States as a naval or military factor in the World War. The lessons of our Civil War had never been suspected, much less learned, by the formal school of the German General Staff.

The excellence of the American armies of both the North and the South, which had been so quickly produced in the white heat of that extraordinary war, had never been understood. Consequently, the German leaders were unable to realize that an intelligent people,

---

[1] "If matters came to a breach, it was not to be assumed that America would make her influence felt in the war before the submarine campaign had taken effect." — "The German General Staff and its Decisions." Falkenhayn.

absolutely united in a just cause, would be capable of a great uprising for warfare.

The result proved how entirely the spirit of America had been misunderstood — and the proof of this was shown in short sequence. It is enough to state the following. War was declared on April 6. Before the end of May, three measures had been adopted which sealed the doom of Germany in the World War. President Wilson had signed the seven billion dollar War Bond Bill; the largest Army and Navy Bill in the history of nations had reached a total of nearly four billion dollars; and the President had signed the draft bill, calling upon all men between twenty-one and thirty. These quickly enacted measures meant that the United States was to make the greatest effort that had ever been made in war by a united people.[1] Thus early was inscribed upon the wall the writing that foretold the fall of German militarism.

[1] "I will tell you about America. She came into the war at a time when the need for her coming was most urgent. Her coming was like an avalanche. The world has never seen anything like it. Her great army of all ranks gave service that no man would, in 1917, have believed possible." — Lloyd George.

CHAPTER III

THE FIRST SHOCK OF THE U-BOAT CAMPAIGN

(See Map at page 22)

THE note from the German Imperial Government, which was suddenly given to Ambassador Gerard on the afternoon of January 31, 1917,[1] began as follows: "From February 1, 1917, sea traffic will be stopped with every available weapon and without further notice in the following barred zones around Great Britain, France, Italy, and in the Eastern Mediterranean." These zones were described, as indicated on the map on page 22. In this German note the sinister phrase "and without further notice" meant "the commencement of ruthless submarine warfare" [2] to sink enemy and neutral ships alike without warning in these prohibited areas.

The delay in delivering this note until the eve of the beginning of the campaign, although the decision for unrestricted U-boat warfare had been made long before, was a deliberate effort to spring a sudden surprise.[3] Admiral Scheer has quoted a telegram from the German

---

[1] "The Secretary of State of the Foreign Office, Zimmermann requests the honor of the visit of his Excellency, the Ambassador of the United States of America, this afternoon at six o'clock in the Foreign Office, Wilhelmstrasse 75/76. Berlin, the 31st January, 1917."

[2] Ambassador Gerard.

[3] "A further condition is that the declaration and commencement of the unrestricted U-boat war should be simultaneous, so that there is no time for negotiations, especially between England and the neutrals. Only on these conditions will the enemy and the neutrals be inspired with 'holy' terror." — Mem. of German Chief of the Naval Staff, December 22, 1916, given in full in appendix.

Emperor (January 9, 1917): "I command that the unrestricted U-boat campaign shall begin on February 1 in full force. You are to make all necessary preparations without delay, but in such a way that neither the enemy nor neutrals can obtain information of this intention."

But, as has been stated in the preceding volume of this work, at the time Germany yielded to the United States after the *Sussex* ultimatum as to the U-boats in April, 1916, Ambassador Gerard had warned the State Department that "the rulers of Germany would at some future date, forced by public opinion and by the von Tirpitz and Conservative parties, take up ruthless submarine warfare again, possibly in the autumn but at any rate about February or March, 1917." And, concerning the time just preceding this new U-boat campaign of 1917, Ambassador Gerard has also written that, before January 6, the American Embassy "had begun to get rumors of the resumption of ruthless submarine warfare, and within a few days I was cabling to the Department information, based not upon absolute facts but upon reports that had been collected through the able efforts of our very capable naval attaché, Commander Gherardi." The truth was, it was the Germans themselves who were surprised, as Ambassador Gerard has left no doubt that they were taken aback by the fact that the United States broke off relations so promptly.

However, this did not in the least affect the overweening confidence of the Germans in the U-boat campaign.[1] It was regarded as a foregone conclusion that unrestricted U-boat warfare would force Great Britain to

---

[1] "So the Chief of the Naval Staff, von Holtzendorff, thought himself in a position to promise that England would be ready for peace after a six months' submarine campaign." — Admiral Tirpitz.

make peace in 1917. A most striking illustration of the overconfidence, which prevailed at this time throughout Germany, has been given in Admiral Scheer's frank complaint: "It is a great pity that the calculations of the Naval Staff were published throughout the country: they had assumed the success of the U-boat campaign within a fixed period of time, and were meant for a narrow circle only." And here again it should be emphasized, as explained in the preceding volume, that these German calculations for the U-boats had been founded upon results in 1916,[1] when the Entente Allies had not yet made use of the best available defense against submarines. This error of the Germans, in not making allowances in their calculations for the offset of new counters that would be found against the U-boats, must always be kept in mind when studying this much discussed campaign. These adverse elements were destined to overthrow the German calculations, even to the extent of swaying the balance against the U-boats.

But, although thus foredoomed to failure by the new forces which were to be aroused against them, it is also a fact that the U-boats were at their strongest in the very area of the main object of this campaign, the attack upon Great Britain. The reason for this will be evident at once. In the waters about Great Britain, vast volumes of vital sea traffic were constricted into small spaces. This meant that great numbers of ships must necessarily be crowded into narrow waters — and these narrow waters were near the bases of the German U-boats. These conditions made the German submarines more formidable in the waters about Great Britain than anywhere else in the world. It was for this reason that the

[1] Mem. of German Chief of the Naval Staff, December 22, 1916.

new attack upon seaborne commerce was the most dangerous in history — and the first disastrous effects of the U-boat campaign of 1917 must be fully appreciated.

Admiral Scheer has stated the German object in impressive terms: "With the unrestricted U-boat campaign we had probably embarked in the most tremendous undertaking that the World War brought in its long train. Our aim was to break the power of mighty England vested in her sea trade in spite of the protection which her powerful Fleet could afford her."

Admiral Scheer's description of this change of German strategy is also impressive: "The strategic offensive passed definitely to the Navy on February 1, 1917. U-boats and the Fleet supplemented one another to form one weapon, which was to be used in an energetic attack on England's might. Our Fleet became the hilt of the weapon whose sharp blade was the U-boat. The Fleet thus commenced its main activities during the war to maintain and defend the new form of warfare against the English Fleet." The new mission of the German Battle Fleet could not be more clearly defined. And, with this, there is no mistaking the vital importance of the German Battle Fleet as an essential element in carrying on the new German strategy. If the Germans had lacked this necessary factor of their Battle Fleet, the U-boat campaign could not have been undertaken. All this measured the result of the tragic failure of the British to destroy the German Fleet at Jutland, and gave proof of the fallacy of the comforting theory that the German Fleet "never came out," which was so widespread in British writings after the Battle of Jutland.

This prevailing error of the British, that the German High Sea Fleet was inactive, and the consequent failure

to appreciate the change of mission of the German
Battle Fleet, went so far that it amounted to an error in
strategy on the part of the British. Aside from not per-
ceiving that the invasion idea could be dismissed, the
attitude of the British Navy, in continuing the same
policy of watching an inactive enemy to guard against a
resumption of activity, did not lead to the use of the
British Grand Fleet in active anti-submarine efforts
against an enemy Battle Fleet whose whole effort was
being devoted to carrying out the new German naval
strategy of the U-boat offensive.

The fact was, the German Fleet was "out" constantly. As Admiral Scheer stated, "it found plenty of
continued and exacting occupation in combating the
means that England had devised to prevent the U-boats
from getting out." The German Admiral has written:
"Only our Fleet could make such efforts useless." Instead of being idle at its bases, as was so often stated, the
German Fleet was all this time occupied in keeping
clear wide areas of egress and entrance for the U-boats.
This duty not only implied maintaining the minefield
outworks about the German bases, which have been
described in the preceding volumes and which kept the
enemy at a distance from the German bases, but it also
comprised clearing the way through the British mines,
which were being laid in the North Sea in constantly increasing numbers.[1]

Admiral Scheer has stated that, in coöperation with
the successful use of the U-boats, "the battleships, together with the cruisers and torpedo-boats, and especially the mine-sweepers, assisted in overcoming the

---

[1] "The number of mines laid in the North Sea by the enemy grew constantly greater." — Admiral Scheer.

enemy's defence. Their efforts were primarily directed
against the belt of mines which the English had laid in
the North Sea to prevent our boats from getting out."
And the German Admiral has added: "In spite of all the
difficulties we managed to prevent anything from stop-
ping the U-boats from going out. There were altogether
very few days when for safety's sake we had to avoid the
direct route into the North Sea and take the roundabout
way through the North Baltic Canal and the Kattegat."
This was a very different state of affairs from the fiction
of an inactive German Fleet confined at its bases, which
was given credence at the time.

Admiral Scheer has stated, in contrast to the inadequate preparation for the U-boat campaign of 1915:
"When the U-boat campaign was opened on February
1, 1917, there were 57 boats already in the North Sea."
With the great opportunities for them in the waters
about Great Britain, which have been stated, and with
the inadequate means of protection and of attack then in
use against them, the first success of the U-boat campaign was so great as to be a shock to the Entente Allies
— and this should be emphasized in any naval history of
the World War. Admiral Jellicoe has called this "the
gravest danger that has ever faced the Empire." "Allied Shipping Control" has thus summed up this menace
beyond any misunderstanding: "The opening success of
the new campaign was staggering . . . The continu-
ance of this rate of loss would have brought disaster upon
all the Allied campaigns, and might well have involved
an unconditional surrender."

The mere statement of the totals of these first losses is
enough to show the magnitude of the threat against Sea
Power. In the first three months 1,000 ships of all classes

had been sunk, including 470 ocean-going vessels. In one fortnight in April 122 ocean-going vessels were lost. "The rate of the British loss in ocean-going tonnage during this fortnight was equivalent to an average round voyage loss of 25 per cent — one out of every four ships leaving the United Kingdom for an overseas voyage was being lost before its return." [1] Before the opening of this campaign on February 1, 1917, losses of shipping through acts of the enemy had been as follows: November, 1916, 311,508 tons; December, 1916, 355,139 tons; January, 1917, 368,521 tons. These were serious losses, but they did not actually threaten an overturn. But, after February 1, the totals of shipping destroyed mounted to these astounding figures: February, 1917, 540,006 tons; March, 1917, 593,841 tons; April, 1917, 881,027 tons.

At the time, the British nation and the world at large had no idea of these totals of losses, and did not realize the seriousness of the situation.[2] As Admiral Jellicoe had stated, "The facts could not be disclosed without benefiting the enemy," and the published lists of arrivals and departures, with losses, disguised the truth.[3] For this reason, at the present time, most people retain the impression of these optimistic reports, and do not have an inkling of the actual facts which the British officials were facing. These easy-going ideas must be

[1] "Allied Shipping Control."

[2] "It is perhaps as well that the nation generally remained to a great extent unconscious of the extreme gravity of the situation which developed during the Great War, when the Germans were sinking an increased volume of merchant tonnage week by week." — Admiral Jellicoe.

[3] "The statements published were not false, but they were inconclusive and intentionally so. They gave the number of British ships sunk, but not their tonnage, and not the total losses of British, Allied, and neutral tonnage." — Admiral Sims, "The Victory at Sea."

put aside, in order to get the true perspective of the war.

In this regard, the first dispatch of Admiral Sims to the Navy Department from London (April 14, 1917) at once sounded the alarm: "The submarine issue is very much more serious than the people realize in America. The recent success of operations and the rapidity of construction constitute the real crisis of the war. . . . Supplies and communications of forces all fronts, including the Russians, are threatened and control of the sea actually imperilled." When war with Germany appeared inevitable, in March, 1917, Rear Admiral William S. Sims, U. S. N., President of the Naval War College, had been sent to London "to get in touch with the British Admiralty, to study the naval situation and learn how we could best and most quickly coöperate in the naval war." [1]

As soon as this American officer arrived in London he was welcomed by Admiral Jellicoe, to whom he was well known. Admiral Jellicoe, who was then First Sea Lord of the British Admiralty, at once took Admiral Sims into full confidence, and showed him the actual figures of sinkings. These were a great surprise to Admiral Sims,[2] and his account of the interview needs no addition, to show the British official view of the situation. He has quoted Admiral Jellicoe as saying: "Yes, it is impossible for us to go on with the war if losses like this continue." In answer to Admiral Sims' exclamation, "It looks as though the Germans were winning the war," Admiral

[1] "The Victory at Sea." "I was to remain ostensibly as head of the War College."

[2] "It is expressing it mildly to say that I was surprised by this disclosure. I was fairly astounded, for I had never imagined anything so terrible." — Admiral Sims, "The Victory at Sea."

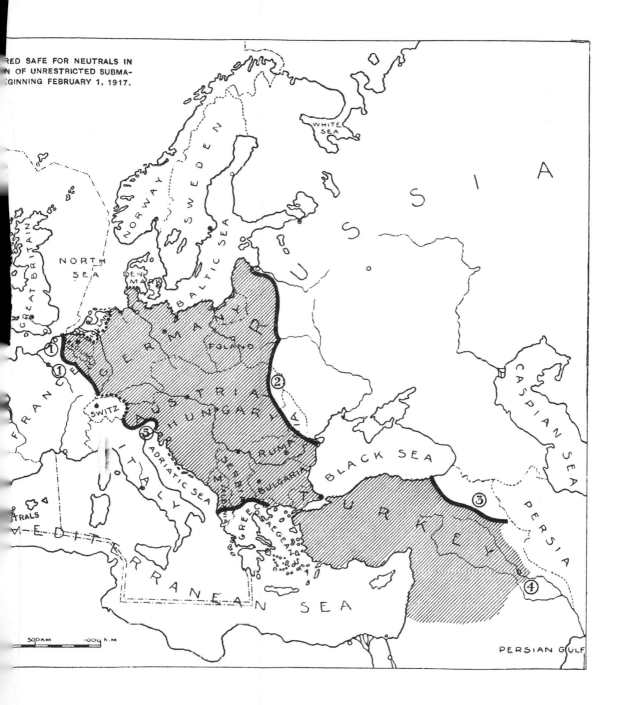

THE SITUATION AT THE BEGINNING OF 1917

(This map is diagrammatic only)

The shaded areas were controlled by the Central Powers
——— Battle Fronts . . . . . . neutral frontiers.

The Central Powers had again improved their situation in
1916. Rumania had been defeated, and the Entente Allies
had not been able to make military gains. At the beginning
of 1917, the Central Powers had deliberately chosen to defend their gains on land, but to make their whole offensive on
the sea by means of unrestricted U-boat warfare. The dotted
lines indicate the prescribed areas on the sea and the areas
proclaimed safe for neutrals.

The Entente Allies were optimistic at the first of 1917, not
realizing the collapse of Russia. They had a concerted plan
for early offensives on all fronts in 1917.

(1)(1) A double offensive by the British and French on the
 Western Front.

(2) Renewed attacks by the Russians against the Austro-
 German armies.

(3) Russian offensive in Asia Minor.

(4) British attack on Bagdad.

(5) Renewed Italian offensive.
 On the Western Front these British and French attacks failed. On the Eastern Front the Russian Revolution ended all hopes of success.

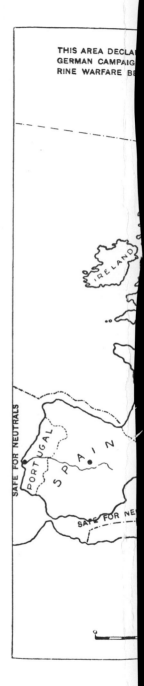

Jellicoe said: "They will win, unless we can stop these losses — and stop them soon." The American officer asked: "Is there no solution for the problem?" Admiral Jellicoe replied: "Absolutely none that we can see now." This must be accepted as the opinion of the British officials.[1]

"But the black fortnight of April was perhaps a blessing in disguise. The certainty of Allied disaster under the existing conditions was so obvious that those who had advocated the institution of convoys were at last given their chance." [2] An account of the adoption of the convoy system, and the progress of the fight against the U-boat campaign, will be given in later chapters.

[1] "According to the authorities the limit of endurance would be reached about November 1, 1917; in other words, unless some method of successfully fighting submarines could be discovered immediately, Great Britain would have to lay down her arms before a victorious Germany." — Admiral Sims, "The Victory at Sea."

[2] "Allied Shipping Control."

CHAPTER IV

THE OBJECT OF THE UNITED STATES IN THE WORLD WAR

THE Government of the United States had soon realized that a colossal task confronted our nation in the World War. In the last half of April, British and French special commissions arrived in this country for an international war conference. The British Commission was headed by Mr. Balfour, the French Commission by M. Viviani and Marshal Joffre. They were cordially received by the people of the United States, but their message to our Administration described the serious situation of the Entente Allies. They reflected the reaction of the leaders of the Allies from their ill founded optimism at the first of the year 1917 to their gloomy realization of the actual facts of the case. Not only were they depressed by the threatening situation as to the U-boats,[1] which had been reported to the Navy Department by Admiral Sims, but both the French and British military offensives on the Western Front, from which so much had been hoped, already bore the stamp of failure. Even without a full understanding of the loss of Russia from the ranks of the Entente Allies, it was evident to the Allied leaders that the expected "series of offensives on all fronts" [2] had broken down. Instead of there being

---

[1] "'Things were dark when I took that trip to America,' Mr. Balfour said to me afterwards. 'The submarines were constantly on my mind. I could think of nothing but the number of ships which were sinking. At that time it certainly looked as if we were going to lose the war.'" — Admiral Sims, "The Victory at Sea."   [2] See Chapter I.

any chance for the Entente Allies "to inflict a decisive defeat" [1] in 1917, which at the beginning of the year they had been confident of accomplishing, the truth had forced them to perceive that the Entente Allies themselves faced defeat, if help were not forthcoming from the United States. And this help must consist of national resources and national manpower on a scale of which the magnitude had not hitherto been estimated.

It would be well, at this stage, to define this assistance to the Entente Allies, which must be the object of the United States in the World War, in order to understand the history of the rest of the titanic struggle.

The obvious first pressing need was naval assistance to the Entente Allies in the crisis of the U-boat campaign. This help of the United States was indispensable in the effort to overcome the menace, and the coöperation of the United States Navy must be kept in mind as a constant factor in the fight against the German submarines, the course of which is to be narrated. The financial aid and supplies furnished by the United States were also essential elements of assistance that must be provided by our nation, as in each of these necessary factors for maintaining the war the Entente Allies were becoming exhausted. But all these were only a fraction of the task of the United States.

The inexorable forces of the World War, which had burst all bounds of former wars, were then molding a situation that would make a call upon the United States so urgent that all else would be cast into the shade. Threatening as was the menace of the U-boat campaign, it was not the crisis of the World War. The actual crisis was destined to come when the collapse of Russia al-

[1] See Chapter I.

lowed the Central Powers to concentrate all their forces on the Western Front, and to establish a military superiority that would have won the World War, if it had not been for the military reinforcement provided by the United States.

Behind the war clouds which obscured all Europe, events were moving as inevitably as a Greek tragedy to the climax when the United States must be present on the field of battle — or else German militarism would win the war. Consequently, to provide that necessary military reinforcement must be considered the great object of the United States in the World War. But what an unprecedented national effort was implied by that phrase!

For the United States there was one great advantage, that the problem of the nation was to furnish a reinforcement against a contained enemy — with no danger of any serious attacks to disturb us in our task. But this problem was complicated by the condition that transportation overseas, which would normally have been provided by the Allies, had been so curtailed by the Allied losses of shipping that we were compelled to provide a large part of the transportation ourselves. In addition, the submarine campaign, and the resultant diversion of Allied naval forces, made it imperative for us to furnish a great proportion of the necessary naval protection.

Consequently, the impending crisis demanded an effort on the part of the United States that would comprise: raising and training an army; transporting a great part of that army overseas; providing supplies and transporting them overseas; constructing and maintaining terminals and bases overseas to receive and handle these troops and supplies; and providing naval protection for the transportation of these troops and supplies. All this must be done in the haste demanded by the approaching crisis — or the war would be lost. And this condition also implied that everything at the outset must be on the vast scale set by the unprecedented demands of the World War. There was no time for the gradual development of forces, as in the case of other nations.

No nation in history ever faced such a task, and a miracle was accomplished when the peaceful United States was able to coördinate the functions of its military, naval, and industrial forces, to gain its full strategic object, in the time thus set by a crisis and on the enormous scale of the World War.[1] To study the great causes that brought about this result will be one of the most interesting things in connection with the war, and especially a most important part of the naval history of the World War. For, as it was evident that our nation's objective must be an operation overseas, the naval factor was absolutely essential.

In fact our whole effort, in this main object of the United States, should be considered one great concerted operation, performed by our combined naval, military, and industrial forces. All these elements were necessary parts of the whole, but it will be at once apparent that this great operation overseas could never have been thought of without the use of Sea Power. Our reinforcement on the battlefield of the Western Front could never have played its saving part in the war, if the conditions had not been provided, as indispensable in carrying out the operation, that we should have the ability to trans-

---

[1] "Her coming was like an avalanche. The world has never seen anything like it." — Lloyd George.

port troops and material overseas, the ability to transport their maintenance overseas, and the ability to give naval protection to the transportation of both overseas. Without these fundamental conditions, the whole national concerted effort would have been anchored at the start, and these conditions, which put the great surge of our people into active offensive operation, could only be provided by Sea Power.

Thus Sea Power became the indispensable and driving agent of what was destined to be the decisive operation of the World War.[1] Moreover, it was the American contribution of naval and shipping forces that alone made possible the necessary superiority on the seas that would provide these conditions. This situation should be made clear beyond any misunderstanding in a naval history of the World War.

It is most impressive to sum up the situation at this stage, and the reader will no longer doubt the importance that Sea Power had assumed in the World War. First, Sea Power, by means of the preponderance of the British navy, was exerting the pressure of the blockade upon Germany, the one element of damage to the enemy that counterbalanced the military defeats of the Entente Allies in the past, and their continued military defeats in 1917. Secondly, the Germans themselves were attempting to win the war on the seas, instead of on land, by concentrating their offensive on their U-boat campaign. Thirdly, and most important of all, in the United States the great uprising had begun which was to provide the decisive reinforcement to the Entente Allies by means of

[1] "The United States Army in France was a decisive factor in obtaining a speedy victory. The transportation of this army overseas under naval protection was, therefore, a major operation of first importance." — Admiral Gleaves, "The History of the Transport Service."

Sea Power. This bare statement of facts should be enough to show that Sea Power was beginning to dominate the World War.

It should also be emphasized that, from the naval point of view, the great united operation of the United States should be measured as follows: The greatest result attained by the Central Powers was the elimination of Russia. The effort of the United States not only took the place of Russia, but went beyond that in assuring victory. This reversal of the greatest result obtained by the Central Powers could only have been accomplished by means of the component naval operation. Consequently, with this just measure from results, we must believe that the year 1917 saw the inception of the most important naval operation of the World War.

CHAPTER V

THE ADOPTION OF THE CONVOY SYSTEM

AT the beginning of 1917, Admiral Jellicoe had become First Lord of the British Admiralty, and Admiral Beatty had been given the command of the Grand Fleet. With the German High Sea Fleet still in being, Admiral Jellicoe has pointed out that the British "could not afford to deplete the Grand Fleet of destroyers, which could under other conditions be employed in anti-submarine work." Added to this was the old idea of invasion, which still had strength enough in Great Britain for the War Cabinet to state that one of the main objects of the British Navy was "to stop invasion or raids upon the British coasts." [1] This influence also restricted the use of destroyers for anti-submarine work.

At the time the Germans began their campaign of unrestricted U-boat warfare, the system of defense against submarine attacks was founded on the general idea of dispersing trade on passage over wide tracts of ocean, instead of using regular lanes, and, when this traffic necessarily converged in the waters about the British Isles, to have it pass through patrolled approach areas. "To carry out such a system it was necessary to give each vessel a definite route which she should follow from her port of departure to her port of arrival; unless this course was adopted, successive ships would certainly be found to be following identical, or practically identical, routes, thereby greatly increasing the chance of attack." [2]

[1] The War Cabinet, Report, 1917.   [2] Admiral Jellicoe.

For this reason, each sailing master was only given the orders affecting his particular ship by the Shipping Intelligence or Reporting Officers, stationed at the various ports at home and abroad. The orders included the warnings as to areas in which submarines were known to be operating, with instructions as to timing for traversing dangerous areas at night and for zigzagging.

Admiral Jellicoe has described the approach areas as follows: "The traffic of the United Kingdom was so arranged in the early part of 1917 as to approach the coast in four different areas, which were known as Approach A, B, C, D. Approach A was used for traffic bound towards the western approach to the English Channel. Approach B for traffic making for the south of Ireland. Approach C for traffic making for the north of Ireland. Approach D for traffic making for the east coast of Ireland via the north of Scotland." He has added that "they were changed occasionally when suspicion was aroused that their limits were known to the enemy, or as submarine attack in an area became intense."

Admiral Jellicoe has also stated the drawback that these areas were of great length, and, with the limited numbers of destroyers, trawlers, and small craft available for patrolling, the protection was inadequate. Definite lines in each approach area were also tried, shifting from time to time, so that patrolling craft might cover the shipping more easily.

But "Allied Shipping Control" has bluntly stated: "This system was ineffective from the beginning, and in time proved a positive death trap. The approach areas covered an immense expanse and the protective craft were utterly insufficient to defend it. The areas and places of rendezvous became known. Sometimes perhaps an indiscreet master would talk at his loading port. Sometimes a rendezvous would be missed — through bad weather or other causes — the ship would wireless in the mercantile code, which was learned by the enemy, and a submarine instead of a protective escort would answer her call. Probably, too, the sight of a protecting craft informed the submarines where shipping was to be found. In the end, the protected areas became more dangerous than the open seas, and perhaps a master who took his own route without protection had the best chance of escape. The chart which showed the sinkings in the area off the south of Ireland became a tragic sight. The protecting craft rescued most of the crews; but they could not save the ships."

Arming the merchantmen had also not proved to be an adequate protection. In the earlier phases of the fight against the U-boat, guns on the merchantmen had been of value in forcing the submarines to submerge and thus restricting their attacks. But the situation had changed. "A specially disquieting factor was the increasing ascendency of the submarine over the defensively armed merchantman . . . not only were the submarines now definitely committed to a policy of ruthlessness which led to two-thirds of the vessels sunk in April being torpedoed without warning, but the more recent types were provided with an artillery armament superior to that of most merchant steamers. . . . It was obvious that defensive armament, though it might mitigate the perils of a voyage, no longer afforded any reasonable prospect of keeping down the rate of loss to a reasonable level." [1] It is also a fact that none of the

[1] "Seaborne Trade."

many devices which had been submitted for use against U-boats gave promise of being a panacea.

It will be evident at once to the reader that this was a hopeless situation, so far as concerned coping with it by the methods then in use.[1] From this point of view, it is easy to understand why Admiral Jellicoe stated that "the later figures made it clear that some method of counteracting the submarines must be found and found quickly if the Allied cause was to be saved from disaster . . . and in these circumstances the only step that could be taken was that of giving a trial to the convoy system for the ocean trade." Consequently, it was another case of the demands of a crisis evolving a counter against a weapon in warfare. "The certainty of Allied disaster under the existing conditions was so obvious that those who had advocated the institution of convoys were at last given their chance."[2]

The convoy system had been advocated for a long time by a group of naval officers, but so far, although they had fortunately worked out the details for operating convoys, their scheme had been rejected at the British Admiralty as inapplicable in the case of modern steamships.[3] There was, of course, the objection that, with the craft available for patrolling against the U-boats, there were not sufficient protecting vessels at hand to inaugurate a complete system of convoys. But this was no argument against using the existing patrol-

---

[1] "He (Admiral Jellicoe) described the work of destroyers and other anti-submarine craft, but he showed no confidence that they would be able to control the depredations of the U boats."   Admiral Sims, "The Victory at Sea."

[2] "Allied Shipping Control."

[3] "The system had been frequently discussed, and fortunately worked out by those who believed in it, but had hitherto been rejected." — "Allied Shipping Control."

ling craft for convoys, and extending the use of convoys as fast as others became available.

The real reasons for not adopting the convoy system earlier had been the objections raised against it at this time, which strengthened the preconceived attitude of the Admiralty against convoys. Admiral Jellicoe has stated an idea which prevailed among many British naval officers: "There is one inherent disadvantage in this system which cannot be overcome, although it can be mitigated by careful organization, viz. the delay involved." This had strongly influenced naval opinion at the time. The masters of the merchant ships had also objected to the convoy system and preferred to take their own chances without it.[1] Admiral Jellicoe has stated, concerning the attitude of the masters of cargo steamers at a conference with the Naval Staff in February, 1917: "They expressed a unanimous opinion that it was not practicable to keep station under the existing circumstances."

But it had become clear that the use of convoys was the only thing in sight that gave any glimmer of hope. The hand of the group of officers who advocated the convoy system had also been strengthened by the fact that the War Cabinet made important additions to the administration of affairs in regard to shipping. A new Ministry of Shipping had been created in December, 1916, and this organization was also strengthened (May 14, 1917) by the fact that Sir Eric Geddes was made Controller in the Admiralty,[2] a new office to act in co-

---

[1] "The Admiralty has had frequent conferences with Merchant Masters and sought their advice. Their most unanimous demand is 'Give us a gun and let us look out for ourselves.'" — Admiral Sims' Report, April 19, 1917.

[2] He afterwards became First Lord of the Admiralty (July 18, 1917), succeeding Sir Edward Carson, who became a member of the War Cabinet.

operation with the Ministry of Shipping. "The Ministry of Shipping had throughout warmly supported the proposals of the naval officers who advocated convoys, and it had at its disposal a shipping intelligence system which both accurately measured the task and assisted in its execution." [1] The United States Navy Department was in favor of this system, and Admiral Sims threw all his influence for the convoys. [2] He was one of the most ardent advocates of the convoy system abroad at that stage. From the time of his arrival in Great Britain, he had continued to send urgent messages to Washington, couched in the strongest terms, recommending that American naval reinforcements should be sent to British waters as soon as possible. Admiral Sims is on record in many dispatches, as urging that our reinforcements should consist principally of destroyers and that the maximum number of destroyers should be sent.

It is evident that both this attitude in favor of the convoys and the prospect of the assistance of American destroyers had a strong influence in favor of the adoption of the convoy system. In this regard, Admiral Jellicoe has written: "The assistance from the United States that it was hoped was now in sight made the prospect of success following on the adoption of the convoy system far more favorable."

"In order to gain some experience of the difficulties attending the working of cargo ships, directions were given for an experimental convoy to be collected at Gibraltar . . . This naturally took time, and the convoy did not arrive in England until after the middle of May.

[1] "Allied Shipping Control."

[2] "Such influence as I possessed at this time, therefore, I threw with the group of British officers which was advocating the convoy." — Admiral Sims, "The Victory at Sea."

The experience gained showed, however, that the difficulties apprehended by the officers of the Mercantile Marine were not insuperable, and that, given adequate protection by cruisers and small fast craft, the system was at least practicable." [1] With this assurance, the change of naval policy [2] was adopted. [3]

"On May 17 a committee was assembled at the Admiralty to draw up a complete organization for a general convoy system." [4] This committee consisted of four naval officers and a representative of the Ministry of Shipping. At last the means was being used, which was to turn the scale against the success of the U-boat campaign, but it must be stated that there was much delay in putting the convoy system into general operation. On June 29, 1917, Admiral Sims was still obliged to report: "If the shipping losses continue as they have during the past four months, it is submitted that the Allies will be forced to dire straits indeed, if they will not actually be forced into an unsatisfactory peace."

But this dispatch of Admiral Sims was a strong indorsement of the convoy system, and an urgent plea for the coöperation of the United States Navy in carrying out the decision of the British Government "to put the convoy system into operation, so far as its ability goes." The first aid of the United States Navy to the Entente Allies was a reinforcement of the craft most urgently needed in the fight against the U-boats. The destroyer

[1] Admiral Jellicoe, "The Crisis of the Naval War."

[2] "A new feature of the means adopted for the protection of trade against submarines has been a return to the convoy system as practised in bygone wars." — War Cabinet Report, 1917.

[3] "The introduction of the convoy system for the Atlantic trade dates from the early days of May, 1917." — Admiral Jellicoe, "The Crisis of the Naval War."

[4] Admiral Jellicoe, "The Crisis of the Naval War."

was the most dreaded enemy of the U-boat. A destroyer could dominate a U-boat by gunfire, and had the great advantage of high speed. A destroyer could rush at speed to where a U-boat had submerged, to drop into the water over it the newly developed depth bombs. These depth charges were most effective weapons against submarines. The first type was a British invention, and the bombs had been improved by being adjusted to explode at a given depth below the surface. By this means a depth charge did racking damage to any U-boat that was near its explosion. Depth charges were used by different types of anti-submarine craft, but they especially increased the effectiveness of the destroyer against the U-boat, as can readily be understood.

Consequently, to send destroyers overseas was the most practical assistance that could be given. On May 4, 1917, a squadron of six American destroyers arrived at Queenstown. Others followed, and on July 5, 1917, there were 34 destroyers of the United States Navy with the "Mother Ship" *Melville*, based at Queenstown, for anti-submarine work.

Admiral Sims had been made Commander of the United States Naval Forces Operating in European Waters. But, from the first, Admiral Sims had seen that it was unwise to have even an appearance of divided command in British waters. By his advice, the Navy Department instructions to the commander of a destroyer division were: "Report to senior British naval officer present, and thereafter coöperate fully with the British Navy." Admiral Jellicoe has thus expressed the good effect of these instructions: "As is well known, Admiral Sims, with the consent of the United States Navy Department, placed all vessels which were dis-

patched to British waters under the British flag officers
in whose command they were working. This step, which
at once produced unity of command, is typical of the
manner in which the two navies worked together
throughout the war."

In the World War the continued discordant element
of divided command had been a great drawback in joint
operations, and it is gratifying that the coöperation of
the United States Navy was free from its harmful influence. By this sensible policy, of acting as reinforcements
to the existing forces of the British Navy, all craft of the
United States Navy in British waters were put in position to take a full part in the anti-submarine operations
from the very time of their arrival.

The reader must realize that, from this time, the convoy system was proving its case, and was to be adopted
as the best defense of shipping against the U-boats. The
circumstances of its being put into general use will be
told in a later chapter. But a few facts as to the convoy
system should be stated here. Wherever it was put in
operation, there never was any reaction against it, and,
when it came to the test, the masters of merchantmen
were able to keep station and follow the directions of the
officers in charge of the convoys. The main outstanding
advantage of the convoy should be made clear at once.
Its makeup, with the protecting craft actually proceed-
ing in company with the group of merchantmen, automatically compelled any U-boat, attempting an attack
upon these merchantmen, to operate in a dangerous
area. It will be evident that the water around these
merchantmen held armed craft whose mission was to
take the offensive against the U-boats. The scheme of a
convoy in itself put these protecting craft in the very

spot for an attack upon the U-boat, instead of scattering them over wide areas of patrol. This forced any attacking U-boat to operate in danger of attack. It was actually an offensive against the U-boat — and the following narrative will show that this unexpected new factor, which was outside all the German calculations founded upon the results of 1916, upset these calculations and brought about the failure of the U-boat campaign.

CHAPTER VI

THE EPISODE OF THE GERMAN RAIDERS

AT the beginning of 1917 three German raiders of commerce were footloose on the seas. These were three disguised ships of greatly differing types, which had slipped out of Germany, eluded the British patrolling cruisers, and were engaged in destroying merchantmen on the high seas. This episode was of course overshadowed by the all-absorbing events of the U-boat campaign, which was causing such devastation among shipping. For the damage inflicted by these German raiders did not reach a total that would bear comparison with the unprecedented losses caused by the U-boats. But the operations of the German raiders have one especial interest. They might be called, in the World War, the last surviving elements of that naval activity over the wide surfaces of the seas which had been characteristic of former wars.

The new order of naval warfare, brought into being by means of the new naval weapon, the submarine, was fighting its way relentlessly in attack and defense, and was a succession of desperate adventures destined to continue until the end of the war. But the old order of naval warfare was almost at a standstill, so far as actual engagements of the usual kind were concerned. On the surface of the distant seas there was nothing left to fight, because throughout these wide areas the German ships had been destroyed, or cooped up by internment in neutral ports.

In home waters, the dominating British Grand Fleet held command of the North Sea and its approaches, but was unable to venture into the areas around the German bases held by the German High Sea Fleet. Both fleets were thus accomplishing most important naval results. The British Fleet was maintaining the ascendancy of Sea Power, and enforcing the blockade which was at length pressing upon Germany. The German Fleet, as has been described, was actively occupied in keeping clear that egress and entrance for the U-boats, without which their campaign would have been impossible. But these conditions, in themselves, did not tend toward a naval action, and there was very little actual fighting. There were clashes of light craft at times, but nothing that was an index of the great results that were being gained by Sea Power — and this gray background, unrelieved by any conspicuous actions at sea, did not give the world an adequate impression of the mighty forces at work, which were in reality shaping the course of the war. This is one reason why the influence of Sea Power upon the World War has not been more widely understood.

Yet the careers of the three German raiders not only have a picturesque touch of the old years on the seas, but for many reasons are well worthy of study in a naval history.

The first of the three was the steamship *Moewe*, which had made a cruise before, as related in the preceding volume. She was skillfully disguised as an ordinary cargo vessel and painted with neutral colors. Her strong armament (four 5.9 inch, one 4.1 inch, two 22 pounders) was hidden behind a high movable bulwark, which would quickly drop and make the guns available. Thus equipped she had the perfectly innocent look of a merchant steamer on a voyage.

In the last week of November, 1916, the *Moewe* had slipped by the British patrols, aided by a fog and darkness, into the trade routes of the Atlantic. Her first capture was made on December 2, and she captured and destroyed on this second cruise 122,000 tons of shipping.[1] Of these 112,000 tons were British. Of the merchantmen captured by the *Moewe* ten were armed for defense against submarines, but were, as matter of course, overpowered in short order by the heavier armament of the German raider.

Her method was to approach her victim without arousing any suspicion of her hostile character, as she had all the appearance of the usual tramp steamer of about 10,000 tons. Then the German naval ensign would be run up, the high bulwark dropped, and the case would be hopeless. The crews of her prizes were taken on board the *Moewe*, and the ships were sunk, usually by placing bombs on board. When the armed ships attempted to resist, they were in most cases easily overcome. There was only one instance of serious resistance. The *Otaki* (9,575 tons), from London to New York in ballast, encountered the *Moewe*, about 350 miles east of the Azores on March 10, 1917. Taking advantage of a heavy sea and a succession of rain squalls, the *Otaki* fought the *Moewe* for over twenty minutes. With her 4.7 inch stern gun the British ship scored hits on the German raider, killing five and wounding ten of her crew. The *Moewe* was also damaged by a fire that was put out with difficulty. But the *Otaki* herself was set on

[1] "A record comparing very favorably either with that of the *Emden* or *Karlsruhe* earlier in the war." — "Seaborne Trade."

fire and her brave captain (Lieutenant Archibald B. Smith, R. N. R.) was then obliged to order the crew to the boats. Four were killed, nine wounded, one drowned. The survivors were picked up by the *Moewe*. Lieutenant Smith remained on board the *Otaki*, when she sank with colors still flying. For this gallant action Lieutenant Smith was awarded a posthumous Victoria Cross.

In December, 1916, the *Moewe* had captured the British steamer *Yarrowdale* (4,652 tons) by the usual means of drawing near when her character was unsuspected and suddenly revealing herself as a heavily armed German auxiliary cruiser. The *Yarrowdale* was a fine new vessel, with a valuable cargo including motor cars and steel, and Count du Dohna-Schlodien, Captain of the *Moewe*, decided that she was worth the risk of sending in as a prize to Germany. The prisoners on board the *Moewe*, about 400, were transferred to her, a prize crew was put on board, and the *Yarrowdale* was sent to make the attempt to get into Germany. This she succeeded in doing, by passing north of Iceland and using Swedish territorial waters, arriving at the port of Swinemünde on January 1, 1917. The captured British officers and crews were interned in German prison camps. The *Yarrowdale* was afterwards fitted out as a German commerce raider, and renamed *Leopard;* but her career was nipped in the bud, as she was sunk with all hands on March 16, 1917, north of the Shetland Islands, by H. M. S. *Achilles* and *Dundee*.

After sinking nearly 50,000 tons in the North Atlantic, the *Moewe* worked south to a rendezvous with a captured collier, *Saint Theodore*. At the last of December, 1916, after the *Moewe* had met her at this rendezvous and had coaled from her, the *Saint Theodore* was herself armed for commerce destroying, being renamed *Geier*, and parted company with the *Moewe* to cruise on her own account.

In January, 1917, the *Moewe* was operating on the Brazilian route with unbroken success, and had the captured Japanese steamer *Hudson Maru* as an attendant. By January 12 the new captures of prisoners, taken from sunken steamers, on board the *Moewe* had grown to over 300. On this date they were all transferred to the *Hudson Maru*, and the Japanese captain was directed to take the ship with them into Pernambuco, where she arrived safely on January 15.

But a warning had been sent out by the British Admiralty, and few prizes were being taken as the shipping was well scattered in consequence. On January 17 the *Moewe* met the rechristened *Geier* at a rendezvous, and coaled from her. The *Geier* had only taken one small prize, and was once more detached as a commerce destroyer. In February the *Moewe* again coaled from the *Geier*, taking all the coal on board, and on February 14 the late *Saint Theodore* was sunk because she was useless to her captor. After this, in February, 1917, the *Moewe* sank four more British steamers, but by this time every British cruiser in the South Atlantic was searching for her, and her commander decided that the only sensible course was to put for home.

On the homeward voyage the *Moewe* destroyed six more steamers, among them the *Otaki*, after the action which has been described. Again the *Moewe* succeeded in running the gauntlet of the British patrolling cruisers, and she arrived at Kiel on March 20, 1917, in triumph, with the officers and crews of eight British steamers on board. This cruise had been notable as skillfully conceived and ably carried out.

The second German raider of this group was of a different type altogether, in fact one of the most unusual craft that ever took part in warfare on the seas. An old American three-master, *Pass of Balmaha*, had been picked up early in the war, when in charge of an armed British escort for examination, and taken into Bremerhaven. She was fitted out in 1916 to resemble the *Irma*, a Norwegian ship, but given a powerful Diesel engine, which made her able to do 14 knots. She was armed with two 4.2 inch guns and two machine guns, and an efficient wireless plant was installed. A real cargo of heavy timber was put on board, false papers were prepared, and her crew taught to obey orders in Norwegian. So carefully was the disguise carried out, that this raider, which was renamed *Seeadler*, was able to put to sea, and actually underwent an examination by a British cruiser south of Iceland, on December 25, 1916, without arousing any suspicion of her real character.

The *Seeadler's* first capture was on January 9, 1917, when the British steamer *Gladys Royal* saw a harmless craft approach, flying the Norwegian flag and showing the Norwegian colors painted on her hull, with a mild request for a chronometer correction. When the sudden apparition of the German naval ensign appeared, the captain of the *Gladys Royal* put on full steam and attempted to escape the supposed sailing ship by heading to windward. Then the *Seeadler* took in her sails, started the Diesel engine, opened fire, and the affair was quickly ended.

This picturesque impostor was naturally unable to do damage that would compare with the cruise of the *Moewe*. The total of her prizes was four steamers and twelve sailing vessels, 30,000 tons in all. But the *Seead-*

ler must be given the credit of playing her rôle for all there was in it. She had also followed the prevailing fashion by sending the captured crews, which amounted to 300, into Rio Janiero in the French ship *Cambronne*, one of the captures of the *Seeadler*.

One feature of the career of the *Seeadler* was the uncanny long distance she was able to cover, by means of her sailing rig and the use of her engine only at need. She worked her way around Cape Horn into the Pacific, and, after cruising up the Chilean Coast, started across for Christmas Island, reversing the course of Admiral Spee. In the summer of 1917 she was among the archipelagoes, but only was able to capture small fry, as she was obliged to lurk away from the steamer tracks. As the *Seeadler* was growing foul, Captain Luckner took her to Mopelia Island, one of the least frequented of the Society Islands, to clean up her bottom. There she was wrecked on a coral reef by a sudden tidal wave August 2, 1917. Her crew and prisoners had many and various adventures in getting back to civilization.

The third of the German raiders was the *Wolf*, formerly the German merchant steamer *Wachenfels* (5,809 tons, 10 knots). Her mission was entirely different from those of the other two raiders, as she was fitted out to act primarily as a minelayer. For this purpose 500 mines were put on board her. In addition, she was well equipped for destruction of commerce, whenever she fell in with shipping, as she had an armament of five 7.6 inch guns and four 18 inch torpedo tubes. She was also unique in the fact that she carried a seaplane. Commanded by Captain Nerger, the *Wolf* sailed from Hamburg December 17, 1916. She eluded the patrols, broke into the Atlantic by way of Iceland, and proceeded south for the area off Cape Town. Although she was too slow for an efficient commerce destroyer, her large coal capacity gave her a much needed wide cruising radius, for the object of her cruise was to lay mines off the focal points of British trade in distant Eastern waters.

Her first minefields were laid early in 1917 off Cape Town and Cape Agulhas. In February she captured the collier *Turritella*, and sent her also on a minelaying mission off Aden. There this steamer, renamed *Itlis*, was stopped by H. M. S. *Odin* on March 5, 1917, and was blown up by her crew when escape was seen to be impossible. In the meantime, the *Wolf* had gone across the Indian Ocean, after laying minefields off Colombo and Bombay, and, although she captured two more prizes, Captain Nerger knew he was unsafe in the Indian Ocean on account of his low speed. Accordingly, after some narrow escapes, in March, 1917, he headed for the Pacific with the object of continuing his mission of minelaying in Australian and New Zealand waters.

By this time Captain Nerger was in straits for coal, and he also needed engine repairs. He had laid two minefields off New Zealand, and from there he proceeded to Sunday Island, in the Kermadic Group, for his necessary refit and repair. He had been on the watch for a collier to replenish his coal, without any success. But, by a lucky chance, on June 2 one passed the very island where he lay repairing. The resourceful German captain sent out his seaplane, which stopped this steamer, the *Wairuna* from Aukland, by dropping a bomb just ahead of her. By this capture an abundant supply of coal, with a large amount of provisions, fell into the hands of the Germans.

With his needs thus provided for, the *Wolf* proceeded

to New Zealand and Australian waters, where more minefields were laid. For protection in dodging the enemy the *Wolf's* appearance had been changed by painting and lowering her masts and stacks, and she made her way toward New Guinea and the Solomon Islands. In this area the *Wolf* captured on August 6, 1917, the *Matunga,* under Admiralty charter with coal and supplies. With this steamer in attendance, the *Wolf* took shelter in a hidden lagoon on the north coast of Dutch New Guinea. There her bottom was scraped and she took on board the coal and stores from the *Matunga,* which Captain Nerger sank on leaving his hiding place August 26, 1917. In September he was back in the Indian Ocean. A minefield had been laid at Singapore Straits, which had exhausted the German raider's supply of mines; and it only remained for the *Wolf* to make the best of her way back to the Atlantic.

The *Wolf* had captured a Japanese steamer, *Hitachi Maru,* which she kept with her as an attendant with prisoners on board. This ship Captain Nerger was obliged to sink for lack of coal, but just afterwards he was fortunate enough to seize a Spanish steamer, *Igotz Mendi,* with the coal he needed. By keeping in the middle of the Atlantic, and by coaling from the *Igotz Mendi,* the *Wolf* was able to make her way to Kiel, where she arrived safely in February, 1918. On her way in, the attending Spanish steamer *Igotz Mendi,* with the sick prisoners, old men, women, and children, from the various ships which had been destroyed, ran ashore in Danish waters. She was afterwards returned to her owners, and all the prisoners sent to England. The *Wolf* herself, with the rest of her prisoners on board, was given an enthusiastic and well deserved welcome at Kiel.

Thus ended what must be considered a most remarkable cruise. By captures and losses caused by her mines the *Wolf* had destroyed 120,000 tons of shipping. In addition, 37,500 tons of steam merchantmen had to be laid up and repaired, on account of the damages received from her mines.[1] To show how astonishing was this achievement, it is enough to state that this steamer of only 10 knots had been able to remain out over 450 days and cover 64,000 miles, in waters controlled by the enemy, while obliged to maintain herself entirely by means of captured fuel and supplies.

This last emphasizes the reason for stating that the cruises of these German raiders should be given consideration in any naval history of the World War. They showed the possibilities of operating, not only without naval bases, but also without any service of supplies whatever. The dramatic career of Admiral Spee's German cruisers, at the beginning of the World War, had been made possible, as shown in the first volume of this work, by the fact that, in spite of the closing of the great German base at Tsingtau, these cruisers had reaped the benefit of a carefully organized German service for supplying at sea. But, by the time these three German raiders went out, there was no German service of supply to rely upon, and, moreover, the German naval leaders were devoting all their energies to the U-boat campaign. Consequently, these German raiders were thrown absolutely on their own resources.

In view of this, their performances should be given high praise. In addition to the losses inflicted by these

---

[1] "It was an aggravation of her success that the majority of the ships sunk by the minefields were liners from 5,000 to 6,000 tons." — "Seaborne Trade."

raiders, the disturbance and delays for shipping, caused by their presence and the diverting of vessels to avoid them, must be counted for them. Thus their total of destruction of shipping was impressive, when summed up. These three German raiders had destroyed 272,000 tons of merchantmen, and had caused disabling damage to 37,500 tons in addition.

Earlier in the war these would have been considered heavy losses. But nothing is more instructive, as to the vast proportions that were rolling up in the World War, than to note the fact that these figures of damages were small compared with merely any one month's toll taken by the U-boats in the spring of 1917. And these results of the cruises of the German raiders were almost lost to sight, as all eyes were focused on the fortunes of submarine warfare.

CHAPTER VII

CONTROL OF SHIPPING

AT the beginning of 1917 long strides were being
taken in Great Britain toward the necessary national control of resources. This had been too much delayed, in view of the development of the World War into
a long drawn struggle between all the resources of nations, instead of a contest of armies and navies as in
the former European wars. In the British change of
administration to the War Cabinet, which has been described, control of Labor, Food, and Fuel, had been provided by new ministries, and the new Ministry of Shipping at once began to exert a control of shipping, which
was an important influence upon the conduct of the war
on the seas.

The Report of the War Cabinet (1917) has stated:
"The issues depending on our shipping were of such importance that the War Cabinet, as one of its first acts,
decided on the formation of a separate ministry charged
with the sole duty of securing the most effective utilization of our mercantile fleet in the interests of the whole
Allied effort."

This last phrase well described the importance of the
new departure, in coördinating the control of the great
volume of British shipping, for using it to the best advantage for the cause of the Entente Allies. And it was
a good move toward Inter-Allied control, which was
eventually to follow. An Inter-Allied Chartering Committee was formed in January, 1917, and the British
Government had proposed that the purchase of ships as

well as the chartering of ships should be put under joint control. But there was opposition among the Allies, and the matter was dropped for the time being. However, as the most efficient use of the preponderating British merchant marine was the main question of this whole matter, the new effort of the British Government became an important phase of the naval history of the World War.

This Government control of British shipping was soon made much more effective through the coöperation of the new branch of the Admiralty, created, as described, by the appointment of Sir Eric Geddes as Controller [1] (May 14, 1917). The importance of this new office will be apparent from the description of its powers in the Report of the War Cabinet (1917). The Controller "was made responsible for fulfilling the shipbuilding requirements of the Admiralty, War Office, Ministry of Shipping, and all other Government departments, and also for the production of armaments, munitions, and material of all kinds for the Navy." Under the Controller, thus invested with plenary powers, this new branch of the Admiralty was organized in three departments, with a Deputy Controller for each. These departments were: 1. Dockyards and Shipbuilding (Naval), 2. Auxiliary Shipbuilding, 3. Armament Production. Coördination with the Ministry of Shipping was maintained by making the Controller an *ex officio* member of the Shipping Control Committee.

The program of the Ministry of Shipping was thus given a strong executive administration. "The out-

---

[1] ". . . an additional member of the Board of Admiralty with the title of Controller and the honorary and temporary rank of Vice Admiral." — War Cabinet Report 1917.

standing effort of the Ministry has been to organize and re-distribute the nation's ships that, in conjunction with the policy decided on for the restriction of import of nonessentials, ample supplies should be maintained for civilian and war needs." [1] The War Cabinet Report cited, as the strongest proof of the good effect of this organization, the fact that in the summer of 1917 Great Britain "actually imported more grain and flour into the country than in the summer of 1916."

The first means taken for establishing this national control of British shipping comprised the "drastic treatment of the problem" [2] by wholesale requisitioning of British ships for the State. Up to the end of 1916 less than half the whole British tonnage had been so requisitioned. These requisitioned ships were mostly tramp steamers, and the greater part of the liners had remained free to trade in their accustomed routes and in private control. Under the new regime in 1917, "practically the whole of the British ocean-going mercantile marine had been brought under requisition at Blue-book rates." [3] This meant an increase of tramps on requisition of about 500, and the requisition of the whole ocean liner service of about 800 ships.

The first and foremost benefit of this Government control came from the systematic withdrawal of ships from the long trade routes and their transfer to shorter voyages with a quicker turnaround, thus insuring more cargoes, even with a lessened number of ships. The reason for this will be seen at once, for instance, in the advantage to be gained by transfer of a liner to a North Atlantic route, instead of keeping it on its long Far Eastern or Australian route. The same ship could carry

---

[1] War Cabinet Report, 1917.   [2] Ibid.   [3] Ibid.

three times the quantity it would have been able to transport in an equal period on its former long route.

As this Government control of British ships became more complete, a Tonnage Priority Committee was set up to adjust the apportionment of tonnage to the various needs of the Departments. It will be at once evident, also, how great an advantage came from this Government control in the organization of the convoy system, which was going into effect at the time the requisitioning policy became operative.

The following from the War Cabinet Report is interesting in its suggestion of the shipping details improved by this control: "The strongest efforts have been made to avoid any waste of carrying power, and to ensure that every vessel bringing imports should be completely loaded. Amongst other changes has been the utilization of the ballast tanks and bottom decks of cargo steamers to supplement the work of the tank steamers in the transport of mineral oils, and hundreds of thousands of tons have been imported in this way."

The immense proportions of the fleets of shipping thus under control will be appreciated when it is understood that the task of this great service of ocean shipping comprised not only feeding and maintaining Great Britain, but also transportation of supplies to the armies and to the Allied nations. The following statement, as to fuel alone, gives an impressive illustration: "The collier fleet responsible for the provision of coal to the Navy, dockyards, the British army in the field and army depots, troop transports, etc., and also the coal imports of France and Italy embraced 584 ships with a carrying capacity of 2,340,000 tons." [1] All former ideas of war-

---

[1] War Cabinet Report, 1917.

fare maintained over the seas were dwarfed by totals like these.

A Government control was also instituted over the coastwise trade, and a separate branch of the Ministry of Shipping was formed to deal with it. This included Channel craft as far south as Bordeaux, and meant the oversight of 1,200 vessels. The gain in efficiency by a redistribution of these craft was shown by their carrying to Ireland important food supplies "estimated in 1917 to be 1,000,000 tons in excess of 1916." [1]

The far reaching good results obtained by this Government control of shipping, which the reader must keep in mind as being developed throughout 1917, have been thus epitomized in the War Cabinet Report: "To sum up the policy adopted and the energies devoted to this vitally important question have been directed to centralizing control, concentrating shipping on the shortest and most essential routes, and securing fullest utilization of all cargo space. By these means we have in a year of increased difficulty, been enabled to meet the largely increased requirements of our fighting forces, to continue rendering assistance to our Allies and to maintain the nation's supplies for military and civil needs, whilst preventing the exploitation of the people by excessive freights."

The second important part of the great work undertaken by the Ministry of Shipping was the Shipbuilding Program, and this project was especially benefited by being put on a strong executive basis through the institution of the new Department of the Controller of the Navy in the Admiralty. [2] One of the great difficulties

[1] War Cabinet Report, 1917.

[2] ". . . but the Navy Controller, by the fact that he was a member of the Board of Admiralty and responsible for all shipbuilding, naval as well as

had been the conflict between warship construction and mercantile shipbuilding, and this new branch of the Admiralty was the one power that could end this. "The first decision by the Controller of the Navy was to separate as far as possible naval from mercantile work. The two are not harmonious. . . . Acting on this decision the Controller devoted a number of yards wholly or partially to warship construction, the other yards being set apart for mercantile and other shipbuilding." [1] Of course this could not be accomplished at once, with the existing construction to be finished. But it at once put matters on a right footing, and set apart the plans for building cargo shipping under the new Admiralty branch of Auxiliary Shipbuilding.

In January, 1917, the Ministry of Shipping had inaugurated its Standard Shipbuilding Program, and this was pushed forward by the new Admiralty administration. Its purpose was to do away with the various conflicting types of the private yards, and to concentrate energies on producing simplified types of cargo vessels with standardized hulls. And it was most decidedly a move in the right direction, although, again this changed program could not be put into effect all at once, for the same reason that existing construction at the yards must be finished. But it should be stated here that the result of these efforts for the year 1917 was to produce in British yards more than double the tonnage that had been built in 1916.[2] An important influence in bringing

commercial, was safe from some of the principal difficulties which had previously beset the path of the Shipping Controller." — War Cabinet Report, 1917.

[1] War Cabinet Report, 1917.

[2] Merchant vessels from British yards: 1916, 542,000 tons; 1917, 1,163,-000 tons.

about improvement in this situation was the broad Government supervision of labor and steel production.

The two principal designs produced for standard hull ships, "A" and "B," were 400 ft. freight steamers of about 5000 tons, with single and double decks respectively. More ships of these two types were laid down than of any other, but there were three smaller standard types of freighters, as well as tankers. However, it must be understood that this shipbuilding program was necessarily a matter of time, and it did not exert its effect upon the situation as quickly as the other measure of Government control of shipping.

The third means of increasing the amount of shipping available was through Overseas Ship Purchase. Contracts had been made abroad, with the authority of the Ministry of Shipping, by the Director of Overseas Ship Purchase. "By the end of May (1917) the contracts signed or definitely closed by the Director of Overseas Ship Purchase comprised ships with an aggregate tonnage of about 1,440,000 dead-weight, or 960,000 gross, representing an expenditure of nearly £60,000,000. Of the total tonnage about 39 per cent was for delivery in 1917, and about 41 per cent for delivery during the first half of the following year." [1]

Of these new ships, which had thus been contracted for, some were under construction already, and were taken over from the original owners. But the greater part were ships to be constructed. Of all the ships under contract, 24 had been ordered in Japan, 31 in Canada, and 171 in the United States. It is interesting to note that, as it was impossible for the British Government to purchase shipping direct in the United States without

[1] "Seaborne Trade."

raising questions of neutrality, all the contracts placed in the United States were made in the name of the Cunard Steam Ship Company. These were known as the "Cunard contracts," and the bulk of this construction in the American yards was taken over by the United States, on our entering the war. The War Cabinet Report (1917) has given the eventual net result to the British Government of all these foreign purchases as 175,000 tons, but of course the shipbuilding taken over by the United States was also for the benefit of the Entente Allies in the World War.

As to Overseas Ship Purchase, it should be understood as in the case of the British shipbuilding program of 1917, that its benefits were a matter of time, and the actual first aid to shipping, in conjunction with the convoy system, came from the Government control of shipping through requisition. The War Cabinet Report has stated: "The result of this mobilization and organization of our shipping resources was, that, despite the heavy submarine losses, British imports during September, October and November were equal in quantity to those of February, March and April, notwithstanding the fact that great quantities of shipping were employed on directly military and naval duties, and that over 1,000,000 tons were lent to France, 500,000 tons were placed at the service of Italy, and much shipping was used for meeting the needs of Russia, Portugal and Greece as well."

In conjunction with this new coördination of shipping under Government control, there was "a drastic reduction of imports" [1] and this was a great help, as it relieved shipping of unnecessary burdens and left the

---

[1] War Cabinet Report, 1917.

space available for actual necessities. Early in 1917 a
Committee was appointed, and cargo space was re-
served "for goods carried directly or indirectly for Government account," [1] restricting the use of shipping to
imports "of essential foodstuffs, raw materials required
for the manufacture of national necessities and military
needs or of munitions of war." [2] This aspect of the case
was also greatly helped by increased production of food
and raw material at home, and careful regulation of the
consumption of food by the Ministry of Food. This last
even went to the extent that "the difficulties in distrib-
uting equally the restricted supplies, compelled the introduction of a system of rationing." [3]

All of this reflected vividly the extraordinary aspect of
this stage of the World War, when the whole struggle
seemed to concentrate on shipping, with the enemy's
main offensive directed against it, and the Entente
Allies, after all their widely extended plans for military
offensives had ended in failure, reduced to the position
of standing or falling according to the determination of
the fate of shipping. This was the essential of the naval
warfare of 1917 — practically a cessation of the naval
activities of old, but a new warfare waged on the seas,
upon the result of which depended the ability of Great
Britain to continue the war.

[1] War Cabinet Report, 1917.   [2] Ibid.   [3] Ibid.

CHAPTER VIII

THE BLOCKADE

THE British War Cabinet Report thus defined the situation as to the British Navy in 1917: "The Navy has continued to hold its predominant position at sea, has denied the oceans to the enemy for the purpose of transporting troops or supplies, and has exerted an ever-growing pressure upon him through the blockade." In the preceding volumes of this work the development of this blockade has been traced, through the first ineffective measures which allowed such large quantities of goods to pass into Germany, to the eventual adoption of the principles established in the American Civil War, which at last enabled the blockade to accomplish its object of shutting goods out of Germany.

These two cardinal principles have been explained, that the ultimate destination of goods for the enemy settled the status of the goods,[1] and that the normal consumption of a neutral country should be the measure for determining whether goods were passing through that country for belligerents. The following from the War Cabinet Report showed how completely the blockade had become founded on the application of these ideas by the beginning of 1917:

"Turning to Blockade, by the end of 1916 the system of the Blockade had reached a high point of elaboration. It was based upon —

(a) Vigilant scrutiny of the transactions of all suspect

---

[1] "The doctrine of the continuous voyage."

neutral traders and the listing of all who habitually assisted enemy trade.

(b) Rationing schedules showing the normal requirements of all European neutrals in respect of all the more important commodities which they obtain from overseas.

(c) Agreements with neutral shipowners, traders and associations of traders under which the contracting neutrals gave certain undertakings in consideration for special facilities for their shipments. Many of these agreements contain rationing clauses which make it possible for His Majesty's Government to detain automatically any excessive shipments of the articles in question."

By means of the adoption and enforcement of these policies, the British had practically barred goods from passing into Germany through the neutral states which bordered on Germany, a traffic which had added greatly to the resources of the enemy in the first two years of the war. It should be noted also, as an assistance for the Entente Allies in the enforcement of these policies, especially the rationing system for restricting imports, that the way was made easier for them by the irritation that Germany had aroused against herself among the neutral nations through the U-boat encroachments of 1915 and 1916. The attitude of the German Government, in this respect, had been so extreme and overbearing that the blockade measures of the Entente Allies had seemed reasonable by contrast. As a result, the objections of neutrals, which at one time threatened complications, had been almost wholly dropped.

The agreements with neutral shippers were a great help toward carrying out these measures of the blockade, as the "special facilities" included the important item of fuel from British bunker control. And this made neutral shippers desirous of being in good standing, instead of being excluded from fuel by the fact that they were listed as assisting enemy trade. These agreements even went to the extent of bringing ships into British ports for examination, in return for "special facilities." All this meant that the great harm, which had been done to the Entente Allies by shipments into Germany through neutral states, was a thing of the past. The War Cabinet Report was enabled to state truthfully: "We could in fact claim that the German attempt to interpose the border countries for the purpose of pursuing the great overseas trade which they had previously carried on from German ports was definitely defeated."

By these methods the main evil had been eradicated. But of course the lesser evil, trade between Germany and the border countries in their own commodities, was a different matter altogether, which could not be stopped by the same means. But this was also restricted by trade agreements between Great Britain and these neutral countries, "to use such means of economic pressure as we had to induce the neutrals to forego their German trade." [1] The British Government also pursued the policy of purchasing surplus products of these countries, with the purpose of keeping them out of Germany. In addition, this situation was much improved by tonnage agreements, particularly with Norway and Denmark, for the employment of their tonnage in Allied interest in return for British coöperation, especially in coal supply.

As has been stated, these effective policies of blockade

[1] War Cabinet Report, 1917.

were at last putting Germany under pressure. This was being brought home to the German people by the experience of actual hardship, and the deprivations in what was called the "turnip winter" were telling upon the nation. "Worst of all, the cumulative effect upon the productivity of Germany herself, of a long-continued stoppage of imported fodder and fertilizers, had now made itself felt with terrible severity." [1] In April the German flour ration was reduced, and throughout the country living conditions had become difficult. It was not alone a shortage of foodstuffs, but of materials necessary to carry on the war. The shortage of metals had even led the German Government to melt down church bells and kitchen utensils. Other materials, in which there were notable shortages, were wool, leather, cotton, and rubber.

The above was the situation, as to the blockade, when the German Government was entering upon its campaign of unrestricted U-boat warfare. The blockade was slowly but unrelentingly constricting the resources of the Central Powers, and, so far, there had been no compensating damage done to the resources of the Entente Allies. But at the beginning of 1917 the word was passed broadcast throughout Germany that their main enemy was to be subjected to this new form of blockade — that, instead of a slow process of deprivation, Great Britain was to be starved quickly into a peace on Germany's terms. It was no wonder that a new confidence spread among the Germans. Their own hardships seemed an index of what was to happen to their enemies. It was also no wonder that they thought success certain. For, as quoted from Admiral Scheer, many had been

[1] "Seaborne Trade."

given the assurance of the Chief of the German Admiralty, who had stated in his official memorandum: "Under such favorable conditions an energetic powerful blow against the English tonnage promises to have an absolutely certain success. I do not hesitate to declare that under the prevailing conditions, we may force England into peace within five months through the unrestricted U-boat war." Consequently, at this stage in 1917, the Germans felt sure that the damages inflicted upon them by the blockade were to be offset by so much greater harm done to their enemies that it would bring victory in the World War.

CHAPTER IX

THE CONVOYS IN OPERATION

AS has been quoted, the British War Cabinet Report called the new counter against the U-boat "a return to the convoy system as practised in bygone wars." This was a true description. For it was a remarkable fact in the naval warfare of the World War, that the best move against the newest and most revolutionary naval weapon was found to be this return to a system which had been in use in the days of oars and sails. Roman galleys, Spanish treasure ships, British sailing ships, all had found that their best safeguard against enemy attacks lay in voyaging in groups escorted and protected by fighting ships.

In this connection, it was another notable fact that the "return" to the usages of bygone days was not a reaction of any conservative element. But it was brought about by the new element overcoming the conservative opinion in the British Admiralty.[1] However, these two facts were not in reality anomalies. They only afforded another proof of the axiom that an old idea, which is sound in itself, may have a very modern application, and often the most inventive minds have been the first to find new uses for old principles.

The convoy system, to describe it in the shortest terms, consisted in gathering merchantmen in groups near their loading ports. The numbers of ships in the groups varied greatly according to circumstances. Each

[1] As has already been stated, it had been decided in the British Admiralty years before the World War that the convoy system was unsuited to modern steamship conditions.

65

group was then escorted over the high seas by one or more cruisers, or other well armed ships, thus providing protection against raiders and the comparatively few U-boats on the high seas. On approaching the dangerous areas infested by the U-boats, the group would be met by destroyers and other small anti-submarine craft, and thus given special escorts adapted for immediately taking the offensive against attacking U-boats. As has been explained, this had a marked advantage over the approach area scheme, because the patrolling craft were actually always in company with the endangered ships, instead of being engaged in patrol of a wide area through which individual ships were passing.

In order to show the dangers for shipping in the approach areas before the change to the convoy system, it will be enough to state the prohibitive totals to which sinkings in these areas had mounted just before the adoption of this new naval policy. The most valuable element of British shipping at this time consisted of ocean-going steamers of 1600 tons gross and larger. Of these ships, in April, 1917, 53 were sunk in the three approach areas, 35 of them in the Fastnet area alone. "Now that every effort was being made to bring the largest proportion of British shipping into the North Atlantic trade, such losses assumed a special and most sinister significance." [1]

It was upon these disastrous losses in the approach areas, under the former system, that the question of the adoption of the convoy system on a large scale hung. The two experimental convoys, from Gibraltar (May 10, 1917) and Hampton Roads (May 24, 1917), had arrived. The Convoy Committee had presented its report

[1] "Seaborne Trade."

advocating adoption of the convoy system, and the new scheme was being put into practice. But the Admiralty could not yet promise escort sufficient for an extended use of the convoy system. At a series of meetings in July, the War Cabinet investigated the subject, in conjunction with the Admiralty, the Shipping Controller, and representative shipowners. These shipowners "were clear that unless the losses in the area of approach could speedily be reduced, a complete breakdown must follow." [1] Upon this, the First Sea Lord of the Admiralty at first promised sufficient force to provide four escorts every eight days, "provided eleven American destroyers continued to be available," and by July 20 the Admiralty announced that "it was hoped shortly to have eight convoys every eight days."

Consequently, it is a matter of record that the American reinforcement of destroyers was the factor which made possible this vitally necessary change. As has been stated, at this stage (July, 1917), there were available, of American destroyers, three times the number specified by Admiral Jellicoe as necessary for the adoption of the convoy system, in order to cut down the heavy losses in the approach areas. And this greater number of American destroyers actually "continued to be available." Destroyers were so necessary against the U-boats in these dangerous areas particularly, that nothing could have been accomplished without them. But, with destroyers to take up the escort of the convoys in the infested areas, the tables were turned against the U-boats. There is no need to add anything, to show the vital necessity for the United States Navy's reinforcement of American destroyers at the crisis of the U-boat campaign.

[1] "Seaborne Trade."

In addition to the principal factor in the convoy system of the presence of armed escorts ready to take the offensive against the U-boats, there were many other advantages in this system. Instead of there being any real difficulty in keeping station, the organization of the vessels in groups was in itself a great benefit. The sailing masters individually were relieved of the necessity for coping with the submarines, and could devote all their attention to navigating their ships under instructions. This relieved officers and men of a great deal of strain. It also helped morale to know that they were in company, with rescue at hand. A convoy could be diverted from a region where U-boats were known to be operating. Secrecy was easier to preserve, for, with each assembled group of ships, only the commander of the escort and the controlling office of the Admiralty would know the route and destination of the convoy. The assembled merchantmen thus proceeded, according to the directions signaled to them by their escort, without information of the voyage being shared by many people.

The groups of merchantmen usually consisted of 20 to 25 ships. Groups of transports carrying troops were much smaller. Aside from the greater security, the losses of time, from collecting the convoy group and the reduction of speed to that of the slowest ship, could be largely made up by the fact that the groups would take more direct routes than the separate scattered courses which the individual ships had been taking to dodge danger.

It should also be noted that the Admiralty had been partly influenced in their ideas of scarcity of escorts by their figures of sailings and arrivals, which had been given out to disguise losses from U-boats. These had included coastwise and short voyages, and, when face to face with the situation, the Admiralty found it was only a question of some 20 arrivals per day of actual ocean-going vessels. This allowed a more rapid extension of the convoy system than had been thought possible by the Admiralty. But, at the start, the convoy system could only be applied to the more vital homeward voyages. Outward voyages could not be so protected in the first months.

The arrangements for operating the convoy system were based upon four main geographical divisions of the world: (1) Mediterranean, which included the convoys starting from Gibraltar; (2) South Atlantic; (3) Gulf of Mexico, including ships from Panama Canal and United States southern ports; (4) United States northern ports and Canada. This last was the most important of all, as its assembly ports included Hampton Roads, New York, Halifax and Sydney, Cape Breton. In this division the first regular sailings of convoys were established; from Hampton Roads, beginning July 2, 1917; from Sydney, Cape Breton, beginning July 10; from New York, beginning July 14. The first regular convoy left Gibraltar July 26. In this way the system was extended throughout the geographical divisions, the regular convoys from the South Atlantic having been at length established in August. These last were the Dakar and Sierra Leone convoys.

In addition to the vital aid of the American destroyers, the United States Navy was soon furnishing ocean escort for the convoys over the Atlantic. The problem of ocean escort was also simplified for the British Admiralty by arming, as auxiliary cruisers, selected vessels which flew the British Naval Ensign. These "Commissioned Escort Steamers" had strong batteries of 6 inch guns, and had on board naval details to man their guns. These armed ships still carried cargo, just as the ordinary merchantmen in the convoys, and consequently there was no loss of freight carrying tonnage through using them as armed escorts.

With ocean escorts thus being provided on an increased scale, and with the Admiralty making great exertions to increase the numbers of destroyers and anti-submarine small craft, it was also found possible, in August, 1917, to extend the protection of the convoy system to outward voyages. This was very necessary, as, naturally, the losses of shipping on the unprotected return trips were growing serious. "Seaborne Trade" has stated: "By one means or another sufficient force was collected to enable the Admiralty, during August, not only to complete and extend the original scheme of homeward convoys, but to furnish escort for outward sailings."

Another difficult problem in the operation of the convoys was to gain efficiency by regrouping the ships into convoys of different speeds. Although the speed of the individual ship, in itself, "unless it approached 20 knots," [1] was only partial protection against the new U-boats, and the slower convoyed group was much safer from attack, yet obviously it was a waste to group together ships of widely varying speed at the one dead level of the slowest; and a great improvement was made by classifying the ships for the convoys according to their speed.

Keeping pace with these developments of the convoys, there were also long strides forward in organization and administration of this system. With the energetic back-

---

[1] "Seaborne Trade."

ing of the War Cabinet, both the Ministry of Shipping and the Admiralty worked in constant close coöperation, and new elements of administration were established in both. Each had a Convoy Section, and at the Admiralty the control of the convoys was placed under an Assistant Chief of the Naval Staff, Rear Admiral A. L. Duff. The manifold details of this new department in the Admiralty were taken care of through the creation of the new offices of Organizing Manager of Convoys and Director of Mercantile Movements. By these means, supervision was exercised over the complications of arranging the programs for assemblies, sailings, routes, assignments of escorts. All this was in co-operation with the great Chart Room, where there were plottings of the various convoys on their routes, and changes of routes could be arranged in case of information of enemy movements.

In addition to all this exacting service for arranging the details of the programs of convoys, there were many details of instruction, which must be given to the Navy and Mercantile Marine alike, in order that officers and men might be fitted for the naval duties of this interlocking system. Lectures had to be prepared to give instruction in keeping station, zig-zagging, etc. and in the new duties for the special signaling gear and other apparatus installed on the ships to equip them for voyaging in groups. It will be evident that a great deal of instruction was necessary when groups of ships must be ready to execute movements which, in reality, amounted to fleet maneuvers. That all this organization and control must be worldwide was another striking example of the vast dimensions of the war of nations, which had in every sense of the name grown into the World War.

On this great scale the war on the seas became, at this stage, "the long contested struggle between the two blockades," as it has been well designated by "Allied Shipping Control." And the convoy system was proving itself to be the decisive factor which saved the blockade of the Entente Allies from being overborne by the blockade of the U-boat campaign. The British official "Seaborne Trade" was enabled to state: "From the first the success of the convoys was unmistakable. The losses of British shipping in July amounted to over 360,-000 tons; but out of twelve convoys, comprising 205 ships, which had arrived at British ports up to August 4th, two vessels only had been torpedoed. One of these was an oil tanker which, though severely damaged, ultimately reached port, the other was a wheat-laden vessel from Montreal, which had parted company in a fog."

Yet, as has been stated, and as was evident from the above losses for July, there was no quick deliverance. The margin of safety provided by the convoys was attained barely in time. This will be evident from the list of the sinkings of shipping, after the peak of disaster for April, 1917, which rose to 881,027 tons. The monthly totals of the gross tonnage of merchant shipping lost through enemy action in the ensuing months were: May, 596,629; June, 687,507; July, 557,988; August, 511, 730; September, 351,748; October, 458,558; November, 289,-212; December, 399,111. These would have been incredible figures, from first to last, before the World War. The least of these monthly totals went far beyond any former ideas. But, even at these large figures, the decrease in losses in the latter part of 1917 meant a percentage in favor of the convoy system, which was destined to defeat the U-boat campaign.

CHAPTER X

THE SHIFTING CONDITIONS OF 1917

ALL through this period the Germans persisted in their air attacks upon Great Britain. In fact, these must be considered an adjunct of their U-boat campaign. Admiral Scheer has stated: "While the U-boats were in full swing at their work of destroying English commerce, the airships with dogged perseverance did their best to contrive their attacks on the island." These Zeppelin attacks had been begun again in March, 1917, and the Germans hoped to win better results than in the past. In 1916 the development of British anti-aircraft defense by means of searchlights, anti-aircraft guns, and attacking airplanes, had made this defense effective against Zeppelins, even at night.

As a result, the Germans have stated that the only way to escape being shot down was for the German airships to fly at so great a height that their attacks became impossible, and consequently there was a cessation of raids from November, 1916, until this renewal of attacks in March, 1917. The reason for this new effort with the Zeppelins was the fact that the Germans had designed a different type of airship, which would be able to operate at a height of 18,500 feet. At this height, the Zeppelins in night attacks would be free from the observation of the most powerful searchlights. As the Zeppelins would thus be in darkness, not only would the anti-aircraft guns be neutralized, but protection would be given against airplanes. The attacks of these defending British airplanes were especially dreaded, as many Zeppelins had been shot down by them, and this danger would be abated if the British airplanes must attack in the dark.

But this German plan, to obtain better results by means of airships flying at great height was defeated by the new difficulties which were experienced at these altitudes. The intense cold and the strong winds encountered were too much for engines and crew. When the Germans attempted to operate at this height, the crews would be overcome, and the airships would drift off helplessly before the strong currents in the air. In one raid five airships were lost, out of eleven which took part. In this case, the airships flying at a great height met so strong a head wind that four were blown into France. The fifth was blown into Germany, but was lost in landing.

The Germans have admitted that this failure of the airships at great height finally defeated their efforts. Admiral Scheer has stated this beyond misunderstanding: "Ultimately the airships were forced up so high that it was beyond the limits of human endurance (altitudes of more than 6000 m.). That meant the end of their activities as an attacking force." [1] Consequently, it can be written that the German airships failed to be a decisive factor in the World War.

The Germans also attempted to gain results by increased use of airplanes in raids over Great Britain throughout 1917 and in the first half of 1918. As in the case of the airship raids, there were a great many killed and wounded among the civilian population,[2] but again

[1] Admiral Scheer, "Germany's High Sea Fleet."

[2] By airplane raids: in 1917, killed 655, injured 1553; in 1918, killed 182, injured 430.

it can be said that they did not accomplish the result of inflicting military damage, and whatever interruption there was in the industries did not amount to a serious element of the situation. Of these German airplane raids, as of the other German attacks with aircraft against Great Britain, the same statement holds true, that the only actual military result the Germans obtained by aircraft was the diversion of British forces for anti-aircraft defense.

But, in this respect also, the situation remained the same as in 1916. The military forces used for anti-aircraft defense were still only a small part of the British forces retained for Home Defense. These troops were to be kept in Great Britain in any event to repel invasion. For the prewar idea of a German invasion of Great Britain had yet remained strong enough to hold thousands of troops in Great Britain. As stated in the preceding books of this work, this policy had maintained a useless cofferdam of troops at home, which impeded the flow of troops to the battlefields abroad. In spite of all the experience of the war, this influence of the invasion scare continued throughout 1917, with its harmful and restraining effect upon British military strategy.

This influence also continued to exert a restraint upon British naval strategy in 1917. The dispositions of the British Battle Fleet were still, to a great extent, dictated by the assumed necessity for guarding against German expeditions in force with the object of making landings on the British coasts. The British War Cabinet Report for 1917 has explained this phase of the dispositions of the British Fleet by stating: "It must always be borne in mind, in considering the relative calls upon the British and German Fleets, that Great Britain has 7,700 miles of coast line to defend, while there are only 290 miles of German coast on the North Sea."

In other respects this point of view, that the Grand Fleet must always be on guard against enemy attempts, remained in evidence. Of course the patrol of the great northern entrance of the North Sea had always been a necessary task — and an exhausting task, as the distance to be patrolled from Scotland to Iceland and Greenland was over 600 miles, with most difficult conditions of wind and weather. Keeping this guard over the passages through the North Sea to Germany, and thus maintaining naval forces in so great strength that this control of the North Sea could not be overthrown by the enemy, constituted the whole main support of the blockade. And this constant unbroken service of the British Grand Fleet must always be recognized at its full value.

But the continued British naval policy, of always keeping the Grand Fleet devoted to the mission of defending against enemy attacks, was all the time militating against harassing the enemy by British naval attacks. After all, there was only one enemy for the British Grand Fleet to take into account. This was the weaker German High Sea Fleet, with its auxiliaries, operating from the strong German bases. As has been explained, at this stage of the war the entire mission of this German Battle Fleet had been changed to the task of keeping clear the gates for the U-boats, to which the Germans had intrusted their whole offensive strategy. The fact that the Germans were staking all their hopes for ending the war in 1917 upon this U-boat campaign was almost a matter of common knowledge — and yet there was not a corresponding change in the strategic use of the British Battle Fleet.

Consequently, in Home Waters, the naval situation existed that the German Battle Fleet was wholly dedicated to forwarding the U-boat campaign, as has been explained, and this Battle Fleet must be considered an operating factor, and an essential part of the united naval effort of Germany to win the war by means of the submarines. This condition, of which Admiral Scheer's description has been quoted, must be accepted as a matter of fact. On the other hand, in the British naval effort against the U-boat campaign, which at this stage had grown to be the main issue of the naval war, the British Battle Fleet did not become in the same sense an integral factor in anti-submarine operations. Instead, the British Grand Fleet, to all intents and purposes, was still retained in its former dispositions for acting against the German High Sea Fleet, if it "came out." Its mission remained, as before, to defend against sorties of the German High Sea Fleet into the North Sea, and against attempts at landing on the British coasts. Consequently, it cannot be said that the British naval strategy in 1917 was as closely coördinated as that of the Germans — and this tended to restrict British offensive anti-submarine operations.

In regard to this lack of offensive on the part of the British Grand Fleet, it must not be inferred that there was any possibility of attacking the German Battle Fleet at its bases, or that it would have been wise to expose the British battleships to the dangers of the Heligoland Bight. Either of these operations would have implied a prohibitive risk for the British Battle Fleet.

But for the light forces of the British Battle Fleet it was a different matter, and yet these British light forces were not disposed for anti-submarine attacks and for supporting the British minelayers, in order to make it more difficult for the U-boats to break out through the British minefields laid about the German bases. In response to a demand in the Admiralty for a greater use of the British light forces, in October, 1917, there had been a tentative operation of these destroyers toward the Bight, but it was not repeated, and the destroyers were retained in company with the Grand Fleet. This seemed a needless restriction of the British destroyers in taking them away from the anti-submarine fight. The very act of moving out the light forces from the Grand Fleet for anti-submarine operations, would have meant, in itself, an advanced screen between the British Battle Fleet and the enemy and it would have been possible to make provision for these light forces to rejoin the British battleships at need of their protection. But keeping the destroyers with the British Battle Fleet rendered them inactive, at the very time when the German light forces were most active. In other words, at this stage, when the German Battle Fleet had changed its tactics to the one object of giving close and active aid to the U-boats, the tactics of the British Battle Fleet remained unchanged in standing aloof, and waiting to oppose an enemy naval strategy which had been dropped by the Germans.

In this way, the unchanged routine of Admiral Beatty's Grand Fleet was kept up. The Harwich Force was also maintained as before. For the Dover Patrol the mission remained unchanged, and this was for the best, as its task remained the same only on an increasing scale as the war went on. The magnificent work of this naval force, in protecting the constant stream of transportation between Great Britain and France, continued to maintain this all-important factor in the World War without impairment by the enemy. There were occasional breaks into this area, but nothing happened, even at the height of the U-boat campaign, which threatened any serious interruption. The above sums up the situation in Home Waters, at the stage when the fight was being waged against the German submarines.

As a means of shutting in the U-boats, the Navy Department of the United States had advocated in April, 1917, the use of mine barrages on a large scale in the North Sea between the coasts of Scotland and Norway. This plan comprised a barrier of mines 240 miles long and over 200 feet deep, and it was so unprecedented that at first it met prompt rejection in the British Admiralty. On May 13, 1917, the Admiralty replied: "From all experience Admiralty considers project of attempting to close exit to North Sea . . . by method suggested to be quite impracticable. Project has previously been considered and abandoned. The difficulty will be appreciated when total distance, depth, material, and patrols required and distance from base of operations are considered."

But our Navy Department remained convinced that this plan was practicable, and the Navy Bureau of Ordnance continued to make a special study of means to make this proposed barrier effective, under the able direction of its Chief, Rear Admiral Ralph Earle. The main problem was to increase the area of destruction of each mine. Various methods were tried, but at length a new type of mine was devised in which each mine was equipped with an antenna that insured explosion from an electric current upon contact.[1] This increased the area of destruction of each mine to a "radius of about 100 feet against a submarine." [2] It will be obvious at once that, by means of this new invention for increasing the area of effect of each mine, the number of mines required was greatly decreased. With one main objection thus removed, the Bureau of Ordnance showed energetic resource and enterprise, in going ahead with the complicated production of the vast quantity of material necessary for this project. All of this material was of novel design, and its manufacture, apportioned among many different sources, was a triumph of ingenuity.

With the whole project thus on a practical basis, the plan for the great barrage was submitted again to the British Admiralty through Admiral H. T. Mayo, Commander-in-Chief of the Atlantic Fleet, who was sent to Great Britain in August, 1917. This time, with the assistance of Sir Eric Geddes, a more favorable reception was given to the plan, and in conferences in September, 1917, the British Admiralty was "in accord with the Navy Department in regard to the major features of the project, but differed in respect to some of the details." [3] This brought about a period of delays from discussion, but the plan was at length adopted, and on November 1, 1917, the Chief of Operations United States Navy cabled to the British Admiralty: "Depart-

---

[1] First proposed by Ralph C. Browne of Salem as a device for firing a submerged gun, and adapted to use for mines by the Bureau of Ordnance, U. S. N.

[2] "A Spherical mine case carrying a charge of 300 pounds of T. N. T. having a destructive radius of about 100 feet against a submarine." Letter of Chief of Bureau of Ordnance to Chief of Naval Operations, July 18, 1917.

[3] "The Northern Barrage and Other Mining Activities." Historical Section, U. S. N.

ment concurs in project for mine barriers Scotland to
Norway and has already taken steps to fit out eight such
mine planters to sail February 1. . . . Expect begin
shipments of mines January 15. Will send officers to
confer and arrange details in a few days." The project
thus became a matter of the naval operations of 1918.
Two officers of the United States Navy, Commander
O. G. Murfin, and Commander T. L. Johnson, were sent
to Great Britain November 13, 1917, to arrange details
for the American participation in this operation. On November 27, 1917, the first draft of men arrived from the
United States. These were to be the nucleus of the Mine
Force of the United States Atlantic Fleet, which carried
out the project, as will be narrated.

The American destroyers, as they arrived overseas,
had been based in the Queenstown area, and put under
the orders of the British commanding officer, Vice Admiral Bayly, thus insuring a united command as has
been explained. But it must be kept in mind that the
administration and maintenance still remained with the
United States Navy. These and the other American
naval vessels sent overseas remained and were designated "a task force of the Atlantic Fleet," and, where-
ever they were put under British command, it was in the
same sense that unity of control was afterwards secured
on the Western Front by placing the British and American armies under Marshal Foch.

The Queenstown area comprised 25,000 square miles
west and south of Ireland, and up to this time had been
badly protected. In this zone, which was so vital a focus
of trans-Atlantic shipping, the United States Navy thus
at once began, and continued to render, a most needed
service against the U-boats in British waters. Another

much desired assistance was soon being given by the
United States Navy. When war was inevitable (March
23, 1917), Ambassador Page had cabled from London
that Admiral Jellicoe had "privately expressed the
hope" that the United States would relieve the British
Navy of the patrol of the western Atlantic. In conference with the Entente Allies, soon after the United
States entered the war, it was agreed that the United
States Navy would assume the patrol of the Atlantic
from Canada to South American waters. This was to include supervision of the Gulf of Mexico and Central
American waters, through which great quantities of oil
were transported to the Entente Allies. The United
States Navy also took over Pacific waters. These agreements released many British ships for other duties.

This was a great help, as, aside from the U-boat campaign, there were urgent calls upon the British Navy
from many directions. The expeditions against the German Colonies were supported by the British Navy —
and the last of these colonies, German East Africa, was
conquered in 1917. Naval assistance was also provided
for the operations in Mesopotamia and Palestine. But,
outside of British home waters, the Mediterranean area
made the greatest demands upon the British Navy and
upon British shipping. In coöperation with the French
and Italian Navies, not only must the great services of
supply be maintained, but the Salonica Army must be
kept at full strength.

The importance of the Salonica Army, established and
maintained by Sea Power, and the great value of its
guardianship of Greece for the Entente Allies, had received signal proof in June, 1917. The pro-German
King Constantine had been obliged to abdicate on June

12, a new Greek Government had been formed with the pro-Ally M. Venizelos at the head, and on June 27 Greece had declared war on Germany, Austro-Hungary, Turkey, and Bulgaria. This had been, in reality, the one favorable event for the Entente Allies in the southeast — and the situation that brought it about must be credited to the presence of the Salonica Army, which was only made possible by means of Sea Power.

Elsewhere the military situation was very bad for the Entente Allies. Their military offensives on the Western Front had broken down completely. So seriously had the French suffered in the defeat of General Nivelle's ambitious plan to break the German line, that the French armies were unable to undertake any serious offensive in the rest of the year 1917. The British had also lost heavily, without gaining any decisive results, in their assault against the Hindenburg line, which was their part of the joint Allied offensive in the first half of 1917.[1]

But the British were able to call upon fresh troops, and they attempted another military offensive in the latter half of 1917. This was an effort to advance along the Flanders coast. A thrust in that area had often been urged, as a favorite plan of British strategists. Moreover, at this time, there was the additional stimulus that driving the enemy back in Flanders would force the Germans out of the Flemish U-boat bases. In fact, this object of curtailing the German U-boat campaign was the main reason for the offensive on the left, which has been called the Battle of Flanders.[2] But in this difficult terrain the British attacks were smothered in a sea of mud, and, as in the other Allied offensives, the long pro-

[1] Battle of Arras.   [2] Begun July 31, 1917.

tracted assaults fell away to affairs of ridges and piecemeal trench fighting. Also, as in the other Allied offensives, this mode of fighting consumed troops as fast as they were poured into the trenches. The result was, these unsuccessful military operations on the Western Front had become so great a drain upon the Allied armies that they were sapping the offensive strength, not only of the French but of the British. It is a great help towards understanding the sudden change in the military situation as 1918 approached, to realize that the military events of 1917 were thus working to deprive the French and British of the power to take the offensive on the Western Front early in 1918. This was one of the serious elements in the military situation that was being evolved in 1917.

Of course the most unfavorable element was the Russian Revolution, which, as has been said, was utterly destroying Russia as a military factor on the side of the Entente Allies. After a feverish advance in Galicia (July, 1917) under Kerensky, the Russian armies had disintegrated under the Bolshevists, who in the latter part of 1917 were preparing to make peace with Germany. As has also been stated, this total collapse of Russia was not soon realized by the Germans, but its effects were becoming unmistakable in the latter part of 1917.

The following German comment sums up not only this unexpectedness of the Russian Revolution, but also the complete military revolution which it brought about. "Contrary to all expectations, an event occurred at that time which offered the German Empire once again the chance of coming through victoriously out of the war. This was the Russian Revolution, which eliminated the numerically strongest opponent and gave us the numerical superiority on the Western Front, notwithstanding the enormous numbers of our enemies." [1]

The first great event of this overturn in the military situation came with startling suddenness. Profiting by the release of the armies which had been arrayed against the Russians, troops were sent to the Austro-German armies on the Italian Front, and a surprise concentration of men and guns was effected against the Italians. By a sudden and unexpected assault [2] the Italians were driven back to the Piave River, with the loss of 250,000 prisoners and 2,000 guns. By this complete overthrow, not only were the Italians rendered incapable of taking the offensive early in 1918, but they were compelled to obtain assistance from the already depleted ranks of the British and French. There is no need to add anything, to show these great dangers which were growing into being through the last half of 1917, but they should be clearly set forth in their relation to the naval war.

On the one hand, Germany was failing in the attempt to win the war in 1917 by means of the U-boat campaign. With the convoy system, the right means were being used to defeat it. We can see that there was much delay in adopting these measures against the U-boats — and more delays in carrying them out. In addition to the indecision abroad, it is evident that American naval reinforcements in greater numbers might have been supplied more promptly. But, by and large, the result had been attained, and the menace of the submarine was being overcome. So far as concerned proving itself a de-

---

[1] General Hoffman, German Chief of Staff, "The War of Lost Opportunities."

[2] Battle of Caporetto, October 24, 1917.

cisive factor for winning the war, the U-boat campaign was already a dead cock in the pit. In this result the United States Navy had played an indispensable part, and had attained America's immediate naval objective in the war.

But, on the other hand, while one danger was passing, the new and infinitely greater menace was arising, as the year 1917 ran its fateful course. With the condition becoming established that France, Great Britain, and Italy, all would not be able to take the offensive early in 1918, Germany was preparing for the most formidable military offensive of the World War. All her forces were to be massed on the Western Front, with an assured numerical superiority and with "once again the chance of coming through victoriously out of the war." All this was not apparent at the time, but it is now evident that the whole fate of the Entente Allies lay in the question, whether the United States would be able to provide sufficient military reinforcement at the approaching crisis of the World War.

CHAPTER XI

THE EFFORT OF THE PEOPLE OF THE UNITED STATES IN THE WORLD WAR

WITH the whole outcome of the World War thus depending upon the solution of the great problem for the United States, which was then being formulated in the concealing war clouds of 1917, the right solution was actually being worked out in America long before this problem itself became visible to the world. It might be said that there was some instinctive sense awakened in advance, to call into immediate action vast unmeasured American forces, to counteract the overwhelming hostile forces which were being accumulated against the Entente Allies in the World War.

In 1917 something was happening in the United States, so extraordinary that it must be classed as one of the great uprisings which have shown the world that human forces united by some powerful fusing impulse can be stronger than artificial military conditions. To find a comparison, with the exception of our Civil War, it might almost be necessary to go back to the great movements of northern races which overran Europe. France, after the Revolution, has always been considered an outstanding example of a united uprising of humanity finding in Napoleon the required leader. Yet, with all the years of enthusiasm for the Emperor, only the military and industrial forces reached full strength — Napoleon was never able to vitalize the naval arm. The wonder was that the peaceful United States was able in a year and a half to coördinate its industrial, military, and naval forces, into a decisive military reinforcement on the distant battlefield of Europe.

This is written in no boastful spirit. In fact, there is every reason against any individual American complacency. It should be bluntly stated that, in every military sense, we were unprepared — and this retarded everything at the start. For a time it looked as if European prophesies as to our helplessness in war would prove true. Then from confusion and delays emerged the miracle, the Army and Navy forces of the United States projected into their mission on the European Western Front.[1] It is true that many kinds of mistakes were made, but all details of individual errors were cast into the shade by the one dominating fact, that behind our operation was the thrust of strong impelling forces which had not been measured since the Civil War.

As has been said, the Civil War offered the only basis for comparison, and it should also be stated that having the Civil War behind us was one of the component factors in our national structure. The extraordinary influence of that epoch-making war was still strong with Americans, transmitted through those who took part in it. In fact, the veterans of the Civil War, North and South, must be given the credit of having been the most valuable elements, throughout the communities of the United States, for inculcating the national spirit. This had been continued through the long interval of years, in which there had been a stream of immigration into the United States.

Beyond any mistaking, the outstanding feature of the

[1] "These hordes of American troops on the continent which turned the balance against us on the Western front in 1918." — Admiral Tirpitz.

uprising of our people, after this long interval of peace, was the instant surge of united Americans which made it at once evident that the United States had become united in every sense of the word. It was the prevailing European opinion that a nation made up of so many elements from immigration could not be fused into a united whole at the crucial test of war. The same opinion had been held as to the North at the outbreak of the Civil War. That opinion was shown to be erroneous in 1861, and students of the Civil War had no doubts of the unity of our people in 1917. At the great summons in 1917, it was again self-evident from the very beginning that the same spirit was vital in our nation, and that all who had come to us had alike become Americans with us. At the touch of war, there was no disintegration. On the contrary, all differences of races and creeds, and all divisions of parties, were forgotten — and it is no mere figure of speech to say that the American nation rose as one man to its appointed task.

The Germans had shared this mistaken opinion that our nation was made up of elements which had not coalesced, and, in the years of preparation before the World War, the German Government had made use of much propaganda to align with Germany racial groups among our population. After the outbreak of war in Europe, the German Government had also organized an elaborate system of German agents for hostile plotting throughout our country. But, upon the declaration of war by the United States, all this was swept away like a cobweb. Our citizens of foreign origin at once showed themselves to be loyal Americans, and throughout our communities there was so universal a spirit of aroused and vigilant Americanism that the efforts of the German plotters did not make headway. For, with each American community on the watch, their agents could not get foothold. Far from having the effect, on any serious scale, of impeding the effort of the United States, they only scored failure. There was, of course, some sabotage. But, taken altogether, it is probable that so great pains and so great expense had never produced such small results, and all the ramifications of the German spy system merely counted for a percentage of delay and damage that was negligible.

In addition to this assured impulse of the surge of the united people of our nation, there were other factors in the national life of the United States which had paved the way for a great national effort. In the forty years preceding the World War our industries had grown beyond localized units. They had expanded into nation-wide organizations, and our people had begun to think in nationwide terms. The natural result followed in legislation and government. There was a corresponding advance from state to national control. The Interstate Commerce Commission in 1887 had been the first step, followed by the Department of Agriculture in 1889. Afterwards came the Departments of Commerce and Labor, and, most important of all, the Federal Reserve Board (1913). This last created a national control of finance and currency, with a system of Federal Reserve Banks throughout the country. Aside from the far reaching benefits of this system for our country in peace, it was providential for our nation destined to be at war, as will be explained.

Through this progress in our national development, we had grown into a national strength that had not been estimated abroad. There existed, in fact, an actual preparedness innate within the United States, for thinking and doing things on a large scale and for national control on a large scale. All this had come into being before there was any thought of the World War. But there had also been other developments, which were the results of the state of war in Europe, and which strengthened the United States for its part in the World War.

In the first place, there had been an expansion of American industries for furnishing war material and supplies at the order of the Entente Allies. This had grown on a large scale, and it had produced the result, in the years before the United States was at war, of stimulating American industries in the very direction most necessary for the United States at war. Consequently these three years had made a great difference in our ability to produce war material and supplies, and in this respect we were not in the predicament of a great peaceful nation suddenly hurried into war.

In the second place, with the great devastating war going on before our eyes, its object lessons were gradually arousing our people to the need for a national defense, and this idea grew, as the German Government made it clear that it was possible we ourselves might be drawn into the World War. After the sinking of the *Lusitania*, and in consequence of the truculent attitude of the German Government, the President of the United States had written to the Secretaries of War and Navy (July 21, 1915), calling upon them to prepare adequate programs for national defense. For a long time this did not lead to much except debate. But there was one notable exception. The Secretary of the Navy in October, 1915, had created the Naval Consulting Board, of civilians whose scientific and trade affiliations made them of value, and this Board appointed an Industrial Preparedness Committee which did useful work in gathering data from over 18,000 industrial plants. This may be considered one of the first steps in industrial mobilization.

But public opinion was being aroused, and there emerged the National Defense Act (June 3, 1916), the greatly enlarged Naval Program (August 29, 1916), and, attached to the army appropriation bill of the same date, the creation of the Council of National Defense. The measure constituting the United States Shipping Board was passed September 7, 1916. These bodies were at the first stages of organization when the United States declared war against Germany, and they must not be considered as machinery ready at once to carry out the nation's program. But they were the first stages of the chemistry that was to produce the mobilization of the nation's resources of food and fuel, shipping and transportation, finance and trade, which must be behind the armed forces of the United States in order to enable them to accomplish their mission in the World War.

That all this was in reality a potent chemistry will be at once apparent when the reader realizes what this meant. The significant element lay in the fact that it comprised a call from the Administration summoning our financial and industrial leaders for consultation as to the national emergency, which had unmistakably become a possibility. Consequently, at this stage in 1916, the Administration had already associated with itself these leaders from our civil life. And, although the definite bodies had not then been formed which were to control our industrial mobilization, yet the activities of these industrial leaders were already making themselves felt throughout our nation. They not only brought men from our industries to work with the War and Navy Departments, but they also stimulated the industrial centres to work in the right direction. The result was a real beginning of leadership and control from the top down, and the uprising of our people was thus given intelligent direction from the start.

It was only this well directed surge of all classes of our people that made our industrial mobilization possible, on the vast scale and in the limited time set by the approaching crisis. In fact, it was the quick recourse to our self-governing communities themselves that was the most notable feature. Just as the strength of our Government was derived from these, so the strength of our resources came direct from our American communities.

The outstanding example of this was shown in the finances of the United States. The financial problem of the United States was unprecedented in the vast sums required. Not only was it a question of the enormous cost of our own war expenditures, made heavier by the urgent necessity for haste, but we must also make great loans to the Entente Allies, who were all at extremity financially. War taxes were imposed, but the bulk of the large amount required to meet this double drain on the nation's finances was actually raised by a series of issues of United States bonds, taken by popular subscription in the different communities throughout the nation. The wise policy was followed of allotting a proportionate part of the bond issues to each community in the country. Each city and town knew the amount of its share, and local pride was joined to patriotism to make sure that each did its part in carrying on the war.

The success of this appeal to our communities was never in doubt — and thus the financial part of our nation's task in the war was assured from the first. It should be emphasized, beyond any misunderstanding, that, no matter how great the zeal of our people might be, the complicated machinery of these loans and the war finances of the United States could not have been operated by any conceivable means except by the system of Federal Reserve Banks. But, through this new agency which had been created by our national development, our American communities were enabled to provide the first essential motive power for our mission in the World War.

The same direct appeal to each American community was the foundation of the success of the urgent call upon the manpower of the United States for our armed forces. In this case conscription was not a last resort, but an immediate first appeal to every city and town to do its share in the war. Each district of each community had its own local board — and again local pride was joined with patriotism. It was in fact, as the name implied, a Selective Service — and this tremendous factor also was never in doubt.

In the same way, the great question of the control of food and fuel had its roots in every community of the country. There is no need to state the self-evident fact that it was a colossal undertaking to apportion these products of food and fuel among our armed forces, our people at home, and the needs of the Entente Allies abroad. The first step of the President was to start a plan of volunteer food administration by the appointment of a Food Administrator (May 17, 1917). This was Herbert C. Hoover, whose name became a household word all over the country. Drastic powers were afterwards given to the Food Administration, through

the President, by means of the Food and Fuel Control
Act (August 10, 1917). These included a strict license
system and fixing of prices. But always these powers
were used to supplement the appeals for voluntary co-
operation among our people.

From this intense nationwide effort of our people
there gradually emerged the elements of actual national
control. Leading men from our various industries
placed their services at the disposal of the United States
Government, and from this was evolved the possibility
of putting the different industrial activities under the
control of recognized experts. It was all an evolution,
not the product of well ordered machinery. We must
realize that things did not go like clockwork. On the
contrary, there was confusion confounded for a long
time, and everything was months too late in being
started, in the chaos at Washington. But, with the national elements in the situation which have been described, the trend was leading toward doing the right
things in the right way, and from the vague supervision
of the Council of National Defense, there were being
evolved national agencies of control which were to take
over industrial administration, each with its own corps
of experts in its own branch.

The railroad organizations of the United States had
promptly offered their services to the Government, and
on April 11, 1917, the Railroad War Board was created.
But this most important matter of transportation was
not coördinated, and there was so much congestion, that
at the end of the year the President took over by military control all the railroads in the country, and the
United States Railroad Administration was constituted,
which, from this time on, ably administered as one great

whole all the railroad systems of the nation. This was an
example of the working out of our tasks — a period of
confusion, and then drastic control under expert management.

This same drastic executive control provided the
means for our attaining at length a real mobilization of
our national industries, after a like period of congestion
from misdirection and confusion. The first stride in this
direction was by means of one of the various bodies
which were the offspring of the Council of National Defense. This was the General Munitions Board (March
29, 1917), which served until July 27, 1917, when the
War Industries Board was constituted. The new board
was still a subsidiary of the Council of National Defense,
and was a smaller organization made up from members
of the General Munitions Board.

But early in 1918, the President of the United States
by executive authority reconstituted the War Industries
Board as an independent body, with extraordinary
powers to control all the industries of America. These
plenary powers included absolute authority, derived
from the Executive, over allotment, priority, and fixing
of prices. In fact, it would be hard to find another example of such widespread national control given to any
similar body of men. This marked the culmination of
the uprising of our people, prepared by our national development for stringent national control. And from this
time the coördination of our mobilized industries with
our Army and Navy forces was assured.

As has been stated, this wonderful result was no matter for American complacency — quite the contrary,
when we look back at our faulty execution of its details.
It is rather a cause for solemn thanksgiving, that there

existed in the United States such great national forces to overcome our faults as individuals, and that such strong currents were running to carry everything along in the right direction.

It is outside the scope of this book to give any long account of this mighty effort of the American people, which was behind our Army and Navy in the World War. But, in a naval history of the World War, this brief summary of the forces at work in the United States is needed, in order to show the impelling power which was absolutely necessary for the joint operation of the United States. In truth, this industrial mobilization was as much a part of the naval grand strategy of the World War as any movement of ships, and these activities of the people of the United States were as much a part of the operation of the United States Navy as if each hand engaged in them had been working on board ship.

CHAPTER XII

THE PRODUCTION OF ARMED FORCES

AT the same stage, when the great financial and industrial forces were thus being developed into the strong impelling powers behind the armed forces of the nation, the United States also faced the problem of actually producing these armed forces. This task was of unprecedented magnitude, because, as has been explained, armed forces were to be demanded of the United States in so short a time and on so vast a scale. Concerning these armed forces also, it is another self-evident fact that the development of the military arm must be considered a part of the naval history of the World War, as the United States Army was the weapon which the United States Navy hurled at the enemy. Consequently, from the beginning, the forging of that military weapon was inevitably a most important factor of our great joint operation in the World War.

In the first place, it must be understood that, from the European military point of view, a military impossibility was accomplished, when this American Army was evolved from such small beginnings. Newton D. Baker, the Secretary of War, has quoted Marshal Joffre, when in America with the French Commission in May, 1917, as speaking of our "great army which may some day be as great as 500,000 men." This is notable, because it reflected the most optimistic view that a European soldier could take of our military possibilities. In this country, those who had studied the Civil War came nearer the truth as to our ability to produce armed forces on a large scale. But it cannot be said that any-one, in America or abroad, had at that time an adequate conception of the enormous numbers of American troops which must be called into battle to meet the im-pending crisis of 1918.

At the outset, it would be a good thing to place this before the reader's eye by stating the totals of what can only be called a miracle. At our declaration of war in April, 1917, the United States Army had consisted of 200,000 officers and men. Of these, 133,000 were Regu-lars, 67,000 of the National Guard. At the time peace was forced upon Germany in November, 1918, 2,086,000 officers and men of the United States Army had been transported to Europe. Of these, 1,390,000 had been in active service on the battle line of the menaced Western Front in France. This unusually large proportion was the determining test of the efficiency of the American troops sent overseas. And it was possible to accomplish this extraordinary result solely because the military effort of the United States had culminated in the unex-pected ability of the United States to rush 1,500,000 troops overseas in the crucial six months of 1918. This was in response to the desperate call of the Entente Al-lies, which urged the United States to make a supreme effort to save the war — and this supreme effort must be made then and there, or the World War would be lost.

The ability of the United States to respond by pouring this great stream of troops into France, and thus to pro-vide so strong a reinforcement at the crisis, implied a gathering of our military resources akin to the industrial mobilization which has been described. In truth, it may be said that the underlying cause for success lay in the fact that we had taken pattern from our habit of mind in our industries, and, at the very beginning, instinctively built up great plants for producing our armed manpower on a vast scale. This treatment of our military problem as akin to that of our industries grew from the actual presence in Washington of the leaders from our industries, who had been summoned by the Administration, as explained in the preceding chapter.

These men had grouped around them voluntary associates and assistants, and, even before we went into the war, their presence was felt in every bureau and activity of the War Department. From the day of our entering the war, these men were multiplied and given commissions throughout the War Department, where the influence of their experience in the larger industries of the country was most valuable. It is to the credit of the Army that it was able to coöperate with these men of experience in solving this problem of the vast enlargement of the Army. The result of this coöperation had, from the start, given us the ability to turn out our product of troops on the necessary vast scale, instead of dribbling them into the war, as would have been the case if we had not at once provided these adequate facilities at the source.

The raw material of American manhood for this enormous expansion of our armed forces had been at once assured by the successful operation of conscription, in the form of Selective Service and an appeal to each community, as has been described — and our success was due to the fact that this was so quickly enacted.

One of the fortunate elements of preparation, long before the World War, had been the establishment of an efficient General Staff of the United States Army when

Elihu Root was Secretary of War in 1902. The value of this organization was soon proved in the emergency of 1917. A month before our declaration of war, the Chief of Staff, General Hugh Scott had brought to the Secretary of War the suggestion for the Selective Service form of conscription. Secretary Baker was so converted to the idea that he laid it before President Wilson. After a short explanation, the President had said: "Baker, this is plainly right on any ground. Start to prepare the necessary legislation so that if I am obliged to go to the Congress the bills will be ready for immediate consideration."[1] The Secretary at once called a conference. "In that conference we laid out the main lines of the bill, which was thereafter drawn by General Crowder in more or less conference with us."[2] In this direct and businesslike way was the Selective Service Bill prepared for its immediate and efficient operation.[3]

With this unusual basis secured for our American conscription, there was no trouble in the operation of the Selective Service Act throughout the nation. And this fact furnished striking evidence of the futility of hostile propaganda in the United States, as the German agents concentrated great efforts against the operation of this measure.

Instead of resistance to this law, there was universal acceptance. The men inducted took pride in feeling that they were representing their communities in this service for their country, and their morale was consequently very high. The first registration was on June 5, 1917, of men from 21 to 31. The total of this first registration

[1] Newton D. Baker, Secretary of War.   [2] Ibid.

[3] "The administration of the act under General Crowder was as splendid a piece of executive business as I have ever seen in public or private life." Ibid.

was over 9,500,000. To fix the large numbers eventually at call for service, it is only necessary to state that of the 54,000,000 males in the United States, after the subsequent registrations had been extended to ages from 18 to 45, 26,000,000 were either registered or already in the service of the United States. With these great resources of manhood at command, recruits for the necessary large expansion of the Army were thus available in abundant supply, and our military problem was reduced to the terms of manufacturing this raw material into an army. It had become a problem of training and organization.

But, even with the supply of recruits thus assured, the difficulties of this strenuous task can be summed up by the mere statement that this enlarged United States Army in the World War reached the total of 4,000,000. In this mighty expansion of forces, the Regular Army had been increased to 527,000, the National Guard to 382,000, and the National Army from the Selective Service comprised 3,091,000. It will at once be apparent that the training and organization of these enormous numbers, with the enforced necessity of making soldiers of them in so short a time, was a tremendous problem. In fact, it was unlike anything in the world's history, except our experience in the Civil War when efficient armies were created in a wonderfully short time.

The working basis for the accomplishment of this gigantic undertaking lay in this immediate and business-like grasp of the idea that it was to be on a vast scale, and in following out this idea by promptly starting construction of plants [1] for receiving and training enormous numbers. The country was divided into training areas, and large camps and cantonments of standardized

[1] Authorized May, 1917.

buildings were rapidly established. These reached a capacity for some million and a half men, and by the autumn of 1917 the great task of training and organizing our troops on a large scale was well under way. This was the characteristic American solution of our military problem, by treating it as if it were a question of great manufacturing plants prepared to turn out greatly increased products at need. It was only by these means that we were able to make our numbers available for the crisis of 1918.

Not only was this solution of our military problem similar to that of our industries, but our industries played an important part in making this solution possible, as the average time for constructing the cantonments was only ninety days. The result was, these great plants for the manufacture of soldiers were ready to begin operating in a surprisingly short time.

But war conditions before our entrance, which had given so great a stimulus to our industries, had not been equally stimulating in the direction of military preparedness. Public opinion had moved slowly, and it was not until the United States declared war that we providentially thus began to think in large figures.

There was one notable exception in that period of unformed ideas and unreadiness for the actual measures of military preparation. The trouble with Mexico had put a large part of the United States Army in the field, and this had given the opportunity to mobilize the National Guard on the Mexican border long before we entered the World War. This was of actual practical benefit, as the mobilization had a marked influence on the National Guard, and unquestionably increased the efficiency of this branch of the Army, as was evident when its Federalized units were called into service for the World War.

Another practical benefit, in this period before our entrance, had its origin in the first awakening of public sentiment for a National Defense, which was all too sluggishly taking form in the United States. The so-called "Plattsburg movement" had been given a start, and the first Reserve Officers Training Camps had been established. The results attained at these camps had quickly shown the ability of American young men to profit by a short intensive course in military instruction. They became the successful models for the many Officers Training Camps which were soon organized in the United States. This system of Officers Training Camps became the principal means of supplying the great increase of officers needed for the expansion of our Army. How much they were needed will be apparent from the totals of officers in the United States Army at the declaration of war, Regulars 5,791, National Guard 3,199, compared with the enormous total of 200,000 officers required for our enlarged Army of 4,000,000. Of these 200,000 officers, who held commissions in the United States Army in the World War, one in every six had previous military training in the service, three in every six were from the Officers Training Camps, and two in every six came directly from civil life. It will be evident from these proportions that practically three quarters of the line officers of the enlarged Army came from the Officers Training Camps, as the greater part of the officers from civil life were physicians in the Medical Corps, and the rest comprised men of special business or technical equipment, who were taken into supply services or staff corps. It should be stated here that the physicians all over the country offered their services willingly, and through their generous efforts the Medical Corps of the United States Army made a record of high efficiency, which marked an era in the care of armies.

These were the different elements which were to be fused into an American Army. The process, as in the case of the American industries, was an evolution — not the result of methods prepared in advance. Here again, as had also been the case with our industries, there was a chemistry at work which rescued us from what would have been the natural result of our shortcomings. This brought forth a spirit that redeemed the faults of our sluggish minds and unready hands. For there was a zeal that was intuitive in finding the right means to the end, both for teachers and pupils. By September, 1917, there were already 500,000 under instruction, and the number steadily mounted to the great totals. Through the fall and winter the stream of troops began its steady movement overseas, which grew into the mighty flood of 1918.

The great causes of this achievement lay deep within the national structure of the United States. It was soon shown that the personnel of our new Army possessed unusual adaptability for military service. This had been the object lesson of the Civil War, and it was repeated in the World War, when these new Americans at once proved that they had the same gift for absorbing knowledge with uncanny quickness from contact with trained men. It was in this relation that our Regular Army was an invaluable asset, as it was a highly organized force of picked men, with officers well adapted for instructing their fellow Americans. Their influence was all that Grant described, when he pointed out the marked effect upon the soldiers of the Civil War of the presence of the Regular Officers who had been scattered among their State troops. Grant stated: "The whole loaf was leavened." He was a keen and sound military critic, but this was one of the wisest sentences he ever wrote, as it was to be proved equally applicable to the World War.

This "leaven" was helped in 1917, as it had been in 1861, by the absence of disuniting strata of class distinctions among the American people. With us, teachers and pupils, officers and men, were thinking and speaking in the same terms — and this gave a quicker coördination throughout all ranks. Added to this was the fact that, instead of laying undue stress on formal drill, the doctrine of the United States Army instinctively turned to the fundamental American idea, that intensive drilling in open order fighting was the chief essential that should be taught.

All this tended to cut away the deadwood of nonessentials, and to open shorter paths to military efficiency. As a result, it is no exaggeration to state that in these American camps and cantonments the methods of making armies were revolutionized, in comparison with European military doctrines. But for Americans, it was in fact merely a repetition of the result obtained in the Civil War. This has been reiterated here, as it has only been after the World War that the sound doctrines of the Civil War have been appreciated.

As in the preceding chapter, long details would have been out of place concerning military matters. But, without this summarizing description, the perspective of the picture would have been lacking. This perspective must be kept in mind throughout the ensuing narrative of the expansion of the United States Navy, and the preparation of naval forces to carry out the naval part of our mission in the war — always remembering that these processes of financial, industrial, and military mobilization were component parts with the naval strategy of the United States in the accomplishment of the great undertaking of America.

NOTE AS TO CHAPTER XII

"In the years prior to our entrance into the World War the United States became a highly organized industrial society. The results of invention and scientific research had been accepted by business and industry, and great organizations had come into existence, presided over by men of vision and power. The whole country had caught the impetus of this development and when we went into the war, there surged over Washington not only the unanimous approval of the people, but also the urgent desire of the great masters of business and industry to throw into the national service the experience they had acquired in private pursuits. All this great organizing and constructive talent was eager to serve the country, and our problem was limited to its assimilation rapidly into the mechanism of the Government."

"From a purely institutional point of view, the four fundamental elements of American preparation for the World War were:

1. The establishment of the General Staff by Secretary Root, which was the greatest single contribution to our military efficiency made by any Secretary of War.
2. The establishment of the office of Chief of Operations in the Navy in 1915.
3. The passage of the Federal Reserve Act in 1912.
4. The establishment of the Council of National Defense by act of Congress and the Navy Consulting Board by the Secretary of the Navy. The implications of these two latter establishments were of tremendous importance and practically all that grew up later in the industrial mobilization was the final fruiting of these seeds."

Newton D. Baker, Secretary of War throughout our participation in the World War.

CHAPTER XIII

NAVAL FORCES AT THE ENTRANCE OF THE UNITED STATES

IN the period of the World War before the entrance of the United States, it is true that the naval arm had received more attention in America than the military arm. But the reader should understand at once that this condition did not mean that plans and preparations had been made which would in any degree correspond to the part the United States was destined to play on the sea. In fact, it was absolutely the reverse. The minds of men had not conceived that the World War would sweep away all usual world conditions and mold a new creation, a situation unlike any other in the history of naval warfare, which would enforce undreamt demands upon the naval arm of the United States.

On the other hand, it was natural that public opinion began to be aroused earlier in regard to our naval needs, as the course of the great war made it more and more clear that the United States was a nation which must recognize the necessity for its defense "to be strong upon the seas." This had been the phrase which was emphasized in President Wilson's message to Congress in 1914.

But what followed was a matter of the slow growth of public opinion, and it did not at all keep pace with the onrushing events which were inevitably bringing us into the World War. The American public was only gradually awakened to the need of a naval defense, as Germany broke away from the usages of the seas and encroached upon our rights. There were, however, definite strides taken in 1915, which were of real value in preparing our Navy. A Naval Reserve was constituted, and this was to be the germ of our future great Naval Reserve Force. As has been explained, the Naval Consulting Board had begun its work, which went far ahead of any Army preparations, in actual arrangements with industrial plants to furnish naval material. There was also a most important provision in the Naval Bill of 1915, by which the office of Chief of Naval Operations had been created in the United States Navy.

By this provision the bill had constituted one of the most powerful offices of Chief of Staff in the world, and at one stroke had eliminated an outstanding defect in the organization of the United States Navy. For no other word should be applied to the former system of the different bureaus functioning independently under the Secretary of the Navy, with only advisory functions assigned to the Aide for Operations and the General Board. Under the new act, the Chief of Naval Operations was to be appointed by the President with the consent of the Senate, for a period of four years, and would, "under the direction of the Secretary of the Navy, be charged with the operations of the fleet, and with the preparation and readiness of plans for its use in war."

By this means was created an actual operating office of Chief of Staff, and its value cannot be emphasized too strongly, as the change came at the time when the approaching enlargement of the United States Navy and the extension of its scope of operations were destined to bring about the greatest need in our history for a strong administrative organization.

The *Lusitania* crisis, in May, 1915, as has been stated

in the preceding book of this series, had suddenly changed the whole aspect of the war in the eyes of the United States. The long interval of doubt, before Germany yielded to the United States, had thoroughly aroused the people of our nation to the need of a strong naval defense against aggression. Consequently, even after Germany had given the promise that merchantmen would not be sunk without warning, American public opinion remained aroused to such an extent that the time was propitious to propose, in the naval bill for 1916, the recommendations of the General Board of the United States Navy. These stated: "The Navy of the United States should ultimately be equal to the most powerful maintained by any other nation of the World. It should be gradually increased to this point by such a development, year by year, as may be permitted by the facilities of the country, but the limit above should be attained not later than 1925."

With the urge of popular opinion behind it, Congress passed this naval bill (August 29, 1916) carrying the unprecedented appropriation of $312,678,000, and authorizing the Naval Building Program of 1916, which marked an epoch in the United States Navy. In view of events after the World War, it should be noted here that this was a measure for national defense only, with no hint of imperialistic policies, and incorporated in the measure was a provision for abrogating this program upon any satisfactory international agreement.

In regard to the actual effect of this bill upon the World War, it should also be stated here that its main feature, the construction of capital ships for the Battle Fleet, was held in abeyance. This authorized construction, ten battleships of advanced design and power of armament and six battle cruisers, was promptly begun, but it was not pressed for completion after the declaration of war, as the urgent need of the United States Navy in the World War was for other types. Consequently the efforts of the Navy were concentrated on other construction, especially of destroyers, and these projected capital ships did not influence the World War. On the other hand, this construction of destroyers and other units of light forces was very important, as will be shown.

But, in its other provisions, this act of August 29, 1916, was of great benefit to the Navy. The President was given the authority to increase the Navy in case of emergency to over 100,000 officers and men, the Marine Corps to 17,500. The Naval Reserve was changed to a Naval Reserve Force unlimited in numbers. These provisions gave a basis for the great increase of the personnel of the United States Navy which was to be necessary upon our declaration of war.

All this had received a very marked stimulus at the time of the *Sussex* incident. As has been narrated in the preceding book of this work, the United States had sent an ultimatum to Germany in April, 1916. This had brought us to the verge of war, before Germany capitulated in her note of May 4, 1916. Things had even gone so far as a designated plan for mobilization of the United States Fleet, and the preparatory order for this mobilization at a rendezvous in Chesapeake Bay had been issued April 27, 1916. Consequently, not only had the United States Navy made a great deal of preparation for a war emergency, but many details of administration had been worked out. It was at this time of the tension over the *Sussex* case that arrangements were made for the mobilization of the radio, telegraph, and telephone communications of the United States. The Naval Communication Service was created to prepare these for war, and, as a result, this important Service for coördinating communication could be put into operation the very day that diplomatic relations with Germany were severed in 1917.

In the same way, plans of the General Board had been prepared and provision made for administration in a war emergency. These were brought to a head on March 20, 1917, the day that President Wilson and his Cabinet came to the decision to call Congress into earlier special session on April 2, 1917,[1] and war with Germany had become inevitable. The President's proclamation summoning Congress bore the date of March 21, 1917, and the "confidential mobilization plan" of the United States Navy was of the same date. Upon declaration of war on April 6, 1917, orders were at once sent out for mobilization of the Navy in accordance with this plan.

In the confidential memorandum of the General Board (February 4, 1917), submitted shortly after the break of diplomatic relations with Germany, "to meet a possible condition of war with the Central European Powers," was the following recommendation for an increased personnel in the United States Navy: "Establish additional recruiting stations and increase personnel of the Navy and Marine Corps to the total number required to supply complements for all the ships built, building, and authorized, and to maintain shore establishments and naval defense districts, including aviation service, with 10 per cent additional for casualties as follows: Enlisted force — Navy, 150,000; Marines, 30,000;

[1] The original date for the Special Session had been April 16.

officers in the proportion prescribed by law." After the decision of March 20, through the authority granted by Congress to the President, a campaign of recruiting for this increase of the Navy was begun throughout the country.

The same memorandum had recommended that the American Battle Fleet should be mobilized in the Lower Chesapeake. At this time of the diplomatic break, the Atlantic Fleet under Admiral H. T. Mayo had been at practice off Guantanamo, Cuba. It was at once ordered to the Gulf of Guacanayabo on the southern coast of Cuba, a large bay with easily defended entrances. This was used as a base until the Fleet was ordered north on March 20. At the declaration of war the Fleet was mobilized at the Yorktown base in the Chesapeake, as a Battle Fleet prepared for action with all its auxiliaries.

At the beginning of March, 1917, Congress had voted an emergency fund of $100,000,000 for the Navy, which had made it possible to order guns, ammunition, depth charges and all sorts of material which began to be delivered for use in April and May.

On March 12 the President had by executive authority ordered the arming of American merchantmen. This measure had been contemplated for some time, and the United States Navy had assembled guns and gun crews for this purpose. But it had been delayed by a filibuster in Congress, and could only be put into operation by executive authority. As guns and gun crews had thus been made ready, it was possible to go ahead at once with the installation of guns for defense on board merchantmen.

Preparations had also been made to follow out the recommendation of the General Board: "Establish immediately the guards at all navy yards, magazines, radio stations, powder factories, munition plants, bases, shipbuilding yards, and naval store utilities in accordance with the mobilization plans." In this way these important adjuncts of naval operations were at an early date safeguarded from damage. The other means of security advised, nets and obstructions to protect naval bases and ports, had also been provided. And a patrol of the coast was built up from the existing patrols, which had been constituted to preserve the neutrality of our waters, including the Coast Guard and Lighthouse service.

These precautions also covered our outlying possessions which might be exposed to enemy attacks. The most important of these was the Panama Canal Zone, and there the guards were doubled, with special protection for the canal.

The foregoing summarized the preparations of the United States Navy, and unquestionably these preparations were of great benefit for what was to come. But there can also be no question of the fact that all this was not, for practical purposes, even a beginning of what must be undertaken to carry out the future exacting tasks of the United States Navy, in order to accomplish our main naval object in the World War. In all these prewar plans and preparations there was not a trace of the main object for the United States Navy, which was to provide the motive power of the great joint naval and military offensive operation of the United States.

There has been much misunderstanding in this regard, but an unbiased review of the actual naval conditions abroad at this stage will give the reasons for our actual situation at the time of entering the war, which has been too often judged in the light of the knowledge of ensuing events. As will be evident to any reader of this work, British naval policy had been defensive from the first of the war. Undoubtedly great results had been accomplished by defending the established naval supremacy. But there had been a lack of offensive counters against the enemy, and even the fight against the U-boat was defensive at the time of our entering the war. The convoy system, which brought about an offensive against the U-boat, had not yet found favor. All naval information from abroad, and it is obvious that all data to work upon must come from abroad, reflected this situation. Consequently, although the trend of mind of the United States Navy and of the Administration was for offensive use of naval forces, there was nothing in sight but this general defensive situation abroad. Not an inkling of our future vast offensive undertaking, so different from anything in the past, had so far been revealed. As a result, it was natural that the mobilization of the United States Navy should follow the usual formulas, with our Battle Fleet assembled at our principal base. In this sense of the word, and for the reasons that have been given, the United States Navy was in a much better state of preparation than was realized at the time.

This gave a good foundation for the development of the future huge increase of our naval forces. But we must realize that the actual plans and preparations for the new and all-important offensive of the United States were not made until after the curtain had been raised for another and different act of the great dramas, as will be described in the following chapters.

CHAPTER XIV

THE NEW CALL UPON THE UNITED
STATES NAVY

IT will be clear from the foregoing that the mobilization of the United States Navy included concentrating, at our main base in Chesapeake waters, our Battle Fleet intact with its attendant destroyers, submarines, and train. Yet the very first demand for our naval forces in the World War put an end to that idea. This first demand upon the United States Navy was the urgent call for American destroyers to be sent abroad, as has been described, to take part in the fight against the U-boats. There was no prewar plan to send any American destroyers abroad. In fact, up to the time British representatives in our country gave information of the exact situation, particularly as to the submarine successes, there had been very little to go on, very little data upon which to base any definite plans. But, upon our entering the war, the true situation was revealed, and the pressing need for anti-submarine forces was shown at a conference with the naval representatives of the Entente Allies (April 10, 1917).

This critical situation abroad, and its necessities, with the circumstances of the arrival of the American destroyers overseas, have been described. But this sudden revelation to America had at once shown the need for a new departure in our naval strategy. The representations of the Allied naval officers were soon confirmed by Admiral Sims' first report of the situation from London,[1] in which he recommended "maximum number of destroyers to be sent, accompanied by small anti-submarine craft."

Sending the American destroyers overseas had at first seemed a radical step to some of the more conservative officers of the navy, who were wedded to the idea of the Battle Fleet in being. For the very act of stripping the Atlantic Fleet of its destroyers, as a matter of fact, stripped it of its organization as a Battle Fleet in being. But the necessities of the case brought drastic action, and the decision was made to take away American destroyers from the Battle Fleet and send them abroad for anti-submarine work with the British Navy.

The orders to this effect were promptly given, but, as has been stated, there were delays in getting the destroyers overseas,[2] These delays were caused by the time required to prepare them for their new special mission overseas. The American destroyers were ready for service in the sense of being prepared for duty with our Battle Fleet, but the sudden call to send them overseas was an entirely different matter. Consequently, fitting them out for this special service away from the Battle Fleet meant a great deal of time in special preparation at the navy yards before the successive divisions of destroyers could get across. And, at the height of the U-boat ravages, these delays must be measured by the heavy losses of shipping.

However, as has also been stated, it is a matter of record that the eventual presence of 34 American de-

---

[1] This first cable from London was sent April 14, 1917.

[2] The instructions to Commander Taussig, in command of the first division of six destroyers sent overseas, were dated April 14, 1917. They sailed April 24, 1917.

stroyers in British waters in July, 1917,[1] was the deciding factor to clinch the matter of the convoy system,
which then hung in the balance.

As a result of this revelation of the true naval situation abroad, and after this first call for naval forces to be
sent overseas, there followed a changed conception of
our naval aims, and the Navy turned to a new point of
view, of which the principal object was the building up
of the greatest possible anti-submarine forces, consisting
of destroyers and other anti-submarine craft abroad,
and Naval District coast defense at home. This included turning out as many new destroyers and submarine chasers as the country could build. At a conference in February, 1917, the decision had been made to
concentrate the efforts of the steel shipbuilding facilities
of the country upon the production of destroyer type of
new construction, and to use the available wood shipbuilding yards for the largest type of submarine chaser
which could be built of wood and propelled by gasoline
engines.

The wisdom of the decision to devote the steel shipbuilding yards to the production of destroyers had been
at once confirmed by the necessities of the new situation,
and a program for building 250 destroyers was adopted
in May, 1917. This was made operative in June, and the
construction of these destroyers was pushed to completion as rapidly as possible.

The use of the wood shipbuilding yards produced the
110 ft. submarine chasers with three gasoline engines.
These were successful boats, large enough to be sea-
worthy and to cross the ocean under their own power,

---

[1] ". . . providing that eleven American destroyers continue to be available." — Mem. of First Sea Lord, July, 1917.

and able to stay at sea for long periods. Their plans were ready in March; contracts for them were let to more than a score of shipbuilding plants in April and early May; and the first deliveries began in June, 1917 — a very wonderful record. Some 400 of these were built, and many of them were sent overseas. They were especially welcomed by the French and Italians, and their best services were on approaches to French ports and in the Mediterranean and Adriatic. But it must be understood that they were no great factor in the anti-U-boat fight, in comparison with the services of the destroyers.

Sending the American destroyers overseas, and the change to anti-submarine operations, necessarily implied the reduction of the Battle Fleet. The dreadnought battleships were conserved as a potential reinforcement for the British Grand Fleet, but many units of the Atlantic Fleet were destined to various services of anti-submarine work, convoying, and becoming training schools on a large scale. This last use of the ships of the Atlantic Fleet was of special value, in view of the greatly enlarged personnel which was pouring into the United States Navy. By these means the new recruits were being brought quickly into contact with the experienced personnel of the Navy, and were adapting themselves to their duties with astonishing quickness. A good beginning, for obtaining the great number of necessary additional officers, had been made at the "Naval Plattsburg," held on a division of the reserve battleships in the summer of 1916. Of 2000 young men who received this naval instruction the great majority became officers of the United States Navy after our declaration of war.

As has been shown, the share of the United States in the fight against the U-boats was of great importance.

The necessity was urgent, and this must be considered an immediate and essential objective of the United States Navy in the World War. Moreover, in addition to the physical effect upon the situation, the act of sending the American destroyers overseas exerted two definite influences upon the existing naval policies of the Entente Allies. First, the presence of the American destroyers was something tangible, which assured them that America would take its part in the naval war. Secondly, the presence of the American destroyers was the factor which brought about the general use of the convoy system, as has been stated.

These results should be scored to the credit of our first effort in providing a naval reinforcement for the Entente Allies. But the one outstanding principal mission of the United States Navy, in order to play its necessary part in providing a military reinforcement for the armies of the Entente Allies at the crisis of the World War, was not yet in evidence. It can be stated positively that, neither before our entering the war nor upon our entrance, did the United States Navy, the United States Army, or the United States Administration, have any adequate conception of the vast scope of this main American objective, and of the gigantic naval operation which was to be our Navy's component part.

But this was not surprising, as the Entente Allies themselves had no conception of the greatness of the danger that was impending. The giant shape was still hidden, and, as it was to be a military danger, it could only be revealed to the Navy through the military information obtained by the Administration. Most fortunately, as will be narrated, the Administration was able to obtain military information that leapt far ahead of that possessed by the Entente Allies. For the President and the Secretary of War, there was thus a gradual enlightenment as to numbers of the military reinforcement which must be given to the Entente Allies, and providentially this grew to a realization that a military reinforcement must be furnished on a vast scale or the war would be lost. Consequently, our main naval strategy must be dictated by the Civil and Military authorities. There must be a mighty American Army on the Western Front. This Army could only be delivered on the Western Front by the coöperation of the United States Navy. Upon its delivery depended the fate of the war. Consequently, all other naval undertakings were of minor importance, and the safeguarded transportation of this American Army and its supplies became the main task of Naval Operations. This summarizes the development of our naval strategy to meet the new development of the World War.

As has been stated, all this was an evolution and not the result of prepared plans. The ensuing situation was so surprising in its overturn of previous ideas that it went beyond all prophesies. It is true that the Allied missions to this country had given the first information of the straits of the Entente Allies, but they had not given any adequate warning of the storm that was rolling up beyond the horizon — for they themselves had no conception of it. To the President and the Secretary of War must be given the credit of going far beyond any information of the Allies, and the following narrative will show how this military information was obtained, which inexorably dictated our naval strategy in the World War.

It had become obvious that an American Expeditionary Force must be sent overseas, although the emissa-

ries of the Entente Allies had not at all grasped the
future size of that force.[1] But, as a result of these conferences, the far seeing determination was made to
select the future commander with his staff, and to send
him overseas in advance, to study on the ground the
whole program of our military coöperation. Another
very wise decision, although of course at this time the
size of the American effort could not be estimated, was
the determination to cast the operation of the Selective
Service upon such a comprehensive scale that it would
work with any size military effort that we might be
called upon to make. This has been described in a preceding chapter.

These two measures may be called the foundations of
the success of our effort. General John J. Pershing was
the choice of the War Department for Commander-in-
Chief of the American Expeditionary Forces. He proceeded at once to France with his Staff, and immediately
upon his arrival began to work out the plans and scale
of American coöperation. It should be here stated, at
the outset, that General Pershing and his Staff from the
very start foresaw more clearly than did the French and
British how great a reinforcement would be demanded
from America.

General Pershing's military vision was in this respect
prophetic of his later able conduct of affairs, as his military information to Washington and his initial plans
were so much more comprehensive of the approaching

[1] "Joffre, in an interview with the Secretary of War in May, 1917, said
that he thought 400,000 would be our limit, and that one French port would
be sufficient to receive them.   How amazed he would have been could he
have looked into the crystal and seen what this country transported to France
in men and material during the eighteen months." — Admiral Gleaves, "A
History of the Transport Service."

crisis than were the military forecasts of the leaders of the Entente Allies, that every aspect of our effort was constantly expanding in response. These broadening views, conceived by General Pershing and his Staff, as to the vast scope of our operation, were confirmed and aided by the great number of American business men from our industries, who were actually on duty with the War Department or were working with the Administration, as has been described.

In this respect, the services of these men from civil life were most valuable, because, both from their training in affairs on a large scale and from their knowledge of European conditions, they were able to foresee the possibility of our effort being required on an unprecedented scale. Consequently, their views were of much assistance to the General Staff, with which they were in contact, for casting military plans upon a basis that would permit expansion, as our program of the necessary reinforcement for the Entente Allies grew into large proportions.

With these elements at work, to stimulate the Administration and the War Department to a conception of the vast scope of the future military task of the United States, the ever growing demands of this military task produced corresponding demands upon the United States Navy. And the response to these military demands was an effort on the part of the United States Navy which attained the full measure of our military necessities, and our main naval strategy became the motive power of our full grown military effort.

CHAPTER XV

THE DEVELOPMENT OF AMERICAN STRATEGY

THE policy of the Administration and the wisdom of the Secretary of War, in sending General Pershing and his staff so soon to France, had been quickly rewarded by practical results, which molded our naval policy into its right form. General Pershing had assumed the duties of his office as Commander-in-Chief of the American Expeditionary Forces on May 26, 1917. He had sailed for Europe on May 28, was in London on June 9, and, after spending some days in consultation with the British authorities, had reached Paris on June 13.

He had arrived on the ground at just the right time to estimate the situation in France after the failures of the Entente Allies in their attacks upon the German lines on the Western Front. The effect of these reverses upon the morale of the Allies had been very serious. The French had placed great hopes upon the over-confident plans of General Nivelle, and their complete defeat had brought about an actual crisis in France. General Pershing in his Report thus described the situation.

"The relatively low strength of the German forces on the Western Front led the Allies with much confidence to attempt a decision on this front: but the losses were very heavy and the effort signally failed. The failure caused a serious reaction especially on French morale, both in the army and throughout the country, and attempts to carry out extensive or combined operations were indefinitely suspended. . . . Allied resources in manpower at home were low and there was little prospect of materially increasing their armed strength, even in the face of the probability of having practically the whole military strength of the Central Powers against them in the spring of 1918."

"This was the state of affairs that existed when we entered the war. While our action gave the Allies much encouragement yet this was temporary, and a review of conditions made it apparent that America must make a supreme material effort as soon as possible. After duly considering the tonnage possibilities, I cabled the following to Washington on July 6, 1917: 'Plans should contemplate sending over at least 1,000,000 men by next May.'"

"A general organization project, covering as far as possible the personnel of all combat, staff, and administrative units, was forwarded to Washington on July 11. This was prepared by the Operations Section of my staff and adopted in joint conference with the War Department Committee then in France. It embodied my conclusions on the military organization and effort required of America after a careful study of French and British experience. In forwarding this project I stated: 'It is evident that a force of about 1,000,000 men is the smallest unit which in modern war will be a complete, well-balanced, and independent fighting organization. However, it must be equally clear that the adoption of this size force as a basis of study should not be construed as representing the maximum force which should be sent or which will be needed in France. It is taken as the force which may be expected to reach France in time for an offensive in 1918, and as a unit and basis of organization. Plans for the future should be based, especially in reference to the manufacture of artillery, aviation, and other material, on three times this force — i. e., at least 3,000,000 men.'"

Thus early, and far ahead of all European conceptions, was the Administration at Washington given the vast scale of the necessary American reinforcement, and, as a result, the American effort, industrial, military, and naval, was being cast in this mold. This great effort was soon given its corollary program, of which the naval part was so important.

To quote again from General Pershing's report: "While this general organization project provided certain Services of Supply troops, which were an integral part of the larger combat units, it did not include the great body of troops and services required to maintain an army overseas. To disembark 2,000,000 men, move them to the training areas, shelter them, handle and store the quantities of supplies and equipment they required, called for an extraordinary and immediate effort in construction. To provide the organization for this purpose a project for engineer services of the rear, including railways, was cabled to Washington August 5, 1917, followed on September 18, 1917, by a complete service of the rear project, which listed item by item the troops considered necessary for the Services of Supply."

"In order that the War Department might have a clear-cut program to follow in the shipment of personnel and material to insure the gradual building up of a force at all times balanced and symmetrical, a comprehensive statement was prepared covering the order in which the troops and services enumerated in these two projects should arrive. This schedule of priority of shipments, forwarded to the War Department on October 7, divided the initial force called for by the two projects into six phases corresponding to combatant corps of six divisions each."

"The importance of the three documents, the general organization project, the service of rear project, and the schedule of priority of shipments should be emphasized, because they formed the basic plan for providing an army in France together with its material for combat and supply."

The dependence of this whole enormous scheme of operations upon the naval part of its program has been most vividly set forth in another paragraph of General Pershing's Report. Whole volumes could not depict the fundamental necessity of the naval factor more clearly than the following: "For all practical purposes the American Expeditionary Forces were based on the American Continent. Three thousand miles of ocean to cross with the growing submarine menace confronting us, the quantity of ship tonnage that would be available then unknown and a line of communications by land 400 miles long from French ports to our probable front presented difficulties that seemed almost insurmountable as compared with those of the Allies."

The reader must realize all that this implied from the naval point of view. It meant an undertaking of a magnitude without parallel in all history, and the statement of its difficulties, in comparison with the problems of the Entente Allies, has become merely a matter of fact. In view of the event, it should be reiterated here that an impossibility [1] was accomplished, according to all former

[1] Admiral Gleaves has quoted Admiral Beresford as saying (July 19, 1917), "I am also distressed at the fact that it appears to me to be impossible to pro-

ideas, when the United States achieved its mission in the World War. But, at this stage, the main naval object of the United States had become defined beyond any misunderstanding. Our effort must be a military reinforcement on a large scale for the Western Front. There was no purely naval operation in sight that could possibly have an equal effect upon the course of the World War. Consequently, the United States Navy must forego all its hopes of taking part in a decisive naval operation fought on the seas, but, instead, must devote its energies to pushing home the military weapon. Admiral William V. Pratt, who was Assistant Chief of Operations in the World War, has very ably expressed this changed function which the exigencies of the World War imposed upon the United States Navy: "Our total effort in the war consisted less in the operations of forces at the front than in a logistic effort on the rear, in which the greatest problems we had to contend with originated and had to be solved here at home. It must be noted that in this war the main united effort was one of logistics." This was repeating in naval parlance what was meant by General Pershing's statement that the American effort was "based on the American Continent" — with the result that the naval share must be the motive power behind the necessary military force.

Most fortunately, in the solution of the great problem by the Administration at Washington, there was no hysterical hurrying of driblets of troops abroad, which would have actually delayed the flood that was needed. The great plants for producing the fighting men were

vide enough ships to bring the American Army over in hundreds of thousands to France, and, after they are brought over, to supply the enormous amount of shipping which will be required to keep them full up with munition, food, and equipment."

first put into operation, and then the corresponding terminals and forwarding facilities for handling the product abroad were put into operation, as will be narrated. In this way only could the enormous volume of troops have been delivered on the fighting front in France.

But there was one notable exception for very good reasons. While on his mission to the United States, Marshal Joffre had made a special request "that an American combat division should be sent at once to Europe as a visual evidence of our purpose to participate actively in the war." [1] This was held to be of so great importance, as a stimulus to the morale of the French, at the time of great depression in consequence of their military failure, that the First Division was formed of regular regiments and ordered overseas. The transportation of these first fighting troops overseas was the beginning of the new and vital function of the United States Navy in the World War, and an account of it will be given in the following chapter.

[1] General Pershing's Report.

CHAPTER XVI

THE FIRST TRANSPORTATION OF AMERICAN
TROOPS OVERSEAS

THE beginning of the "great adventure," from which was evolved the decisive result of Sea Power bringing to the battlefield on the Western Front the American reinforcement, sprang from the necessity of sending at once to France the advance force of American fighting men, as a stimulus to the failing morale of the Entente Allies. The command of this first transportation operation of the United States Navy was assigned to Rear Admiral Albert Gleaves, who had been in command of the Destroyer Force of the United States Atlantic Fleet. On May 23, 1917, Admiral Gleaves was summoned to Washington, and on May 29 received his formal orders designating him Commander of Convoy Operations in the Atlantic. In his flagship U. S. S. *Seattle*, an armored cruiser, he proceeded at once to New York to expedite preparations for this first expedition to France.

The regular transports of the Army could not be used, as they "were not suitable and ready for trans-Atlantic convoy operations." [1] The United States Navy had only three vessels available for transport work with this expedition, *Hancock, Henderson, De Kalb*. It was typical of the unexpected course of the World War that the *De Kalb* should be the *Prinz Eitel Friedrich*, the German converted auxiliary cruiser, of which the checkered

[1] Admiral Gleaves, "A History of the Transport Service, 1917–1919."

career has been narrated in the preceding books of this work. After sharing the adventures of Admiral Spee's Squadron, and after having been left behind in South American waters to play her last part by deceiving the British as to Admiral Spee's departure, she had come north to internment in an American port — only to be seized by the new enemy of Germany, and re-christened for making war against Germany. As the *De Kalb*, she not only was a useful troop ship, but was also an able vessel for escort duty with the convoys.

As only these three vessels of the Navy were available, "it was necessary to commandeer such ocean-going vessels as could be found and alter them as quickly as possible for carrying troops." [1] The following table shows from what varied sources were collected the extemporized troopships at this sudden emergency:

Name	Gross Tonnage	Line
Saratoga	6,391	N. Y. & Cuba Mail S. S. Co. (Mail Steamer)
Havana	6,991	N. Y. & Cuba Mail S. S. Co. (Mail Steamer)
Tenadores	7,782	Tenadores S. S. Co. (United Fruit Co. Line)
Pastores	7,781	Pastores S. S. Corp. (United Fruit Co. Line)
Momus	6,878	Southern Pacific Co.
Antilles	6,878	Southern Pacific Co.
Lenape	5,179	Clyde S. S. Co.
Mallory	6,063	Mallory S. S. Co.
Finland	12,229	International Merchantile Marine
San Jacinto	6,069	Mallory S. S. Co.
Montanan	6,659	American S. S. Co. (Cargo Carrier)
Dakotan	6,657	American and Hawaiian S. S. Co.
Edward Luckenbach	2,730	Luckenbach S. S. Co. (Cargo Carrier)
El Occidente	6,008	Southern Pacific Co. (Cargo Carrier)

[1] Admiral Gleaves.

It is no wonder Admiral Gleaves stated that "the somewhat motley assemblage of ships finally gathered together for the first expedition did not long survive the duty imposed upon them." And his additional comment vividly depicted the situation: "Looking back to the first expedition of June 1917, it seems indeed that the hand of Providence must have been held over these 'arks' or the task never could have been accomplished. Who would have dreamed at that time that we were laying the foundation of the greatest transport fleet in history?" This last has actually become a matter of naval history, for, from that "motley assemblage" grew the Cruiser and Transport Force of the United States Navy — and it was symbolical of this unprecedented growth that the designation "U. S. S. *Seattle*" was destined to become not only that of the ship which remained Admiral Gleaves' flagship, but also the letterhead of a tall office building in Hoboken. Throughout the "decks" of this building were to be distributed the administrative offices developed from a flagship staff, and from its "bridge" on the high roof were to be directed the movements of many transports laden with the armed manhood of the United States.

The original date set for the departure of the first convoy of transports was June 9, 1917. But Admiral Gleaves changed the sailing to June 14, "not without consideration of the phase of the moon as affecting night submarine attack at the expected time of arrival off the French Coast." [1] The expedition started to sail from New York on June 14, 1917, in a thick fog. The craft were divided into four convoy groups on the commonsense basis of speed. Group I proceeded at 15 knots;

[1] Admiral Gleaves.

Group II at 14 knots; Group III at 13 knots; Group IV at 11 knots. As Admiral Gleaves very clearly explained: "The groups sailed at intervals of two hours from Ambrose Channel Lightship, except Group IV, which was held by the Department twenty-four hours for belated dispatches and stores. As has been stated, Group I was the fastest, Group IV the slowest, and their departure was timed to avoid congestion at the eastern terminus. It is obvious that, as the expedition advanced, the intervals between the groups opened out, thus increasing the difficulties of submarines lying in wait to attack."

Each of the four groups was provided with a very strong escort, in proportion to the number of transports.[1] Group I of four troopships was led by Admiral Gleaves in the *Seattle* with the *De Kalb* and three destroyers. The converted yacht *Corsair* had also started with this group, but poor firing service had obliged her to fall back to Group II, and she was replaced by the destroyer *Fanning*. The other groups were protected in a similar way by the escort of cruisers with auxiliaries and destroyers. For the destroyers, the oil tanker *Maumee* had sailed from Boston, a few days before the expedition left New York, to a secret rendezvous on the route of the convoys, in order that the destroyers might refuel at sea.

"Oiling at sea was one of the manoeuvres which had been developed in the Destroyer Force three months before the war. A division of destroyers had been oiled en route to Queenstown at the rate of 35,000 gallons per hour in a moderate sea, and with the wind blowing a half gale. Without the ability to oil at sea, the destroyers would have had to be towed and the eastward move-

---

[1] The organization of the various groups is given in full at the end of this chapter.

ment correspondingly delayed. Only the newest destroyers, those which could get over to the other side by
one refueling, were designated to go all the way across, [1]
while the old boats, the short-legged fellows, as they
were called, went only half way or as far as their oil
could carry them, and then returned to New York, or in
case of necessity called at St. Johns or Halifax, and as a
rule they had to steam against strong headwinds on the
way back." [2]

Admiral Gleaves' description of the special precautions taken as to these groups of troop ships should also
be carefully studied, as giving the basis of the future
success of the great movement of American troops overseas.

"The work of converting the requisitioned cargo
ships was pressed to the utmost. They were armed with
guns, fitted with lookout stations, a communication system and troop berthing accommodations. The method
of commissary supply and messing was worked out and
the sanitation of the ships improved as far as possible.
Life belts were supplied in a quantity of 10 per cent in
excess of the number of passengers carried. Special measures were taken to protect life in case of casualty, and
sufficient rafts were provided so that if life boats on one
side could not be launched, because of the listing of the
ship or other reason, all hands could still be accom-
modated. Attention was given to the paramount necessity of landing the troops in good health and in good
spirits."

[1] Of the thirteen destroyers with this first expedition, the following were
listed as having gone all the way across: *Wilkes, Fanning, Burrows, Allen,
Shaw, Ammen, Parker.*

[2] Admiral Gleaves.

"The instructions issued to all ships were, in brief, as follows, and every man had to be as familiar with them as with the Lord's Prayer:

1. The use of maximum speed through the danger zone.

2. Trained lookout watches made effective by an efficient system of communication between officers of the deck and fire control watch.

3. Continuous alert gun watches in quick communication with lookouts through the fire control officer.

4. Constant zigzagging.

5. Minimum use of radio; reduction of smoke to a minimum; darkening of ships at night; throwing nothing overboard lest it point to a trail.

6. A trained officer always alert and ready to use the helm to avoid torpedoes.

7. Special prearranged day and night signals between ships on manner of manoeuvring when submarines were sighted.

8. Use of guns and depth bombs by all transport and escort vessels."

"In addition, it was directed that Abandon Ship drills be held daily; that in the danger zone at daybreak and twilight, the hours most favorable to submarine attack, troops be assembled at Abandon Ship Stations fully equipped and prepared to leave the ship; that water-tight doors always be kept closed; that all communication pipes and ventilators be kept closed as much as possible; that the water-tight bulkheads be frequently examined — in short, that everything possible be done first, to guard against disaster, and second to save the ship and to save life if mined or torpedoed."

These terse sentences, from the able officer who com-

manded the first expedition, have in themselves painted
a vivid picture of the new conditions on the seas, and
this picture was destined to remain a true portrayal of
the difficulties and dangers to be encountered throughout the successful operations of Admiral Gleaves vastly
enlarged command. No one can help seeing that such
infinite painstaking, in thoughtful preparation in advance, must inevitably gain results of efficiency in the
trying service which was to ensue. In this respect, the
mere narrative of the American transport service will be
sufficient testimony of the value of a good command and
a good organization from the very start.

In Admiral Gleaves' secret order before leaving New
York it was stated: "Reports of enemy submarine activity indicate that the area of greatest activity is East
of longitude twenty West, and within a circle radius five
hundred miles from Fayal, Azores." On the passage
across the Atlantic the groups had moved undisturbed,
until, as Admiral Gleaves has stated, "at 10.15 P.M.
June 22nd, in Latitude 48° 00' N., Longitude 25° 50'
West, the first group was attacked by enemy submarines." This was when Group I was crossing the line
from North Ireland to the Azores. The lookouts on the
Seattle, which was ahead and to starboard of the troopships, reported "sighting in the extremely phosphores-
cent water the wake of a submarine crossing our bow
from starboard to port toward the convoy." [1] Simul-
taneously the *De Kalb*, ahead and to port of the troopships, sighted two torpedo wakes, one ahead and one
astern, and opened fire. Admiral Gleaves has stated
that two torpedoes passed close to the troopship *Havana*,
and that Captain Gherardi of the *De Kalb* "handled his

[1] Admiral Gleaves.

ship to perfection and disaster was avoided." "The ships of the right and left columns of the convoy turned to starboard and port, respectively, and ran at full speed as per instructions. There were no torpedo hits and no evidence of injury to the enemy. The convoy reformed at daylight and proceeded on its course." [1] Group I was met by American destroyers from Queenstown in the afternoon of June 24 at an appointed rendezvous.[2] The next day this group met the French escort of two small destroyers. There was no further attack, as this group moved toward port.

Admiral Gleaves has stated that Group II was attacked as follows: "The second group encountered two submarines, the first at 11.50 A.M. 26th of June in Latitude 47° 01' N. and Longitude 6° 28' W., about 100 miles off the French coast, and the second two hours later. The group was under escort of six additional American destroyers at the time. Both submarines were successfully evaded, and the destroyer *Cummings*, when sighting the second submarine, headed for it at twenty-five knots. The submarine immediately submerged and the periscope was lost to view, but the course of the submarine was plainly disclosed by a wake of bubbles. The *Cummings* passed about twenty-five yards ahead of this wake and dropped a depth bomb, the explosion of which was followed by the appearance of several pieces of lumber, oil, bubbles and débris upon the surface. There was no further evidence of the submarine, and if not destroyed, it is probable that it was at least badly damaged. Commander Neil, who made the counter attack

[1] Admiral Gleaves.

[2] "We had joined up with them on time at the appointed rendezvous, which was a good piece of navigation on both sides." — Admiral Gleaves.

on the submarine in the *Cummings*, was decorated by the British Government for this exploit."

Admiral Gleaves has stated that Group IV was attacked (June 28) and that the commanding officer of the *Edward Luckenbach* reported: "About 10.30 A.M., this vessel was attacked by a submarine, and one torpedo was seen to pass within about 50 yards of the *Luckenbach*. The course of the ship had just been changed by the Commanding Officer to avoid this torpedo, and the torpedo was seen to come to the surface in the wake of the *Luckenbach* at the point where the change of course took place." Admiral Gleaves has also stated that, at this time, the German U-boat was under fire from U.S.S. *Kanawha*, one of the two armed colliers with the expedition. Of the *Kanawha's* gunfire Admiral Gleaves wrote, after describing its accuracy: "It may well be that those shots so confused the aim of the submarine as to cause her torpedoes to miss." This was playing a rôle far removed from the usually accepted peaceful task of a collier.

There were no other attacks encountered on the passage. All the three slower groups had been met by additional American destroyers at appointed rendezvous, as had been the case of Group I, and all four groups arrived at the small port of St. Nazaire, without any loss. The last to arrive, Group IV, came into port July 2. In France all ostensible preparations had been made with the idea of giving the impression that the convoy groups were to come into Brest, the natural point of disembarkation instead of the small and ill adapted harbor of St. Nazaire. This was undoubtedly a very wise precaution, as it is now known that the Germans at the time had laid many mines off Brest. In fact the French cruiser

Kleber was there sunk [1] by one of these mines, and the inconveniences of disembarking and unloading at St. Nazaire were well worth enduring, in view of the comparative safety.

By this well conceived and well conducted naval operation the first step was taken on the path to the battlefield of France. There was no question of the fact that the actual appearance of American troops in Paris was a great stimulus to French morale, and the request from General Joffre that they should be hurried to France was justified by this result.[2] But it was also a stimulus for us, in our great task, to have this proof that it was feasible to span the Atlantic. In this regard, it should be emphasized that, if the first venture of transporting American troops overseas had met disaster, there would have been a widespread deterrent effect upon our nation, as losses in the first expedition would have confirmed the opinions of the many who thought such transportation of American troops to Europe impossible under the circumstances. But the complete success of the undertaking was also a complete refutation of these pessimistic prophesies, and, from this time on, it was a settled thing that American troops were to be sent overseas in great numbers.

At this time there had also been begun naval preparations for safeguarding the arrival of our troopships in the waters adjacent to France. On June 9 there had sailed from New York a squadron of six converted

---

[1] The French cruiser *Kleber*, 7,700 tons, was sunk by a mine in the Loire June 27, 1917.

[2] "The arrival of the First Division and the parade of certain of its elements in Paris on July 4 caused great enthusiasm and for the time being French morale was stimulated." — General Pershing, Report.

yachts,[1] which were to be the nucleus of a special American naval force, U. S. Patrol Squadrons Operating in European Waters. This force was at first commanded by Rear Admiral William B. Fletcher, who was succeeded on November 1, 1917, by Rear Admiral Henry B. Wilson, who remained in command through the rest of the war. From this beginning, grew an important element in American operations overseas. Brest was the headquarters of this force, and it remained a separate American command to the end. Admiral Sims has described it as "a force which was ultimately larger than the one we maintained at Queenstown; at the height of the troop movement it comprised about 36 destroyers, 12 yachts, 3 tenders, and several minesweepers and tugs." As will be evident in the ensuing narrative of the great movement of American troops, this patrol of the waters about the American bases was an essential factor in the operation.

[1] *Noma, Vedette, Christobel, Kanawha, Harvard, Sultana.*

ORGANIZATION OF THE FIRST EXPEDITION

Convoy Group I

Train Troopships	Escort
Saratoga...........	Armored Cruiser, *Seattle* (Flag)
Havana............	Auxiliary Cruiser, *De Kalb*
Tenadores..........	Converted Yacht, *Corsair*
Pastores...........	Destroyers, *Wilkes, Terry, Roe*

Convoying Group II

Train Troopships	Escort
Momus............	Scout Cruiser, *Birmingham*
Antilles...........	Converted Yacht, *Aphrodite*
Lenape............	Destroyers, *Fanning, Burrows, Lamson*

Convoy Group III

Train Troopships	Escort
Mallory...........	Cruiser, *Charleston*
Finland...........	Armed Collier, *Cyclops*
San Jacinto.......	Destroyers, *Allen, McCall, Preston*

Convoy Group IV

Train Troopships	Escort
Montanan	Cruiser, *St. Louis*
Dakotan..........	Cruiser Transport, *Hancock*
El Occidente.......	Armed Collier, *Kanawha*
E. Luckenbach......	Destroyers, *Shaw, Ammen, Flusser, Parker*

CHAPTER XVII

AMERICAN PREPARATIONS OVERSEAS

(See Map at page 148)

IN addition to the First Division of American troops sent overseas in these first convoy groups, General Pershing's immediate plans also comprised a call for "nine newly organized regiments of Engineers." [1] This was in accordance with the vast service of the rear project, which has been described. It will be obvious that, before developing plans for the American line of communications, it would be necessary to decide upon the sector of American operations on the Western Front. This area of future American operation was determined in advance, and General Pershing's statement of the case was most clear and convincing.

"Our mission was offensive and it was essential to make plans for striking the enemy where a definite military decision could be gained. While the Allied Armies had endeavored to maintain the offensive, the British, in order to guard the Channel ports, were committed to operations in Flanders and the French to the portion of the front protecting Paris. Both lacked troops to operate elsewhere on a large scale."

"To the east the great fortified district east of Verdun and around Metz menaced France, protected the most exposed portion of the German line of communications, that between Metz and Sedan, and covered the Briey

[1] General Pershing, Report.

iron regions, from which the enemy obtained the greater part of the iron required for munitions and material. The coal fields east of Metz were also covered by these same defenses. A deep advance east of Metz, or the capture of the Briey region, by threatening the invasion of rich German territory in the Moselle Valley and the Saar Basin, thus curtailing the supply of coal or iron, would have a decisive effect in forcing a withdrawal of German troops from northern France. The military and economic situation of the enemy, therefore, indicated Lorraine as the field promising the most fruitful results for the employment of our armies." [1]

In view of the enormously increased tonnage of supplies required by modern warfare, the main problem was to find a way to forward the vast volumes of food, munitions, and material to this chosen American sector. It must be done by means of railroads, and the French railroads of northern France were already overtaxed by the demands of the Allied Armies fighting in France. Not only were the British already crowding the Channel ports, but any attempt for the Americans to use these ports on a large scale would have meant that our supplies sent by railroads to the east, would have been obliged to cross the British and French zones of operations. This condition ruled out a line of communications based on ports and railroads in that region. As General Pershing expressed it, "If the American Army was to have an independent and flexible system it could not use the lines behind the British-Belgian front nor those in the rear of the French front covering Paris. The lines selected, therefore, were those leading from the comparatively unused South Atlantic ports of France to the

---

[1] General Pershing, Report.

northeast where it was believed the American Armies could be employed to the best advantage."

"The ports of St. Nazaire, La Pallice, and Bassens were designated for permanent use, while Nantes, Bordeaux, and Pauillac were for emergency use. Several smaller ports, such as St. Malo, Sables-d'Olonne, and Bayonne, were available chiefly for the transportation of coal from England. From time to time, certain trans-Atlantic ships were sent to Le Havre and Cherbourg." [1] Brest was most heavily used for landing American troops in France, as will be seen from the diagram on page 205. Later, at the time of the German offensive of 1918, arrangements were made "to utilize the ports of Marseilles and Toulon as well as other smaller ports on the Mediterranean." [2]

"In the location of our main depots of supply, while it was important that they should be easily accessible, yet they must also be at a safe distance, as we were to meet an aggressive enemy capable of taking the offensive in any of several directions. The area embracing Tours, Orleans, Montargis, Nevers, and Chateauroux was chosen, as it was centrally located with regard to all points on the arc of the Western Front." [3]

These preparations, for receiving and handling the troops and supplies of the future great American Expeditionary Forces, implied a program of engineering construction on a vast scale, which has not been realized by the public. It comprised constructing port facilities at the different ports of unloading, which did not begin to possess adequate accommodations. At these ports construction included docks, railroads, warehouses, hospitals, barracks, and stables. Throughout the southern

[1] General Pershing, Report.   [2] Ibid.   [3] Ibid.

French railroad systems, which were to be used by the Americans, it was necessary to lay 1,002 miles of standard-gauge track, consisting largely of double-tracking, cut-offs, and tracks in the yards at ports and depots. 1761 consolidation locomotives were shipped to France with over a third of these set up on their own wheels ready to run off on the tracks under their own steam. 26,994 standard-gauge freight cars were also sent to France. Rails and fittings shipped to France, for improving the French railroads and for our own construction, aggregated 430,000 tons.

General Pershing has stated that "we assisted the French by repairing with our own personnel 57,385 French cars, and 1,947 French locomotives." He has also given the following summary of another phase of this great work: "The French railroads, both in management and material, had dangerously deteriorated during the war. As our system was superimposed upon that of the French, it was necessary to provide them with additional personnel and much material. Experienced American railroad men brought into our organization, in various practical capacities, the best talent of the country, who, in addition to the management of our transportation, materially aided the French. The relation of our Transportation Corps to the French railroads and to our own supply departments presented many difficulties, but these were eventually overcome and a high state of efficiency established."

"The amount of construction of buildings was enormous. From the French we secured 2,000,000 sq. ft. of covered storage. It was necessary to construct some 20,000,000 sq. ft. in addition. As an example of the great scale of other construction, the hospital at Mars of

700 buildings covered 33 acres. This was practically a city, with the roads, water, sewerage, and lighting plants of a municipality. The refrigerating plant at Gieves had a capacity of 6,500 tons of meat and 500 tons of ice per day. "If the buildings constructed were consolidated, with the width of a standard barrack, they would reach from St. Nazaire across France to the Elbe River, a distance of 730 miles. In connection with construction work, the Engineer Corps engaged in extensive forestry operations, producing 200,000,000 ft. of lumber, 4,000,-000 railroad ties, 300,000 cords of fuel wood, 35,000 pieces of piling, and large quantities of miscellaneous products." [1]

All this was going on overseas to create the facilities for handling the great output which was being produced in the United States. The reader must keep before his eyes this situation of the year 1917, for it contained the whole essential of the main naval strategy of the United States in the World War, which again might be summed up as follows. A strong American reinforcement must be on the battlefield to meet the crisis of 1918, or the war would be lost. It must be produced in the United States; it must be transported overseas from the United States; in France, it must be handled and maintained by the United States. This threefold operation was what was meant when General Pershing, as already quoted, described the American Expeditionary Forces as "based upon the American Continent."

Two factors of this threefold destiny, of which the naval element was essential, were taking assured form in 1917. The mighty processes at work in the United States were producing the men and the material. The

[1] General Pershing, Report.

corresponding preparations for receiving and handling these products in France were being successfully carried out. The third factor comprised the vital question at stake, the naval element. Was it possible to transport the product of the training camps and industries of the United States 3000 miles overseas to be delivered to the prepared facilities in France? Sea Power was the only agency through which this could be done, and the development of this vital third factor of transportation overseas will be narrated in following chapters. Upon this naval factor hung the fate of the World War.

CHAPTER XVIII

THE AMERICAN TRANSPORTS

THIS vital question, as to the possibility of transportation overseas on a large scale, was a problem for which the United States must be the one nation to provide the answer. The need came at the time when shipping had been so reduced, through losses inflicted by the U-boats, that it was impossible for Allied shipping to furnish anywhere near the amount of this transportation. Allied shipping, and of course this meant for the most part British shipping, eventually provided the greater share of the ships which carried overseas the troops of the American Expeditionary Forces, as will be narrated. But it must be stated at once, as an absolute condition of the naval situation, that, if the United States had not also been able to provide a large part of this transportation,[1] the whole great operation must have failed, with fatal effect upon the war.

It seemed a desperate situation, and was in truth one of great difficulties. That the Transport Service was hard put to charter ships for the first expedition was evident from the list of ships given in a preceding chapter. Yet these were the best that could be gathered from American shipping by experts who went over the registry. The Army transports, controlled by the Transport Service, had the fatal defects of being slow with small bunker capacity. They were used for other purposes, but had

[1] By Great Britain 49%, by the United States 45%, by other nationalities 6%.

to be discarded for transportation of troops over the Atlantic.

Consequently, the ships in the first expedition became the nucleus of the fleet of American troopships and cargo carriers of our great undertaking. It should be stated here that, before these ships of the first groups had returned to America, one great drawback in this service had been obviated. For the first expedition, there had been much delay and confusion in getting the troops and their belongings on board ship, and there had been a hectic experience at the piers. But this was not to be repeated, as, from that time, the Army Transportation Service, perfected a system for the increasing volume of transportation, which loaded ships from the piers as fast as the troops arrived at the water-fronts.

But this first beginning of a fleet could only carry some 15,000 troops and 40,000 tons of freight, which was a small percentage of what was needed. It will give a measure of this to state the fact that in one month of 1918 over twenty times 15,000 troops were transported across the Atlantic. But, strangely enough, the element which meant the turning point from failure to success was provided by the enemy. Again, this was an example of the extraordinary overturns of the World War. The German merchant marine, so enthusiastically developed by the controlling German régime, became the decisive weight thrown into the balance which turned the scale against Germany.

On April 6, 1917, when the United States declared war against Germany, there were lying in the harbors of the United States and its colonies 104 ships of German ownership. Of these twenty were German liners, passenger ships, best adapted to be used as troopships, and many of them built with the idea of eventual use as German transports.

Upon our declaration of war, all these German ships were seized by the United States, following the proper precedents of international law. After inspection, it was found that the engines of these German ships had been wrecked, in the opinion of the Germans, beyond repair.

The United States Government had received ample warning, as early as the *Lusitania* crisis in 1915, that the Germans would attempt to disable these ships. But the status of these interned German steamships was all in favor of damage by their own crews. An interned ship remains in the possession of its owners and crew. Possession is not taken by the authorities of the nation in whose port the ship has been interned. It was a parallel to what occurred after the Armistice. Under the terms of this preliminary treaty of peace, the German warships were not surrendered, but were interned at Scapa to await their disposition under the terms of the final treaty. They were thus in the possession of their German crews, and, upon the news of the final disposition of the warships of the German Fleet, the German crews sank all these ships in Scapa Flow.

The damage done to the German steamships interned in America in 1917 had been a definite part of the German naval program, as stated in the memorandum of the Chief of the German Admiralty of December 22, 1916, which is given in full in the appendix. In this memorandum Admiral Holtzendorff expressed absolute confidence that the German steamships interned in American ports could not be used for transportation during the decisive months of the war, and they were thus eliminated from the German calculations as a means of sending American troops to Germany. But here, as often in the World War, German calculations did not take into account any factor outside of the German calculations. All of these German steamships had cylinder engines, except the *Vaterland* which had turbine engines. The German efforts were mainly directed toward wrecking the cylinders, as the greatest harm that could be done to a marine engine, following the idea that the one thing impossible was to run with defective cylinders. To their minds, this meant so extensive a need of replacement that it would involve a delay beyond the decisive period of the war. That these cylinders could be repaired in a short time, to be as good as new, was outside their calculations.

Yet this was what actually happened. At the first inspection the Shipping Board experts had taken the pessimistic view that it was a long replacement job before the German ships could be put into operation. But the United States Navy, in the case of the two German auxiliary cruisers, had recommended that the cylinders be mended by electric welding. Upon this, the Navy Bureau of Steam Engineering was asked to examine all the German steamships, and, after examination, the recommendation was made that all should be repaired by electric welding.[1]

As a result, on July 11, 1917, the unprecedented task of repairing sixteen damaged German steamships was

---

[1] This process of electric welding was first proposed by D. H. Wilson, an electrical engineer, introduced to the naval authorities by Commander A. B. Hoff (U. S. N. retired). Captain E. P. Jessop, engineer officer at the New York Yard, believed in this process, and Admiral R. S. Griffin, Chief of the Bureau of Engineering, sent his assistant, Captain O. W. Koester, for a thorough inspection. This officer was convinced that the process was practicable, and it was at once adopted.

turned over to the United States Navy, and the Navy accomplished this task in an astonishingly short time, and with an efficiency that made the job complete once and for all. It is no wonder that at first it had been considered a hopeless case. Cylinders had been smashed, and in many cases great pieces had been knocked out of them. The German crews had done everything to the machinery that their minds could conceive. There was something almost pathetic in the amount of strenuous work put in by the Germans, and their assured complacency as to the result — only to find that a new element, outside of the German mind,[1] was to upset all their calculations, and the very ships they had deemed useless were destined to transport over 550,000 troops to fight against the Germans at the crisis of the World War.

The success of the new process was never in doubt. The following quotations from Admiral Gleaves' book will give the reader at a glance the picture of what can only be called one of the most remarkable feats in the history of marine engineer work.

"The biggest job, of course, was the work of repairing the main engines. This was most successfully accomplished by electro-welding large cast steel pieces or patches on the parts of the castings which remained intact. This was completed in a few months, whereas to make new cylinders would have taken over a year."

"This electric welding was an engineering feat which the Germans had not calculated on. The enemy had broken out large irregular pieces of the cylinders by means of hydraulic jacks. Where these parts had been

[1] "We were accustomed to attribute to these men a knowledge and ingenuity almost superhuman, and yet they failed to take into account electric welding, to say nothing of Yankee ingenuity, perseverance, and skill." — Admiral Gleaves.

left in the engine room they were welded back into place, and in cases where the pieces had been thrown overboard new castings were made."

"Electric welding is a slow and difficult process and was carried on day and night, Sundays and holidays, to the full capacity of the available skilled mechanics. After each casting had been welded, the cylinders were machined in place, — special cutting apparatus being rigged for the purpose. Finally each cylinder and valve chest was thoroughly tested under hydrostatic pressure. The repairs to the cylinders were perfectly successful. In actual trial they held up perfectly under hard operating conditions and there was not an instance of the welded portion breaking away."

This last is the true measure of this most successful exploit. It was not a temporary makeshift job of repairs, but one that made the machinery as good as new. In fact in many cases these steamships did better with their repaired engines than with the original engines. The other damages to these ships, to machinery, piping, valves, wiring, &c., were repaired with the same ingenuity and dispatch. All were ready in six months, some in a few weeks — and in many cases the damage wrought by the Germans was repaired before the working gangs had completed the alterations necessary to change the ships into transports for troops.

Again a quotation from Admiral Gleaves will give in a short space a résumé of all this: "In addition to the long list of machinery repairs, extensive alterations were effected, including the installation of thousands of 'standees' or bunks; large increases in the bathing and sanitary plumbing arrangements; the enlargement of the galleys and increase of commissary equipment; the installation and equipment of hospitals; the provision of life rafts, boats and life belts for four or five times the normal number of passengers; the installation of guns and ammunition magazines; and scores of other smaller, but important changes necessary to permit the great increase in passenger capacity, and at the same time to keep the ships safe and sanitary."

At our declaration of war, the first idea had been that the Army would man and operate the American transports, with the Navy providing guns and gun crews. But, after it had become clear that a great American army must be produced and sent overseas, and the vast plans for the Army began to take form, it became evident, not only that the United States Army had enough on its hands without operating troopships, but also that the operation of the American troopships at sea was logically entirely a naval operation and should be the province of the United States Navy. Consequently the American troopships were armed by the Navy, manned by the Navy, and operated by the Navy.

Admiral Gleaves has shown how well this worked out, even before the ships were in commission, in the preparations to put into active service this great addition to the Cruiser and Transport Force under his command, and it will be evident that the presence of the naval crews hastened these preparations.

"Before these ships were commissioned, several naval officers and a skeleton naval crew were ordered on board each of them to assist and supervise. Daily reports of progress were made, and each week I held a conference on board the Flagship with my Staff and the officers assigned to the different ships for the purpose of interchanging ideas and devising means to expedite the work. The damage done to auxiliary machinery, piping, and fittings by deterioration from lack of care was, in general, even greater than that done willfully. The boilers, the most sensitive part of a ship, had suffered woefully through neglect, and the ships throughout were dirty beyond description. The naval crews were gradually filled up to strength, and while machinery repairs were going on, they went ahead with scrubbing, scraping, cleaning, painting, disinfecting, and fumigating, to make the ships habitable and sanitary for the troops." The accompanying table will show the importance of this great group of troopships thus acquired by the United States from the Germans, and used against Germany contrary to all expectations of the enemy.

This acquisition of the German ships was the most important factor in the solution of our great problem of transporting troops overseas. For they were available at the very time when troops were to be sent over in increased numbers, and afterwards for the ensuing crisis when the maximum of numbers must be sent. The astonishing totals of 557,788 American troops transported overseas by means of these German ships tell the whole story. This acquisition put the whole matter of troopships on a different basis.

But the work was not yet done, as the demand for cargo ships was growing out of all proportion to prewar ideas. This will be appreciated when the figures are compared. At the time of the Armistice, 500,000 deadweight tons of American shipping were engaged in carrying troops, 2,000,000 deadweight tons of American shipping were engaged in carrying supplies for the American Expeditionary Forces — that is, for every ton carrying troops four tons were needed to carry supplies. The public has thought of this operation too much in terms of ships carrying troops. The great fleet of cargo carriers has not been taken into consideration, but, after

GERMAN MERCHANT STEAMSHIPS USED AS TROOPSHIPS BY THE UNITED STATES

German name	Re-christened	Gross tons	Speed Knots	Date of first departure with troops	United States troops carried overseas
Vaterland	Leviathan	54,282	24	12-15-1917	96,804
Kaiser Wilhelm II	Agamemnon	9,360	23.5	10-19- "	36,097
Koenig Wilhelm II	Madawaska	9,410	15.5	11-12- "	17,931
President Lincoln	President Lincoln	18,167	14.5	10-19- "	20,143
President Grant	President Grant	18,072	14.5	12-26- "	39,974
Barbarossa	Mercury	10,983	14	1-4-1918	18,542
Grosser Kurfurst	Aeolus	13,102	15.5	11-26-1917	24,770
Hamburg	Powhatan	10,531	15	11-12- "	14,613
Friedrich der Grosse	Huron	10,771	15.5	9-8- "	20,871
Prinzess Irene	Pocahontas	10,893	16	9-8- "	20,503
George Washington	George Washington	25,569	18.5	12-4- "	48,373
Martha Washington	Martha Washington	8,312	17.2	2-10-1918	22,311
Prinz Eitel Friedrich	De Kalb	8,797	16.5	6-14-1917	11,334
Amerika	America	22,622	17.5	10-19- "	39,768
Neckar	Antigone	9,835	14	12-14- "	16,526
Cincinnati	Covington	16,339	15.5	10-19- "	21,628
Kronprinzessin Cecile	Mount Vernon	18,372	24	10-19- "	33,692
Rhein	Susquehanna	10,057	14	12-14- "	18,345
Kronprinz Wilhelm	Von Steuben	14,901	23	10-19- "	14,347
Prinzess Alice	Princess Matoika	10,492	16	5-10- "	21,216
					557,788

(The *Princess Alice* had been interned at Cebu, Philippine Islands, all others in United States ports.)

the gain of the German ships had thus helped the troop-ship situation, the most difficult part of the operation was to get hold of enough cargo carriers.

As a first step toward an increase of American ship-ping for this purpose, the United States Shipping Board, on August 3, 1917, requisitioned at the shipyards all steel vessels of 2,500 deadweight tons or over, which were then under construction.[1] This assertion of emi-nent domain, though ultimately of great effect, was not the only official act which immediately added the most tonnage to the Government's merchant fleet. On Octo-ber 15, 1917, the Shipping Board commandeered all commissioned and going American steel cargo steamers of 2,500 deadweight tons or over, and also all American passenger vessels of more than 2,500 gross tons that were suitable for foreign service. "This action added instantly to the federal marine 408 merchant vessels, of more than 2,600,000 deadweight tons." [2]

Every effort was also made to acquire foreign tonnage, by seizure of enemy ships, by charter of enemy ships seized by others in the war, by purchase and charter from neutrals, by granting privileges for export in ex-change for chartered tonnage, and by seizure of neutral tonnage in our ports, as will be narrated. But it should be frankly stated that things were going very badly in respect to cargo carriers in the first six months of our participation in the war, not only from the scarcity of ships, but also from the confused situation as to allocat-ing the available tonnage among the demands of the various industrial activities and the needs of the armed forces.

[1] "Before the armistice, 255 of them were in commission — nearly 1,600,-000 deadweight tons." — "The Road to France," Crowell and Wilson.

[2] "The Road to France," Crowell and Wilson.

CHAPTER XIX

OPERATING THE TRANSPORTS

BY the means described in the last chapter, there was put into being the great operation which was the main object of the United States Navy in the World War, and the reader should understand its relation to the convoy system, which was winning a margin of safety against the German U-boat campaign in the last half of the year 1917. Not only did this great American naval operation join up with the convoy system, but it became even a greater measurement of the defeat of the U-boat campaign. For, with the change of strategy to the new development of the great German military offensive at the beginning of 1918, it should be stated that the logical main object of the German submarine campaign must also be changed to a matter of breaking the American chain of communication across the seas, which was delivering and maintaining the American military reinforcement on the Western Front. For the presence of this reinforcement on the battlefield meant the doom of Germany in the World War.

The American chain of communications was also doing a great deal to maintain the military effort of the Entente Allies and to furnish food and other supplies to their civil populations.

As has been explained the convoy system was at this stage in 1917 winning its way against the U-boats, by its reduction of losses to a margin of safety for Allied and chartered shipping. Losses still were enormous, com-

pared with any prewar ideas, but it must be emphasized that, in this respect, the convoys were rendering a
double service. Not only were they reducing the totals
of actual losses, but they also were increasing the totals
of available shipping, as the confidence induced by this
additional security led the neutral nations to send out
shipping previously kept in port from fear of the U-
boats.

The United States had acquiesced in the obviously
sound doctrine that, in general, British control was best
for the convoys. Not only must the greater part of the
convoyed shipping move to and from the central area of
the British and French ports, which made this focus the
obvious best seat of administration, but the worldwide
maritime connections of Great Britain were all in favor
of British administration of this system. But there was
one exception made on the part of the United States
from the first. While the American cargo ships were
operated under the British direction of the convoy system, the convoys of American troopships were controlled
and operated by the United States Navy, as will be
described.

British troopships carrying overseas American soldiers were, for the most part, under the regular British
control, and these transported a greater total of American troops,[1] especially at the crisis of 1918 as will be told
in the ensuing narrative. But it was a matter of commonsense that American troopships should be under the
control of the United States Navy on account of the
special conditions governing this American naval operation overseas.

[1] The British troopships transported 49%, the American troopships 45%,
of the total number of American troops transported overseas (6% carried by
other nationalities).

So far as regards the United States Navy, the American operation must be considered as follows. The United States Army produced the military personnel for overseas, transported it to the sea terminals, and delivered it at the docks, exactly like goods delivered for export in commerce. The United States Navy received these troops and their equipment on board ship, and from that time took full charge of them, caring for them and feeding them, transporting and safeguarding them overseas, and finally delivering them to the United States Army at the prepared base ports overseas. Again this was like the process of commerce for delivering goods at foreign ports to the consignees. At the ports overseas the United States Army received the troops and again took full charge. The Army then delivered the troops at the fighting front by means of the facilities which had been prepared in advance, as has been described. If the reader will think of the great American joint operation in these terms, the picture will stand out in its true perspective.

It will at once be clear that this sensible agreement, arrived at between the Army and Navy, for handling the ever-growing volume of transportation on American troopships gave a businesslike basis for operation that was better without recourse to the machinery of the British convoy control. With the great task apportioned as described, the movement overseas of American troopships became a convoy system in itself, a thing apart from the other convoy operations, although the arrivals in the war zone of the American troopship convoy system had to dovetail very closely into the general convoy systems. The wisdom of this course received an astonishing proof of success. Of over 900,000 troops transported overseas in American troopships and safeguarded by the United States Navy, not a single man was lost through an act of the enemy. There is no need to add anything to this matter of record.

The conduct of this joint military and naval operation was also a proof of how quickly the minds of our Army and Navy leapt forward to a grasp of affairs, which were suddenly cast on so vast a scale, and with complicated tasks that had never been undertaken before. Both services demonstrated that their high training had fitted them to perform duties which were outside of all former ideas. A notable feature was the excellent teamwork between the two services, and this was a most necessary element, in view of the constantly shifting needs for control and apportionment of the details of the ever-growing operation and its huge volume of supplies. It will be apparent that all this was far afield from the usual demands of the services, but, after the first weeks of confusion, it was done in a business-like way.

The Army had instituted an Embarkation Service, with General Frank T. Hines as Chief of Embarkation, and his relations with Admiral W. S. Benson, the Naval Chief of Operations, were so cordial that they were able to adjust points at issue without cut and dried classifications, which would have inevitably caused delay as the flood of troops poured in for transportation. Matters had to be adjusted man to man. There was no time for tabulating the details of control. The same coöperation existed between General David C. Shanks, in charge of the great embarkation base of New York, and Admiral Gleaves, and between General Grote Hutcheson at Newport News and Admiral Hilary P. Jones, who had charge of the Newport News Division of the Cruiser and Transport Force.

The reader must understand that not only was the actual performance of the new tasks difficult, but these new tasks must also be performed with the constant accompanying call for additional preparation and organization, in order to be able to carry them along to an increasingly greater scale. The Army's task was hard enough, to prepare to transport overland and disembark the great numbers of troops that were to come. But what can be said of these strenuous months for the United States Navy? More and more ships to be operated — more and more men to be trained! The ships must be schools as well as efficient on their jobs. The trained personnel of the Navy must not only perform all kinds of new duties, but must also act as teachers for the new untried personnel that was coming into the Navy in such great numbers. Few of our people have any conception of this phase of our Navy's work. At the very time the personnel of the United States Navy must perform tasks greater and more varied than had ever been undertaken by any navy, the Navy's personnel must also be occupied in training a personnel greater than had ever been in any navy. A very few figures will fix this fact in the reader's mind. At our entry in the World War, the personnel of the United States Navy, Regular [1] and Reserve, was in round numbers 95,000. At the Armistice, the total, Regular and Reserve, was over 530,-000 — a personnel far greater than that of the British Navy at its maximum in the World War.

Of all these varied and exacting undertakings, the

[1] United States Navy, personnel April 6, 1917, enlisted men 68,680, commissioned and warrant officers 4,876.

work of operating the separate convoy system of the American troopships, by the Cruiser and Transport Force, stands out as of unprecedented difficulty. On the one hand, the safeguarding naval forces must be at high efficiency, on the other hand, the troopships themselves must be at high efficiency. Their crews must be well organized, and the whole administration of the troop carrying steamships must be radically changed. This was typified by the structural changes in the troopships themselves. Their decks had become great stretches of standee bunks, and they were run like floating camps, in regard to care, feeding, and sanitation.

Yet, for this American troopship convoy system, success had been in reality assured after the problem of utilizing the German steamships had been so quickly solved. When the coöperation of the British troopship service became also assured, as will be narrated, transportation for American troops was never in danger of being inadequate. The real danger was that the difficulty of obtaining cargo carriers would defeat our effort, as our troops could not be maintained without our own services of supply overseas.

This became the crux of our operation, and success hung in the balance in the last months of 1917. With all the efforts that were being made to gather in cargo tonnage, the supply was far behind the demand — and this in spite of all the seized and chartered foreign tonnage.[1] As has been explained, the amount of tonnage which the Shipping Board could assign for the Army needs must compete with the rival demands of the great industrial

---

[1] The Dutch shipping in United States ports was acquired by exercising the right of angaria — seizure justified in the act by extreme necessity. Of the 500,000 tons thus acquired the Army received 250,000 tons. The Embarkation Service also received 94,000 tons of the purchased and chartered Japanese shipping.

and commodity movement which was also demanding ships. As the needs of the Army increased so enormously, this competition brought about a congestion of shipping, which was only overcome when at length the Shipping Control Committee was constituted early in 1918, as will be narrated.

But the development of the Army cargo carriers in their relation to the convoy system should be here defined. It will be obvious that this was a service entirely differing from that of the troopships. The heterogeneous collection of shipping, partly owned by the United States, partly chartered and operated by the United States, partly chartered by the United States and yet operated by the owners, was not in favor of a closely organized special convoy service, like that of the American troopships. Consequently our cargo carriers became part and parcel of the convoy system under the general British control. But it should be noted here that manning and operating the American cargo carriers became more and more a service of the United States Navy. This came from natural causes. The main difficulty was in finding civilian crews, with all the other demands upon labor. After some cases where cargo convoys were held up until crews were provided by the Navy, there followed a working agreement by which the operation of most of the Army's chartered cargo carriers was placed in the hands of the Navy. This at once implied a great increase in the Navy's herculean task of operating ships and training men at the same time.

It was an astonishing picture of strenuous American effort on the seas, to accomplish what the enemy had deemed impossible, and teachers and pupils of the United States Navy must be given the credit of winning a decisive success.

CHAPTER XX

THE WANE OF 1917

(See Map at page 174)

THE year 1917 was thus running to the end of its course, with these great component elements of the American effort growing into a strength that the world did not at all appreciate. Moreover, even in the last months of 1917, there was still no conception, on the part of the Entente Allies, of the vast scale of the military reinforcement which must be provided by the United States to avert defeat at the crisis of 1918. A striking proof of this last in regard to the Entente Allies was made a matter of record in November, 1917.

This was on the occasion of the Paris Conference, begun on November 29, 1917,[1] from which eventually sprang the Allied Maritime Transport Council, a long step toward bringing about coöperation in the matter of Allied shipping. At this Conference delegates were present from practically all of the Entente Allies, and with these was associated a representative of the United States. In fact, one main object of the Conference was to urge upon the United States greater coöperation with the Entente Allies in the matter of shipping. And it was a most significant sign of the times that, even thus late in 1917, the following was adopted: "That if she (United States) take these steps, however, there is a prospect of her being able to transport and maintain an

[1] "The Paris Conference, which began on November 29, 1917, was probably the most impressive expression in the war of both the range and unity of Allied effort." — "Allied Shipping Control."

American Army of 500,000 by the early summer and of 1,000,000 later in the year." This estimate by the conference of the scope of our effort was only half of the actuality, and it was most fortunate that, as has been stated, in the United States, ideas had leapt far beyond any such estimate as this, and our structure was already being built up to the great scale demanded by the World War.

At this time all minds in Europe were occupied with the great struggle between the U-boats and shipping. The convoy system had already won this fight, as has been described — but this was not yet apparent to the Entente Allies, and at this Conference a gloomy view was taken of the situation on the seas. This was not a matter for wonder, as it was there stated that Great Britain in the war had lost 10,000,000 d. w. tons, which meant a net loss of 4,000,000 d. w. tons over replacements and captured ships, and the world losses of shipping had been 17,000,000 d. w. tons, which meant a net loss of 9,000,000 d. w. tons.

Yet, at this stage, the convoy system had in fact grown into a real system in every sense of the word, and its operation had been developed, as if many regular steamship lines were running from the outlying ports to the central station, which was of course Home Waters and the ports of Great Britain and France. The group sailings of these convoys had become scheduled and regulated in every detail, as to departures, voyages, and arrivals. The ships were not only protected by warships, but they were also trained in the tactics of self-preservation and consequently prepared in advance to cope with the attacks of the U-boats.

This was the picture of the situation on the seas at

this stage of the World War, with these well regulated groups of convoys arriving in due order in the infested zones of Home Waters, where they were picked up one by one by their assigned forces of anti-submarine protection, which made any attacks upon these convoys a matter of operating the U-boats in an area made dangerous for them by the assured presence of enemy naval forces prepared to take the offensive against them. It was altogether a different situation from what had gone before, when scattered ships were taking their own means of protection, and arriving in patrolled areas with no assurance of striking the company of protecting warships.

This revolution in the methods of protecting shipping, by reverting to the ideas of the old convoying days, had produced an astonishing result in relation to losses from the U-boats. It is true that losses of ships in the nearby coastwise traffic, and of ships outside the convoys, still remained large, but the convoy system had reduced the losses of overseas shipping in the convoys to a point that assured the defeat of the U-boat campaign. This is best shown by the simple statement of fact, that, whereas there had been losses of ten unconvoyed ships before the introduction of the convoy system, there was only the loss of one convoyed ship after the convoy system had been put into full operation.

This balance had been swung in the direction of safety only just in time, as the demands of the war upon shipping were growing out of all proportion to former experience. Of course the great joint operation of the United States was the heaviest drain of all, but everywhere else the call was urgent for more ships. The scale of operations in France was constantly increasing, with greater expenditures of munitions and supplies. Troops were still being drawn from Canada, Australia, New Zealand and South Africa. The distant expeditions must also be maintained, and this implied services of supply to Salonica, Mesopotamia, Palestine, and East Africa. In fact, the whole world presented an almost inconceivable picture of shipping and naval activity, which was in itself a complete demonstration of how the result of the World War depended upon Sea Power.

It is hardly an exaggeration to say that at the end of 1917 the whole war was being fought on the seas, especially in view of the Italian collapse and the waning away of the fighting on the Flanders and on the Western Front. And yet there actually was almost no fighting on the seas, in the old fashioned sense of the word, which implied engagements between regular naval forces. There were all kinds of fights and adventures in the course of the U-boat campaign, for the ships that were sought as prey, for the U-boats themselves, and for the anti-submarine forces. But of set actions between naval forces in the old way there was almost no trace left in the war. Occasionally there would be a clash of light craft, but the battle fleets were never near a general action in 1917.

The reason for this lay in the changed naval strategy of the Germans, which has been described. The British Grand Fleet was retained for its same mission of defending the North Sea area, and was prepared to fight the German Battle Fleet, "if it came out." But, from the time of the German decision for unrestricted U-boat warfare at the end of 1916, the German Battle Fleet remained devoted to its changed mission of forwarding the attacks of the German U-boats. Its task continued to be that of clearing the passages beyond the German naval bases for the U-boats. In this task the German Battle Fleet was, in general, successful, but this mission restricted its area of operations to these waters beyond the German naval bases. Consequently, with the German High Sea Fleet operating on one side of the North Sea, and with the British Grand Fleet defending the other side, there was not much chance of an action of fleets.

But the Germans carried out one operation of the High Sea Fleet, which was apart from its task of forwarding the U-boat campaign. This operation was not in the North Sea, as it was undertaken in the Baltic against only the demoralized Russians, in order that the Baltic should be made even more completely a "German lake." [1] After the German army had taken Riga, in September, 1917, the German Supreme Army Command had asked for the coöperation of the German Fleet in a joint operation to capture the Baltic Islands. In this Admiral Scheer acquiesced, and his comment was significant of the naval situation for the Battle Fleets: "This offered a welcome diversion from the monotony of the war in the North Sea."

Of the battleships of the High Sea Fleet, Squadrons III and IV (10 battleships) were detached under the command of Vice Admiral Schmidt, to whom was also assigned the battle cruiser *Moltke* as flagship. With this force were nine cruisers, with full complement of destroyers, U-boats, and a large number of small craft to act as minesweepers. It was evident that in this operation the danger from mines would be the main obstacle. There were nineteen troopships "for the transport of

---

[1] *See* Offensive Operations 1914–1915, page 152.

23,000 men, 5,000 horses, and much material." [1] The transports were gathered at Libau, the capital ships of the Battle Fleet in the Bay of Danzig, with the cruisers and light craft at Libau.

The expedition sailed on the morning of October 11, passed through the mine fields in the night, and the Germans were in the Bay of Jagga, where the landing was successfully made early the next morning. Not much difficulty was experienced with the batteries or with the defending Russian warships. As had been anticipated, the mines were the main danger. While taking position to bombard, the German battleships *Bayern* and *Grosser Kürfurst* struck mines, "which, however, did not hinder them from completing their task." [2]

One of the small steamers engaged in landing troops, the *Corsica*, also struck a mine and had to be beached, but the men on board were taken off and landed. On October 14 the Germans were in Moon Sound, and again the only damage was through mines. By October 17 the Russian ships had been driven to the north, the Russian battleship *Slava* having been sunk and the Russian cruiser *Bogatyr* torpedoed by a German U-boat. In this way the islands of Moon, Oesel, and Dago were easily captured by the joint German expedition, and German control of the Baltic became absolute.

Admiral Scheer has stated: "The fact that our Main Fleet was thus occupied presented a favorable opportunity for us to make an advance with light craft into the northern waters of the North Sea, since under the circumstances the enemy would least expect it. We, therefore, dispatched the light cruisers *Brummer* and *Bremse* to harry the merchant ships plying between Nor-

[1] Admiral Scheer. [2] Ibid.

way and England. . . ." These Scandinavian convoys were naturally the ones most exposed to attack, as the British cruiser forces in the north were too much tied to the Grand Fleet, but it was not until this date (October 17, 1917) that they were first attacked by German surface craft. The German cruisers found an easy prey in one of these convoys of twelve steamers escorted only by two British destroyers, *Mary Rose* and *Strongbow*, and two trawlers. Both British destroyers were sunk, and nine steamers destroyed. This was one of the most severe blows ever dealt to a convoy. A second surface attack was made on a Scandinavian convoy December 12, 1917, when four German destroyers sank six steamers, four armed trawlers, and the British destroyer *Partridge*. The British destroyer *Pellew* was also disabled, but escaped in a shower of rain.

Aside from these attacks to the north, the Germans only made in 1917 what Admiral Scheer called "test-trips," to feel out the British obstructions beyond the German bases, and these were a valuable help in the new mission of the German Battle Fleet for forwarding the U-boat campaign. "Every test-trip group comprised mine-layers and sweepers with their tackle for finding mines, behind them went torpedo-boats with U-boat 'kites' with which to locate nets; these were followed by barrier-breakers, and light cruisers with seaplanes for scouting. Heavy warships protected the test-trip groups on routes that were known to be free of mines." [1]

The British were making great efforts to strew mines in the egresses from the German bases, and British mine-layers were constantly kept at work in these areas. But, as has been stated, these obstructions could not be ex-

[1] Admiral Scheer.

pected to prove as effective as if they had been protected by armed naval forces.

For the British Grand Fleet, there was in 1917 even greater "monotony of the war in the North Sea" than that described by Admiral Scheer's complaint as to the German High Sea Fleet. The bases and areas of patrol of the British Battle Fleet lay to the north, and, for the reasons which have been stated, this British main naval force was not a coördinated part of the U-boat struggle, as was the German Battle Fleet. Admiral Jellicoe, the First Sea Lord of the British Admiralty, had asked that a division of battleships of the United States Navy should be sent to reinforce the British Grand Fleet, and also that these should be coal-burning owing to the great scarcity of oil in Great Britain. Accordingly, under the command of Rear Admiral Hugh Rodman, the following American battleships joined the Grand Fleet in December, 1917: *New York* (flagship), *Texas*, *Wyoming*, *Arkansas*. Later were sent *Florida* and *Delaware*. These American battleships became a division of the Grand Fleet under the command of Admiral Beatty, and from that time took part in its routine of duty.

But, as will be evident from the foregoing, 1917 was a drab year for the main naval forces. It was the reverse of this for the other elements of naval forces and shipping which were on the seas. The World War had brought back the old conditions when all on the seas were obliged to scheme and fight for their ships and their lives. The great currents of the war had swept all seafaring shipping into the struggle, and naval warfare was no longer a question of naval forces. Never in all the history of pirates and predatory nations had captains and crews been compelled to cope with such great dangers — and the vast multiplication of shipping had brought down to the sea great numbers of men to whom seafaring was a new adventure.

This was especially true of the United States — for the greatest expansion must come from her. The necessary constant increase of transportation of our troops and material has been described. In addition, there was the increasing share of the United States in the anti-submarine warfare and the protection of convoys, outside of the protection of the transportation of our own men and material. In July, 1917, the decision was made to establish an American naval base at Gibraltar, and in August began a gathering of American light forces which performed valuable service at this important center of convoys. The establishment of an American naval base at the Azores soon followed.

As has been stated, the American naval forces in the Brest area remained an independent American command. This was natural, because this area had been given over to the bases for American troops, supplies, and material. For this reason, it was apparent that here was one case where putting American naval units under a foreign command would not have produced the best coördination, as their services were devoted mainly to the protection of the arrival of the American Expeditionary Force. This could best be accomplished under the control of the United States Navy, and Admiral Wilson's command, U. S. Patrol Squadrons operating in European Waters, became a necessary element in the success of the American movement overseas.

An important factor in this great operation was another independent American fleet, of which little has been known. It was our Cross-Channel Fleet, which

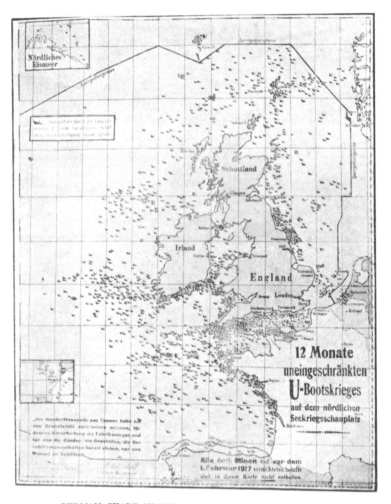

GERMAN CHART SHOWING THE SINKINGS BY U-BOATS

This was a captured chart, prepared in Germany to keep up the faith of the Germans in the success of the campaign of unrestricted U-boat warfare. Sea sinkings indicated were claimed as a result of this campaign, beginning February 1, 1917.

The following is a translation of the statement given over the signature of Churchill: ''By hundreds of thousands of tons have I had to reduce the steel for shells, for which the factories were ready to manufacture, and for which fuses, guns, and gun crews were in readiness, simply for lack of ships.''

was being created at this time for carrying cargoes and men from Great Britain to France. This was a very necessary part of our transportation system, and it grew to 300,000 dead weight tons by the end of the war. All sorts of small steamships were utilized, and it is notable that, with chartered Swedish and Norwegian shipping, were used numbers of American steamships from the Great Lakes — an instance of the unexpected bunkmates brought together by the demands of the World War.[1] The most notable service of the Cross-Channel Fleet, a service which was indeed indispensable, was bringing Welsh coal to the American bases. The ships of this fleet were subject to U-boat attack,[2] and their hazardous services deserves great praise.

The foregoing gives a picture of the strenuous situation on the seas. It seemed that the extreme of effort and activity was being called forth at the end of the year 1917. But, in fact, the new year of 1918 was destined to summon the contending nations to greater exertions, and to bring forth a new situation which changed the whole aspect of the World War.

[1] These were known as Lake boats and their names were *Lake Arthur*, etc.

[2] "The U-boats paid considerable attention to the American Cross-Channel service; and more than one of the vessels launched in grimy harbors of the Great Lakes — in the New World, thousands of miles from the scenes of conflict — came to grief in the English Channel and went down to join the bones of ships sunk in those historic waters in wars fought when America was a wilderness." — The Road to France," Crowell and Wilson.

CHAPTER XXI

THE SITUATION AT THE BEGINNING OF 1918

THE beginning of the fateful year 1918 found the Central Powers in so favorable a military situation that the Germans were preparing the most formidable assault of the World War, in full belief in its power to sweep through the Western Front to a victory that must win the war. The elimination of Russia as a military factor had allowed Germany to concentrate all her forces against France, with the assurance that the Central Powers were not in danger elsewhere.

A survey of this military situation will show at once the domination of Germany over all military factors in Europe at the beginning of 1918. This situation had been wrought by the inexorable grinding processes of the World War, which had consumed the resources of nations as never before in history. In all former wars results had been measured by victories and gains of territory. In the World War all such results had been dwarfed by the toll of lives and the consumption of material resources. This fearful drain had been more severe for the Entente Allies, as must be evident from the preceding books of this work. After the first defeat in 1914 of the German General Staff's "dry-land" plan to win the war by one great military coup, the unsuccessful strategy of the Entente Allies had allowed the Central Powers to concentrate against Russia. This was largely due to the failure of Allied naval strategy to gain control of the Baltic and the Dardanelles, as has been emphasized in this work. There had been no military diversion, as the fighting on the Western Front only consumed men and material, as fast as Great Britain and France poured their resources into the trenches, without dislodging the Germans. As a result, the losses of Russia in men and resources had been beyond anything the nation could endure, and the whole national structure had collapsed.

At the beginning of 1918 all was ended for Russia, so far as concerned any participation in the World War. The ruling Bolsheviki had agreed to an armistice in December, 1917, and this was to develop into separate peace treaties with the Ukraine and Russia early in 1918. Thus the mighty power of Russia had been shorn away from the Entente Allies. Of course, as has been stated, this was the greatest victory for the Central Powers in the World War. But even this was not the total of the unfavorable situation for the Entente Allies. The Italian reverses of the fall of 1917 had at one blow changed Italy from an allied force pressing upon Austria-Hungary to the position of an ally in distress. Instead of being a power in the war on the offensive against the Central Powers, Italy herself needed help from the Entente Allies, and it had consequently become a definite condition in the military situation that there could be no hope of an Italian offensive in the early months of 1918.

Over all the far flung fields of battle, outside of the Western Front, it was the same story. The Central Powers had nothing to fear that would interfere with their great offensive. In the southeast, Rumania, without the support of Russia, was doomed to downfall.[1]

[1] "As a result, the Treaty of Bucharest was signed on May 7th. The terms of the treaty were of extreme severity." — War Cabinet, Report, 1918.

The Allied Army at Salonica was held in check. The Turks had served their purpose for Germany at the Dardanelles. After the downfall of Russia they were outside the German sphere of operations. Left to themselves they had become demoralized, and General Allenby's expedition had little difficulty in capturing Jerusalem (December 7, 1917). But nothing in these outlying regions threatened to interfere in the least with the success of the projected German assault on the Western Front. The reader must realize that the ensuing decisive campaign of the World War must be fought out on the actual battlefield of the Western Front. All else had faded into insignificance.[1]

Of this general military situation there can no longer be the slightest question, and the main interest in the study of the ensuing history of the World War must be concentrated upon the factors which made up the strengths of the two opposing forces in the last desperate fight to a finish.

In the first place it should be stated that by their ability to move troops from the Eastern Front to France the Germans had established an actual superiority in forces.[2] But there were also other especial reasons for the military superiority of the Germans in their initial attacks on their chosen battlefield of 1918. One outstanding reason was the weakness of the Allied armies on the Western Front, in consequence of the drain of losses in preceding years. The year 1917 had been notably

---

[1] "But it never must be forgotten that it was on the Western Front, and in the magnificent resistance there offered to the last violent onset, that victory was secured. Successes on other Fronts would not have availed, save after long years of protracted and costly sacrifice, if the Western line had been broken." — War Cabinet, Report, 1918.

[2] "Numerically we had never been so strong in comparison with our enemies." — "Ludendorff's Own Story."

costly in losses. This can be baldly stated as follows. The unsuccessful French offensive had consumed the remnant of the French power to undertake any offensive operation on a large scale. From this time on it was an arduous task to keep the French ranks anywhere near fighting strength. For the British it was the same situation. 1917 had been a year of heavy British losses, and, when the Battle of Flanders dwindled to its ineffective end in the mud of the late fall, the casualties had reached a total which forbade any hope of increased British armies for the new year. On the contrary, Great Britain was also facing a difficult problem to keep her armies on a fighting basis for 1918. Consequently, there was no chance of a French or British offensive early in 1918, and the Germans possessed the great advantage of being able to make their plans against Allied armies which must act on the defensive. This advantage meant that the German leaders would be able to choose their points of attack, without being in danger of counter attacks.

In addition, the Germans possessed "an element of tactical surprise which had been, generally speaking, lacking in the case of previous offensives on the Western Front." [1] This was a carefully rehearsed system for disposing German divisions so that they would converge upon the objective in successive instalments. It was a practical method of returning to the first principle of a concentration of superior numbers against the point of attack, and it was especially dangerous against the French and British, who looked for nothing beyond their own tactics in what they had grown to regard as "stabilized" trench warfare. As the event proved, this preconceived idea of the limitations of trench warfare

[1] War Cabinet, Report, 1918.

left the Allied armies on the Western Front unprepared for defense against the new German system of attack.[1]

These conditions had unquestionably established a great military advantage for the Germans at the time, and this was beyond the power of the Entente Allies to remedy.[2] Any true analysis of the situation leads to the unavoidable conclusion that a strong reinforcement of fighting troops was necessary to turn the balance on the Western Front. But the Entente Allies were too depleted in manpower to provide this reinforcement. Only the United States could furnish the additional element of military force necessary to overcome the established German superiority. Thus the great objective of the United States in the World War, which has been explained, took definite shape in 1918.

Again the German calculations did not admit defeat. The Hindenburg-Ludendorff régime had won complete control of the affairs of the Central Powers. But Ludendorff had gone over Hindenburg's head and become the military dictator of Germany. Ludendorff's was the guiding will [3] that determined the strategy of 1918, and the German people were again confident of the outcome of his plans.[4] Their leaders were positive in their con-

[1] "By this means the enemy was, during the course of the Spring and early Summer, able to attain a far greater degree of success than had been previously achieved by any army on the Western Front since the commencement of trench warfare." — War Cabinet, Report, 1918.

[2] "When on March 21, 1918, the German army on the Western Front began its series of offensives, it was by far the most formidable force the world has ever seen." — General Pershing, Report.

[3] "The last war period Germany was controlled by one will only and that was Ludendorff's. His thoughts were centred on fighting, his soul on victory." — Czernin, "In the World War."

[4] But the Germans were persuaded that after leaving the Eastern Front they would throw themselves on to the Western Front and that the war would end before the Americans had time to come in. Their reckoning was at fault, as we all know to-day." — Czernin, "In the World War."

viction that the preparations of the United States could not possibly result in the actual presence of an American army on the battlefield.[1] In this respect, the statement of Hindenburg has left no question as to German opinion of the United States: "Would she appear in time to snatch the victor's laurels from our brows. That, and that only was the decisive question! I believed I could answer it in the negative."[2] It was thus frankly a "race," as it has often been called, but one in which the German leaders did not think there was a chance for America to win.

[1] "Why this unexpected defeat following performances so grand? Because a military commander, intoxicated with isolated success, flushed with the omnipotence of Caesar, twice failed to conceive a proper estimate of America as a factor." — Maximilian Harden.

[2] "Out of my Life."

CHAPTER XXII

THE PROBLEM OF TRANSPORTATION

AT this time, the beginning of 1918, when the Germans were preparing for their assault upon the Western Front, with utter confidence that the United States would not be able to produce an army on the battlefield to balk German victory, it must be admitted that on the surface there was every appearance that the calculations of the German leaders were sound as to the helplessness of America. The leaders of the Entente Allies were deeply disappointed at the results of the American effort so far. To them it seemed that failure was inevitable, judging from the small numbers of American troops in France. General Pershing has stated in his Report: "On December 31, 1917, there were 176,665 American troops in France and but one division had appeared on the front. Disappointment at the delay of the American effort soon began to develop."

The confidence of the Germans and the feeling of disappointment on the part of the Entente Allies were both natural enough, in view of the small visible American product of 1917. But neither side realized that this first result was no measure of what was to follow, and that the steps taken, in the earlier days of what seemed to be confusion and delays in America, were to bear fruit in production and movement of troops and supplies on a large scale. An urgent call for this full effort of America had been given in General Pershing's estimate of the situation, which was cabled to the War Department

December 2, 1917, with the following unmistakable warning as to the actual situation:

"The Allies are very weak and we must come to their relief this year, 1918. The year after may be too late. It is very doubtful if they can hold out until 1919 unless we give them a lot of support this year. It is therefore strongly recommended that a complete readjustment of transportation be made and that the needs of the War Department as set forth above be regarded as immediate. Further details of these requirements will be sent later."

It was upon this question of transportation overseas that the success of the American effort depended, and the situation at the first of 1918 was far from satisfactory. As stated by General Pershing "a complete readjustment of transportation must be made," or the American effort would fail. This question, as has been stated, resolved itself into two problems: transportation of troops overseas; transportation of cargoes to sustain the constantly growing needs of our troops abroad.

Transportation of troops was the less difficult problem. As will be seen from the table on page 157, the great fleet of German steamships taken over by the Navy was in full operation at the first of 1918. These seized enemy ships made the best possible transports for troops, and they were the backbone of the Cruiser and Transport Force. Added to these were American steamships and acquired foreign steamships, and transportation of troops already stood on a better basis than transportation of cargoes.

Yet it must be understood that this fleet of American transports could not possibly have been made adequate for the needs of the greater movement of American troops which was to follow. Transportation for these must also be provided by means of Allied shipping — and of course this meant, for the most part, British shipping. The beginning of this additional service of British troopships came in November, 1917, when the Chief of the American Embarkation Service asked the British Ministry of Shipping to assign to us the White Star liner *Olympic*, 46,359 tons gross. This fine steamship, at the time, was laid up in a British port. Under an agreement that the American Government would assume all risks, and that the *Olympic* was to be operated by her owners on this condition, the British Admiralty assigned this ship for transportation of American troops. The *Olympic* made her first trip with American troops in December, 1917. In January, 1918, the *Aquitania*, 45,647 tons gross and *Mauretania*, 30,704 tons gross, both of which had also been in port, were added as transports for American troops on the same conditions. These three British ships at once added a monthly carrying capacity of 15,000 troops, and this was the start of British transportation of American troops on a large scale to meet the emergency of 1918. In the first months of 1918 monthly transportation of American troops overseas increased to the following totals: January, 47,853; February, 49,110; March, 84,882.

After this came the desperate call for help from the Entente Allies, when the first smashing German onslaughts of March, 1918, had revealed the danger of losing the war. The story of the American response to this call will be told in due course. But it should be stated here that a notable factor in the success of this future great movement of American troops was developed in advance, after a conference with British representatives in February, 1918. At this conference the British had not been able to believe in the great numbers of American troops that would be ready to go overseas. General Hines had reassured them by the promise: "We will load every ship you put in our ports." To fulfill this promise, General Hines and General Shanks at once made plans to increase the port facilities of New York. By enlarging Camp Upton and taking over a part of Camp Mills, the Embarkation Service provided additional space, and this enabled the Port of New York to reach its high records in the rush of troops overseas at the emergency of 1918.

By these means the problem of transportation of American troops was well on its way to solution before the crisis. But the question of cargo carriers was a much more difficult and complicated problem, and so remained throughout the war. With every exertion that was made, we were barely able to stagger through to the end. Transportation of troops was a matter that loomed large in the public eye, but transportation of supplies, which meant the life and being of these troops, did not make the same appeal. But, as Admiral Gleaves has stated, "In making our Army in France effective, special mention should be made of the Naval Overseas Transportation Service. Little could have been accomplished without these unromantic, rusty, slow plodding tramps, transporting food, munitions and supplies." [1]

It would be hard to exaggerate any description of the difficulties experienced in collecting enough cargo carriers for the needs of the United States. These difficulties were encountered abroad and at home. The Entente Allies, in their sore straits, could see that every

[1] "History of the Transport Service."

thing must be done to expedite the transportation of American troops to France. But, with the many other calls upon Allied shipping, the needs of America for cargo ships did not stand out in the same proportion, though equally vital, as the decisive American reinforcement of troops must be "based on the American Continent." [1] And this meant that its supplies must come from America by sea.

It was the same story even in the United States. The demands of the Embarkation Service for cargo carriers leapt so rapidly beyond all early ideas that they soon came into conflict with the other requirements of the country. That there should be conflicting demands was natural, with the many Government agencies hard at work, as has been described to develop all the resources of the nation. These activities necessarily implied a great drain upon shipping, and the congested situation as to cargo carriers, in consequence of the confusion among so many demands, has been emphasized in previous chapters.

In 1917 the United States Shipping Board was the controlling body, which allotted shipping among the various claimants. The ships at the disposal of the Shipping Board were not only the American cargo carriers, but also all cargo carriers acquired from foreign owners. It will be readily apparent that there must be heavy demands upon all this shipping from the War Industries Board, the Food Administration, and from the different essential industries of the country. The result was that, in 1917, the practical effect of this sytem had been to permit each of these activities to acquire a definite fleet of cargo carriers for its own particular use. And

[1] General Pershing, Report.

this method, of dividing the cargo carriers into separate groups, had not produced the best results for getting the maximum use out of the whole total of shipping.

A great deal of the confusion and delay in 1917 had come from this cause, and, with the increased demands of the beginning of 1918, the situation was going from bad to worse. The remedy for this state of affairs grew out of one of the typical Government activities which have been described — without any definite powers at first, but suddenly developing into a practical central control. At the call of the Government, there had been a meeting in Washington each week to discuss the shipping situation. At these meetings the Administration officials conferred with eminent American shipping men, who acted as voluntary advisers to the Government. One of these advisers, P. A. S. Franklin, president of the International Mercantile Marine, was consulted by the Secretary of War as to the bad situation in regard to shipping. Mr. Franklin submitted a plan to put the whole ocean marine in one pool under the control of one management.

This plan was immediately adopted by the Secretary of War, with the approval of the Chairman of the Shipping Board. The Shipping Control Committee was at once constituted with Mr. Franklin as its head, who built up its organization, and early in February it was at work in quarters in New York, in the former office building of the Hamburg-American Line — another instance of the irony of events in the World War. By this means a central control of shipping was established. There were no longer different fleets for the different interests. All ships were allotted to their different tasks, as if the whole mass of shipping were one great ocean line. Each allotment was made a matter of tonnage of freight, with local supervision of loading and turnarounds of the ships. In this way the maximum use of the available shipping was obtained, and the results in efficiency were equivalent to a large increase in tonnage of cargo carriers.

This was the turning of the lane. It must not be supposed that any magic cure was found for our difficulties. On the contrary, the quest for cargo carriers for the ever expanding volume of supplies and material to maintain the American Expeditionary Forces in France was a never ending problem. But this fortunate change to a central control of all shipping came just in time to improve the situation, at the very stage when the greatest demands were to be made upon the United States.

Another stride forward was taken as to the cargo carriers early in 1918. As has been stated, it had become evident that manning and operating these ships lay in the province of the United States Navy. Through the last months of 1917 more and more cargo carriers were thus manned and operated by the Navy. At the end of the year, these had increased to such great numbers that on January 7, 1918, a special Branch of Naval Operations was created, called the Naval Overseas Transportation Service,[1] with the sole duty of operating the Government cargo carriers. This grew into the largest merchantman fleet ever assembled under one management. Commander Charles Belknap was Director of the N. O. T. S., in the Office of Operations.

The advantage possessed by the United States Navy, in its ability to receive crews by the appeal to patriotism for enlistment in the Navy, will be easily understood.

---

[1] Usually known as N. O. T. S.

For the difficulty experienced in obtaining civilian crews had been very great. The Navy was also best able to gather intelligent men for officers in the Naval Reserve Force, to train them quickly for their duties, and to give them special practice with experienced officers in the novel requirements of service with convoys. These Government cargo carriers were destined for the convoys as a matter of course. And for this arduous service, so different from anything else on the seas, the Navy, by intensive training for this particular purpose, produced with uncanny quickness a personnel of uncanny skill in convoy seamanship. The test of their efficiency was shown by the small losses in that dangerous service, which must perforce make use of the slow ships, as the ships of speed were taken for troopships. "Of 450 vessels in the N. O. T. S. fleet, only eighteen were lost — 4 per cent of the total; and of the eighteen, only eight fell victims to German mines and submarines. Four went down after collisions at sea, and the rest were accounted for by fire or by stranding." [1]

Hampton Roads was made the main port of departure for the cargo convoys from the United States. It was near the coal fields. The tankers from the south (Tampico) put in there, and great reservoirs of oil were established there. It was also nearer the cotton supply, and it had access to the great resources of the Middle West. This choice of Hampton Roads not only avoided train and shipping congestion, but it also diminished the risk of "too many eggs in one basket."

[1] "The Road to France," Crowell and Wilson.

CHAPTER XXIII

THE FIRST GERMAN ASSAULT OF 1918

THE first great prepared German assault upon the Western Front was launched against the British in the region of St. Quentin in the concealing mists of the early morning of March 21, 1918. This German concentration effected a complete surprise at the point of attack, but the new infiltrating tactics of the Germans gave a still greater surprise, and they broke through the British defenses without a check. "Within eight days the enemy had completely crossed the old Somme battlefield and had swept everything before him to a depth of some 56 kilometers." [1] The most serious feature of this disaster was the dislocation and crippling of the British Fifth Army, with the consequent drain upon available reserves to fill the breach in the Allied defense. As General Pershing expressed it, "The offensive made such inroads upon French and British reserves that defeat stared them in the face unless the new American troops should prove more immediately available than even the most optimistic had dared to hope."

Thus suddenly was the revelation made that there must be a strong reinforcement of American troops to save the situation on the Western Front. This could only be provided by the means of Sea Power, and, then and there, it was settled that the naval history of the decisive stage of the World War would not be an account of naval actions and operations after the old fash-

[1] General Pershing, Report.

ion, but that its main theme would be the narrative of the intense naval effort which placed the American troops on the battlefield. In fact, it is a true statement in a naval history of the World War to say that Sea Power made its fight upon this battlefield of the Western Front. It was there that the United States Navy fought its battle as truly as if its battleships had been present on the fighting line.

After this fearful object lesson of German military strength in March, 1918, the Military Representatives with the Supreme War Council at once made an urgent appeal to the United States (March 27, 1918) in which they stated that they feared a situation in which the strength of the British and French troops in France could "no longer be maintained." They called upon the United States to render help at once by permitting the temporary use of American units in Allied corps and divisions, and to concentrate transportation upon moving overseas infantry and machine gun units.

The American Secretary of War was in France at this time, and he recommended that in compliance there should be preferential transportation for infantry and machine gun units, and that the Commander-in-Chief of the American Expeditionary Forces should use his troops "to render the greatest military assistance, keeping in mind always the determination of the U. S. Government to have its various military forces collected, as speedily as their training and the military situation permits, into an independent American Army, acting in concert with the armies of Great Britain and France, and all arrangements made by him for their temporary training and service will be made with that end in view."

This last was the clear expression of a most wise determination, made at the very start, which eventually enabled our seaborne reinforcement to render its service at full value. The orders given to General Pershing, when he was about to sail from America, had enjoined upon him as an underlying idea that the forces of the United States were "a separate and distinct component of the combined forces, the identity of which must be preserved." [1]

General Pershing, on his arrival overseas, had been confronted by a plan of the Entente Allies for scattering the American troops among the Allied armies. He had stood out against this, as not being the best means of using our troops. As can be seen from the indorsement which has been quoted, Secretary Baker continued to stand squarely behind General Pershing in this regard, and adhered rigidly to the previous decision, in spite of great pressure abroad. The wisdom of this course received a vindication in the event, and it was no matter of national pride, but for practical military reasons.

There can be no question of the existence of these military reasons, which would have rendered the adoption of this scheme of the Entente Allies a most unwise policy. As has been stated, the training and tactics of the Entente Allies had been cramped to their limited ideas of trench warfare. On the other hand, most fortunately, the training of the new American troops had been given the right direction. As General Pershing expressed it, "The development of a self-reliant infantry by thorough drill in the use of the rifle and in tactics of open warfare was always uppermost." With our new troops thus providentially prepared in advance to cope

---

[1] Orders from the Secretary of War to General Pershing, May 26, 1917.

with the very tactics the Germans were about to use, and which were destined to change the whole military situation on the Western Front, it would have been a fatal mistake to identify the Americans irretrievably with the unsatisfactory conditions then existing among the armies of the Entente Allies on the Western Front.

In his report, General Pershing has expressed this beyond any misunderstanding: "While the Germans were practising for open warfare and concentrating their most aggressive personnel in shock divisions, the training of the Allies was still limited to trench warfare. As our troops were being trained for open warfare, there was every reason why we could not allow them to be scattered among our Allies, even by divisions, much less as replacements, except by pressure of sheer necessity." At the pressure of this emergency, all available American troops were freely given to the French and British armies, but it was always with the wise proviso that the ultimate use of our troops was to be as an American fighting army.

Before the first German attack, General Pershing had become convinced that "an early appearance of the larger American units on the front would be most beneficial to the morale of the Allies themselves." [1] Accordingly, four American divisions [2] had been put on the front, and on January 20, 1918, the First Army Corps Headquarters, with Maj. Gen. Hunter Liggett commanding, was organized at Neufchâteau, "and the plan to create an independent sector on the Lorraine front was taking shape." [3] This organization was later to

[1] General Pershing, Report.
[2] An American division was the equivalent of two German or Allied divisions.
[3] General Pershing, Report.

develop into the First American Army. At the time of the first German attack on March 21, 1918, "approximately 300,000 American troops had reached France." [1]

It has been necessary, in a naval history of the World War, to give this summary of the military situation on the Western Front at the time of the first great disaster to the armies of the Entente Allies, in order to show two factors in this situation. First, the American reinforcement, which Sea Power was to bring onto the field, was best adapted, by training and doctrines of command, to meet the actual conditions which so suddenly broke up "stabilized" trench warfare. Secondly, the determination had been made to use this seaborne reinforcement to the best advantage. With these two factors assured, there was no possibility of our military forces being wasted after they had been brought into action by means of the naval forces. In the whole joint operation of the American military and naval forces, one was so dependent upon the other, that this dependence must be reiterated in order to keep the true proportions of the picture.

As a result of the overthrow on the Western Front, and in response to the urgent call of the Entente Allies, then began the most gigantic movement of troops over the sea that the world has ever seen. This was the naval operation which hurled a decisive military force against a victorious and advancing enemy.

[1] General Pershing, Report.

CHAPTER XXIV

RUSHING AMERICAN TROOPS TO FRANCE

(See Map on p. 205)

THE approaching crisis of the war was now revealed beyond any misunderstanding. As General Pershing stated, "Ever since the collapse of the Russian armies and the crisis on the Italian front in the fall of 1917, German armies were being assembled and trained for this great campaign which was to end the war before America's effort could be brought to bear. Germany's best troops, her most successful generals, and all the experience gained in three years of war [1] were mobilized for the supreme effort." The race was on — and it was a race such as the world has never seen.

The first disastrous defeat had at once brought home to the British the realization that transportation of American troops was more important than any other use of shipping. "The losses had been heavy and the British were unable to replace them entirely. They were, therefore, making extraordinary efforts to increase the shipping available for our troops." [2] The Report of the War Cabinet (1918) has stated the result: "At the same time, however, orders were given by the War Cabinet at the beginning of April that every effort was to be made to convey American troops to this country in the largest possible numbers. In order to effect this every available

---

[1] . . . "the advantage in morale, in experience, in training for mobile warfare, and in unity of command." — General Pershing, Report.

[2] General Pershing, Report.

195

ship suitable for the conveyance of troops was taken from every trade route in the world and diverted to the North Atlantic. The number of additional ships put into the service between the 31st March and the end of August was 124. By this means an average of over 150,-000 American troops per month were conveyed on British ships and 10,000 per month on Italian ships (which were placed at the disposal of the British Government by the Italian Government)."

"Until May, 1918, almost all of our troops were embarked in our own Naval transports." [1] But at last the full resources of British shipping were being used, and the monthly totals of American troops sent overseas leapt to astonishing figures. 84,889 had been taken across in March, 118,642 in April. In May, in consequence of the agreements with Great Britain, the number of American troops transported reached the unprecedented total of 245,945, and General Pershing could report: "Following the agreements as to British shipping, our troops came so rapidly that by the end of May we had a force of 600,000 in France." In order to keep in mind the facts as to this gigantic movement of American troops, which grew to such a flood in the ensuing months of the war, the following monthly totals should be stated here: June, 278,864; July, 306,350; August, 286,974; September, 257,457; October, 180,326. This meant that a million and a half American troops were rushed to Europe in the six months of the crisis of the World War,[2] and thus the United States accomplished

---

[1] "A history of the Transport Service." Admiral Gleaves.

[2] "These hordes of American troops on the continent which turned the balance against us on the Western front in 1918." Tirpitz.

her main object in the World War by providing the decisive reinforcement to the Allied Armies in France.[1]

It also should be noted that, in accordance with the agreements for priority of infantry and machine gun units which have been described, the first great rush of American troops provided a maximum strength of fighting men. The general policy as to the American troops overseas, agreed upon with the Entente Allies, had tended toward this direction. By the give and take arrangements, field guns, animals, airplanes, &c., were to be provided at first by the Allies in exchange for raw material, in order that the whole effort of the United States might be concentrated upon the production of fighting men. But the new agreements went far beyond this, and the troopships were all being used for the transportation of armed men, with only their equipment. This was a phase of the situation which the Germans could not understand. From their point of view, a division must be transported with all the impedimenta of its full organization for the field. The chagrined Ludendorff described "bringing over the American masses, crammed tight in transports, to France. The men carried only their personal equipments. . . . The whole operation was a tour de force, uncommonly effective for a short time, but impossible to maintain for a long period. Had the war lasted longer a reaction must have followed. . . . Ruthlessness and energy once again brought success." In their first disappointment at German defeat, the German leaders broke out with frank complaints, which showed their states of mind — and which can never be recalled. The very fact that Luden-

---

[1] "America thus became the decisive power in the war." Ludendorff.

dorff should thus describe the transportation of American troops is an involuntary tribute.

It is also a notable fact that the Germans did not have information of the flood of American troops pouring into France. All this was outside their calculations. Consequently, German agents were fussing over details of information, according to their instructions, and they were missing the one great thing. As to this, Ludendorff has left no doubt: "How many Americans had got across by April we did not know." And he has made an admission which is another involuntary tribute: "But the rapidity with which they actually did arrive proved surprising."

The explanation was, in the spring of 1918 the great machinery of the effort of the United States had begun to work on a large scale with a smooth efficiency, which, in itself, provided secrecy. After the troubles of the hard winter, the United States Railroad Administration had so successfully coördinated the railroads of the nation into one unified system that uninterrupted transportation of troops was secured. In the great training camps troops would know nothing of their approaching departure before they were loaded into trains at the sidings within the camps. These trains would be given special right of way to the great embarkation points, where the troops were secure from observation until they went on board the transports, of which the sailings were jealously guarded. All this was so unprecedented, in its simplicity on a vast scale, that the vastness of the scale was not suspected at the time.

The troopships supplied by Great Britain were retained under British control when transporting American troops. They were operated by their owners, and they were controlled by the British convoy system. But all were brought up to the American Navy standards of health and safety. "Many of these vessels had been cargo carriers, and much of the work of refitting was done at New York under the direction of the Port of Embarkation." [1] "The Port of Embarkation spent $4,000,000 for life-saving equipment alone, either to supplement that already carried on British ships or to replace equipment which our officers condemned. The new equipment was sold to the British ship owners at cost." [2]

The diagram on page 205 shows at a glance the totals and distributions of the transportation of American troops overseas. It will be noted that New York was the great port of embarkation, and, with the subsidiary port of Norfolk, sent out over 1,900,000 of the two million American soldiers. Of the receiving ports abroad, Brest, with St. Nazaire, received the bulk of our troops sent direct to France. Of those sent to Great Britain first, to be relayed to France later, it is shown that Liverpool received the bulk. Of course these last were, for the most part, from the British convoys of troopships.

The American troopships of the Cruiser and Transport Force remained a separate convoy system under Navy control. This American fleet of transports had been increased far beyond the total of the seized German shipping, which at the first had been its main reliance. At the time of the Armistice, 45 American troopships had been put into service with the Cruiser and Transport Force.[3] These had been secured by the

[1] "The Road to France," Crowell and Wilson.

[2] Ibid.

[3] In the great task of bringing back the American troops from overseas, 105 additional ships of the Cruiser and Transport Force carried troops to the United States. These comprised battleships and cruisers, as well as trans-

United States taking over every steamship that could be pressed into the service.[1]

Of these, only two were owned by the Shipping Board, the fine oil burners, *Orizaba* and *Siboney* (late *Oriente*). The rest were taken over from various sources, by requisition and charter or by downright purchase. Of course many were taken over from the International Mercantile Marine and its subsidiaries. Notable among these were the *Finland* and *Kroonland* of the Red Star Line, and the sister ships *Manchuria* and *Mongolia* of the Atlantic Transport Company. Each of these last two had a carrying capacity of about 5,000 troops. Especial mention should be made of two very valuable transports, the *Northern Pacific* and *Great Northern*, secured from the Great Northern Steamship Company. These were new oil burners of twenty and twenty-one knots respectively. "They proved to be the best ships in the transport service — better even than the German ships, built primarily for troop transportation." [2] Three of our troopships were steamships commandeered from the Dutch, which had been taken over by the United States as explained. Four steamships were assigned as troopships by the French Government, and these were grouped with the United States Navy convoys, as were ships assigned by the Italian Government. The French Government also assigned to the Cruiser and Transport Force a division of three cruisers under Rear Admiral Grout,[3]

ports. It was a wonderful operation, but its story is outside the province of this book.

[1] "By November, 1918, the Army had brought into its own service about all the suitable passenger boats that the world could supply." — "The Road to France," Crowell and Wilson.

[2] "The Road to France," Crowell and Wilson.

[3] *Gloire* (flag), *Marseillaise, Du Petit Thouars.* This last cruiser was sunk in the Bay of Biscay.

and these served as a welcome reinforcement in escorting the American convoys.

Admiral Gleaves and the officers under his command were tireless in improving the efficiency of the operation of the ships of the Cruiser and Transport Force. Everything was done to keep the ships at their best for the arduous task of voyage after voyage, rushed at top speed and with no delays in port. Crew repair parties were at work on them day and night. Actual major repairs, which would mean docking, were fought off as well as possible. "It was anything to keep the ships going." [1] All this was fearfully hard on the ships, and they were badly used up at the end. But they were successfully "kept going," and not one vessel broke down under the strain. By constant study of methods for getting the most out of the ships, the turnarounds of the round trip voyages were shortened to an incredible extent, and in this respect the troopships of the Cruiser and Transport Force "outdid any other ships placed at our disposal, and by a wide margin." [2] "The average turnaround of a British ship in the American troop service was 84.4 days, or nearly three months. The American turnaround was 36.3 days, or slightly more than one month.[3]

A great help in producing this result of a much shortened round trip for the American troopship, was the study given to the matter of coaling. In the preceding hard winter, coaling had been a difficult problem. It had even come to a point where Admiral Gleaves, on his own initiative, recruited a working party from the Navy crews in port and commandeered the coaling equipment

---

[1] "The Road to France," Crowell and Wilson.
[2] Ibid.   [3] Ibid.

of the contractors, in order to get a transport to sea without delay. "Thereafter, the Force itself continued to operate the coaling equipment in New York." [1] But the greatest advance in this direction was by increasing the bunker capacity of the troopships so that the necessity for recoaling was reduced. The Navy changed over the adjacent cargo holds into bunker space and connected them with the firing rooms. By this expedient a great deal of time was saved in each round trip. There was also a notable gain in shipping, from doing away with the necessity to transport coal to the ports of debarkation, with the attendant delay of handling the coal at these congested ports.

For the largest transport of all, the *Leviathan*, this could not be done, but, as she could carry more troops than anything else afloat, the British were glad to make a special arrangement for her to load 1,200 tons of Welsh coal each time she reached her debarkation point. After delays on her first two voyages at Liverpool, on account of the tides, Admiral Gleaves recommended that this great troopship should be sent into Brest, where there was deep water at all tides. Thereafter, her trips were made to Brest, with her allotted coal there ready for her by agreement. After this, the turnaround of the *Leviathan* averaged the unprecedented short round trip of twenty six days.[2] As will be seen from the table on page 157, the *Leviathan* alone transported overseas 96,804 American troops. On account of her high speed, this mighty ship usually traveled alone or in company with the *Great Northern* or the *Northern Pacific*. These new

[1] "The Road to France," Crowell and Wilson.
[2] ". . . an increase of 30,000 men in her annual carrying capacity." — "The Road to France," Crowell and Wilson.

American steamships were the only troopships that were able to maintain speed adequate to accomplish a trip with the *Leviathan*. These two American steamships had another advantage, which made them of great value as troopships. Both were oil burners and could be fueled for the round trip on each voyage. Consequently, these two ships held the records for short turnarounds over all other troopships.

It was not only by means of ability to make more frequent trips overseas that the efficiency of the American troopships was increased. In addition, the actual troop-carrying capacity of the American transports was increased, and thus there was a double gain in efficiency. Admiral Gleaves and his officers made intensive studies of the means to increase the accommodations for troops in each ship. All the normal space for passengers had been utilized for berths. Yet, by clearing additional space, from ripping out passages and cabins, and using even mess halls, many more berths were installed. A great gain was also made by utilizing head room to make the standee berths in additional tiers. By these means the carrying capacity of the American troopships was increased some 25 per cent. Admiral Gleaves even went farther than this. He proposed that the troopships should carry 50 per cent above their total berth accommodation, the men to sleep in shifts, each watch occupying the berths for twelve hours. This plan was adopted on nine of the best American transports,[1] and was successful until the influenza epidemic in the fall put an end to overloading. But it has been estimated that "the intensive loadings of transports had landed in France 100,-

[1] *Agamemnon, Mt. Vernon, Great Northern, Northern Pacific, von Steuben, America, George Washington, Orizaba, Siboney.*

000 extra troops." [1] It will be evident from this that Ludendorff's horrified description, "bringing over the American masses, crammed tight in transports, to France," was in truth, all unintentionally, a high compliment to the efficiency of the Cruiser and Transport Force of the United States Navy.

[1] "The Road to France," Crowell and Wilson.

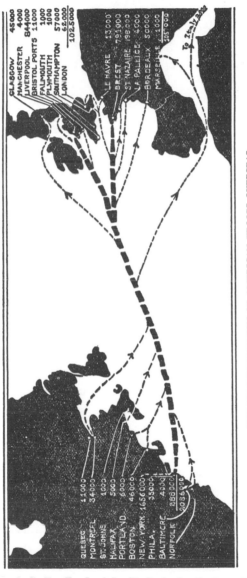

THE TRANSPORTATION OF AMERICAN TROOPS OVERSEAS

Showing the totals sailing from American ports and landing at the various ports overseas

CHAPTER XXV

THE OPPOSING NAVAL FORCES IN 1918

WHILE the great movement of American troops overseas was gathering way, and growing into the main naval operation of the crisis of the World War, the general situation of the opposing naval forces abroad remained unchanged. The Germans had lost their original battle in the U-boat campaign, but they were still making every effort with their submarines. As their main grand strategy had now shifted to their great military assault on the Western Front, from this time, the mission of the U-boats must be held to consist of coöperation with the new main German object, as has been stated. Consequently, the success of this coöperation must be measured by its results in keeping away reinforcements and supplies from their enemies in France. Measured by this test, in what must be considered the principal naval object for the Germans in 1918, the Germans were again failing.

In this case theirs was a double failure. First, the convoyed troopships were proving their ability to bring the great American military reinforcement overseas, in defiance of the U-boats. Secondly, the U-boats were no longer destroying Allied shipping beyond replacement — and this last meant that the Germans no longer threatened to cut off seaborne supplies from the Entente Allies.

The Report of the War Cabinet (1918) has thus recorded the stage when replacements of shipping balanced losses: "About the middle of 1918, mainly owing to the ship building effort of the United States, the world's output of new tonnage equalled the rate of loss." This implied the passing of the peak of peril for the Entente Allies. It was true that the tonnage position of the Entente Allies abroad grew even worse. "The new ships from the United States shipbuilding yards were all required to meet the growing demands of the United States Army," [1] and there was also the drain upon Allied tonnage to provide transportation for American troops and supplies, as has been stated. But all this was putting shipping to the best possible use for the cause of the Entente Allies, and was entirely to their advantage.

By this time the convoy system was working like clock work. As Admiral Sims expressed it, "The Admiralty in London was thus the central nervous system of a complicated but perfectly working organism which reached the remotest corners of the world." Admiral Sims has also written of shipping that "now for the first time it was arranged in hard and fast routes and dispatched in accordance with schedules as fixed as those of a great railroad." He has added: "This comparison holds good of its operation after it had entered the infested zones. Indeed the very terminology of our railroads was used. . . . The whole gigantic enterprise flowed with a precision and a regularity which I think it is hardly likely that any other transportation system has ever achieved." In fact, Sir Eric Geddes, the First Lord of the British Admiralty, who had done so much for this system, was a trained engineer.

As London was the center of this great system, with which were interlocked all the activities of our naval

---

[1] War Cabinet, Report, 1918.

forces abroad, it was the only right move to have the American headquarters in London, in constant touch with the British Admiralty. There Admiral Sims, as Commander of the United States Naval Forces Operating in European Waters, had established a strong administrative staff, of which the late Rear Admiral Nathan C. Twining was the efficient Chief of Staff. As the numbers of American naval units overseas increased, the policy was still continued of securing a united command by putting these American forces on active duty under the local British commanding officers, except that the great patrol area of the Brest American bases continued to be an independent American command. But all these American naval forces overseas remained under American control for maintenance, as was the case with the first contingents sent across.

For this reason, as the American naval forces overseas grew to large numbers, with detachments at Queenstown, Brest, Gibraltar, the Mediterranean area, and the Azores, with detachments with the Grand Fleet, and on other duties over the wide seas, including eventually even northern Russia, the American Headquarters was a busy place, and its activities extended in many different directions. At the end of 1917 a Planning Section [1] of Admiral Sims' staff was constituted, and the first list of special subjects, to be studied "at as early a date as possible," gave a comprehensive view of the development of American naval strategy: "(1) The Northern Barrage; (2) The English Channel; (3) The Straits of Otranto; (4) The tactics of contact with submarines; (5)

[1] Captain N. C. Twining, Chief of Staff and ex officio head of the Planning Section, Captain F. H. Schofield, Captain L. C. McNamee,* Captain D. W. Knox, Captain H. E. Yarnell,* Colonel R. H. Dunlap, U. S. M. C.,* Colonel L. M. Little, U. S. M. C.* (* part time).

The convoy system; (6) Coöperation of the United States naval forces and the naval forces of the Allies; (7) A joint naval doctrine." Numbers 1, 2, and 3 referred to the great American mine project, which has been described. Denying the enemy U-boats access to the English Channel was the necessary corollary of the barrage in the North Sea, and there was also a project for denying the enemy access to the Mediterranean from the Adriatic. It will be obvious that the other subjects were vital to the naval situation.

From this appreciation, and from the widespread dispositions of American naval forces which have been described, the reader can at once realize the many and various missions of the detachments from Admiral Mayo's constantly growing Atlantic Fleet.

These details of American naval forces, as well as Admiral Gleaves' Cruiser and Transport Force, were made more efficient by refueling with oil at sea, as has been described. This had been developed into a system that maintained a reliable service both winter and summer. Under the Office of Operations, and with the greatest secrecy, the positions of the tankers were plotted out to meet the different units which were to be refueled. Broadly speaking, 30° Longitude had been designated as a boundary line. When they had passed to eastward of this line, the different naval details passed into the control of the American Headquarters in London, with Operations directing the policy and prescribing the point where 30° Longitude should be passed. That is, from the United States to 30° Longitude the details were under Admiral Mayo, or Admiral Gleaves. After passing to the east of 30° Longitude, they came under the control of Admiral Sims. In the same way, on trips westward they passed out of Admiral Sims' control on crossing 30° Longitude. This made a very practical basis for the constant long distance activities of the United States Navy, and it worked out well in actual use.

The War Cabinet Report (1918) has stated, of this stage of the war, that the British Navy and the United States Navy "coöperated on terms of close alliance and high efficiency in maintaining the sea communication of the Allies and in transporting from the United States to European battlefields the rapidly growing armies which the American people provided." For the main British Naval force, activities were "necessarily lacking in incident. But, nevertheless, the Grand Fleet was the essential support of all the work carried out by the naval forces of the Allies in all the seas." [1] The attendant destroyers and light forces were still kept in close company with the British Battle Fleet.

The British Navy kept up "the systematic mining of the Heligoland Bight, to prevent the submarines from leaving their bases by the route." [2] Minelaying submarines joined in this task. But, as has been stated, these minefields were not sufficiently covered by armed forces to prevent the German minesweepers from clearing channels for egress of U-boats. With the light armed forces of the Grand Fleet at a distance, support of the British minelayers was confined for the most part to the Harwich Force. The War Cabinet Report has stated: "In Southern Waters the light cruisers and torpedo craft stationed at Harwich were employed in attacking German vessels in the Heligoland Bight and in support of our minelayers. Many operations were undertaken by the Harwich Force alone, or in conjunction with air-

[1] War Cabinet, Report, 1918.   [2] Ibid.

craft and coastal motor boats, but beyond the destruction of a few minesweepers no decisive results were obtained."

On January 1, 1918, Rear Admiral Keyes had succeeded Vice Admiral Bacon in command of the Dover Patrol. The light forces of the Dover Patrol had been increased, especially in destroyers. These comprised on June 30, 1918, 4 flotilla leaders, 29 modern destroyers, 10 older destroyers, and 6 "P" boats.[1] The flotilla leaders were very valuable, as "their powerful armament made it possible for them to engage successfully a numerically greater superior force." [2]

Two of these flotilla leaders, *Broke* and *Swift*, had proved this to be true in an engagement with German destroyers on the night of April 20–21, 1917. Two detachments of German destroyers had broken into the channel, and one of these had fired a few shots at Dover. They had joined at a rendezvous, and were returning to the German base, when they were intercepted by the *Broke* and *Swift*. After a hot engagement, two of the six German destroyers had been sunk, one by torpedoes and one by being rammed by the *Broke*.

The net barriers in the Channel could not be maintained through the winter months, and in 1918 "the Straits were eventually closed by broad minefields extending from the British to the French coast." [3] They were deep minefields, with the mines anchored far enough below the surface to allow the light patrolling forces to pass over them. This was a preliminary to putting into execution the American scheme for closing the

---

[1] Fitted with fish hydroplanes.
[2] "The Crisis of the Naval War," Admiral Jellicoe.
[3] War Cabinet, Report.

northern exits by the great system of mine barrages for which preparations were being made as has been stated.

The efforts of the Dover Patrol against the Germans along the Belgian coasts by means of the bombarding monitors had remained a failure. The German guns distributed in positions on this coast had again shown that guns on shore, if well placed, cannot be dominated by ships' guns. On the part of the Dover Patrol, there had also been a plan to coöperate with the expected advance of the British armies in Flanders, in the last half of 1917, by "landing a force of some 14,000 officers and men with tanks, artillery and transport on the coast of Belgium under the very muzzles of the German heavy artillery." [1] The idea was to put the military force on board specially constructed pontoons, which were to be pushed to the shore by monitors.

A great deal of preparation was made for this scheme of a landing on the Belgian coast. The pontoons were constructed, over 500 feet long, with bridges for landing. There were also specially designed tanks, with which it was intended to scale the sea wall. Detailed forces of the Army and Navy were gathered for this operation, and the proposed landing was rehearsed in every particular and in the greatest secrecy. There was even a model of the sea wall set up at the Headquarters of the British Tank Corps in France, in order to give these tanks practice in scaling. For a long time everything was held in readiness for a favorable opportunity to carry out this scheme, which was to be a surprise descent upon the coast under a smoke screen, with covering bombardment, and bombardments at other points as diversions. But the favorable opportunity never came,

---

[1] "The Crisis of the Naval War," Admiral Jellicoe.

because the efforts of the British Army to drive back the Germans in the Battle of Flanders ended in failure. As there was no advance of the British on land, an attack from the sea would only have been an isolated effort foredoomed to failure. In this regard, Admiral Jellicoe has written that "when it became necessary to abandon it owing to the inability of the Army to coöperate the intense disappointment felt by all those who had worked so hard to ensure its success can be realized."

Another plan against the Belgian coast had also been in discussion since 1916. This was Rear Admiral Tyrwhitt's proposal for the blocking of Zeebrugge. It had not found favor until Admiral Keyes came from the Plans Division to the command of the Dover Patrol. Admiral Keyes at once made the project an important part of his plans, and this was carried forward to execution as a determined attempt to close the egress of the Zeebrugge and Ostend canals from Bruges. An account of this operation will be given in the following chapter.

On the part of the Germans, Admiral Scheer has stated: "The winter months brought no change in the activities of the Fleet, which were directed towards supporting the U-boat campaign." But there was one departure from this program, "in the spring of 1918 when our army was attacking in the west." [1] This was a plan to upset the system of Scandinavian convoys. The Germans realized that these convoys were then so well protected that a repetition of the former raid with light forces would not be successful. Consequently the German plan was to make a sudden attack with their battle cruisers, while giving these "the necessary support from the battleship squadrons." [2] This implied a sortie of the

[1] "Germany's High Sea Fleet," Admiral Scheer.   [2] Ibid.

whole German Battle Fleet toward the Norwegian coast. The Germans chose a time when their information told them that the convoys would be exposed to attack.[1] Every precaution was taken for secrecy, and "it was enjoined upon the officers in command of the subordinate groups to use their wireless as sparingly as possible during the expedition." [2]

"On the 23rd at 6 A.M. the various groups put to sea." [3] The German fleet was delayed by a fog for a short time but "the journey through the mine-fields passed off without a hitch." [4] The morning of April 24 was "fine clear weather." [5] But nothing was sighted on the route of the convoys. "Information received from the Naval Staff at 2 P.M. concerning the times of arrival and departure of convoys indicated that we had not been lucky in our choice of a day to attack them. Apparently the convoys from England to Norway had crossed the North Sea on the 23rd." [6]

One incident of this sortie of the German Battle Fleet was notable. The battle cruiser *Moltke* broke down on the morning of April 24. A remarkable feature in the naval operations of the war had been the fact that, unless there were injuries caused by the enemy, the capital ships of the different navies showed themselves to be very efficient in their ability to keep on going. But this time there was a complete collapse. The *Moltke* threw off one of her four propellers. The turbine raced, and, before it could be stopped, the training wheel had flown to pieces, causing so much damage that two thousand

[1] "So far as could be made out, convoys mostly travelled at the beginning and middle of the week. Consequently Wednesday, April 24, was chosen for the attack." — "Germany's High Sea Fleet," Admiral Scheer.

[2] Ibid.   [3] Ibid.   [4] Ibid.   [5] Ibid.   [6] Ibid.

tons of water flowed into the ship. "Through a curious train of circumstances an accident to a propeller, slight enough in itself, had brought the ship completely to a stand, so that it was powerless to move." [1] The *Moltke* was taken in tow by the battleship *Oldenburg*, and a good deal of difficulty was experienced in getting her in. Off List the *Moltke* had been sufficiently repaired to be cast loose, and to proceed at 15 knots under her own steam. "About an hour after she was cast loose, at 7.50 P.M., she was attacked by a submarine 40 nautical miles north of Heligoland and was hit amidships on her port side. She could not avoid the torpedo, but was able to turn towards its course so that it struck at a very acute angle. The injury did not prevent the ship from entering the Jade under her own steam." [2]

Admiral Scheer has put it on record that this was the last operation at a distance from the German bases undertaken by the German Battle Fleet. Consequently, from this time and for the duration of the war, we must think of the High Sea Fleet as solely occupied in its mission of forwarding the U-boat campaign by keeping a wide area clear for the egress and entrance of the U-boats. But, as before, the British did not estimate this change of German naval strategy, and continued to keep all the forces of the Grand Fleet at a distance, on watch for an incursion into the North Sea which never came.

[1] "Germany's High Sea Fleet," Admiral Scheer.   [2] Ibid.

CHAPTER XXVI

THE ZEEBRUGGE AND OSTEND OPERATIONS

THE British anti-submarine project, which was developed by Admiral Keyes, was a plan for blocking the two canals which gave the German base Bruges egress into the North Sea. Bruges itself is inland, and is connected with the sea by the Zeebrugge and Ostend canals, consequently there was one outlet for submarines at Zeebrugge, another at Ostend. The plan was to run in block-ships by a surprise operation, and to sink these block-ships in the entrances of the canals, to render them useless for the enemy. This was a bold and novel scheme. It implied surprise approaches to the two entrances under a smoke screen of artificial fog, and the difficult problems of getting the block-ships into position where they could be sunk in such a way that they would obstruct the canals.

It will be obvious that this plan was most complicated in its details. It comprised assembling at a distance the two forces which were to operate against the two Belgian outlets, and moving them into positions for their sudden incursions with the nicest adjustment to time and tides. As there were two widely separate points of attack, the undertaking became divided into two distinct and simultaneous operations.

Against Zeebrugge it was much the more difficult attack, as the operation against this canal was complicated by the Mole on the west side of the harbor. This was a mile and a half long, and had a strong German battery on the extension guarding the entrance of the harbor, with also guns on the shore end. Consequently the attack at Zeebrugge must include also an effort to neutralize this defense, while the block-ships were being brought into position to be sunk in the canal.

The block-ships provided for these operations were five old light cruisers, filled with cement and fitted with explosive charges and mines attached to their bottoms, to insure their sinking quickly when they were in place. Three of these were to be used against Zeebrugge, two against Ostend.[1] They were manned by volunteer crews who were specially drilled for their hazardous service. Motor launches were to be in attendance to take off the crews.

The light cruisers and destroyers of the Harwich Force were to cover these operations against any movement of the enemy from the direction of Heligoland Bight. For the two operations there were required monitors for bombardment of the shore batteries, destroyers [2] for a protecting cover, motor launches to lay the smoke screens and rescue the crews of block-ships. Against Zeebrugge there were special preparations to attack the Mole. The old type cruiser *Vindictive* and two large shallow draft Mersey ferryboats, *Daffodil* and *Iris II*, were to carry in a landing force, and two British submarines were detailed to blow up the viaduct connecting the Mole with the shore. It will show the extent of British preparation for this action to state that the striking force numbered 142 vessels. Of these 75 were sent against Zeebrugge, 67 against Ostend. Admiral Keyes was in command of the Zeebrugge operation, in his flagship the cruiser *Warwick*.

[1] *Thetis, Iphigenia, Intrepid,* at Zeebrugge; *Sirius, Brilliant,* at Ostend.

[2] Twenty-three British destroyers, eight French destroyers.

Through April these prepared naval forces waited for the favorable conditions which were necessary to carry out the elaborate schedule of attack. Twice the whole expedition was at sea, and once within thirteen miles of its objective, when weather conditions compelled postponement. At last on the night of April 22–23, 1918, conditions remained favorable. There had been many bombardments of the shore defenses. Consequently, the bombardments to cover the actual operations did not give any special warning of what was to come. Well off shore the two forces separated. At midnight each was before its point of attack.

At Zeebrugge, the *Vindictive* and her two attending ferryboats steamed toward the Mole, under a concealing smoke screen until within 400 yards. On emerging from the smoke they were under fire, but the *Vindictive* succeeded in getting alongside the Mole, which towered over her and protected everything but her upper works from gunfire. She had been fitted with a false top deck and 18 long landing gangways on her port side, to enable her landing party to scale the Mole. She had come into position with her port side along the Mole, but there was so much sea that great difficulty was found in making fast and using the landing gangways. But the ferryboat *Daffodil* pushed her against the Mole and held her there. Then a landing party of over three hundred was put ashore. A landing party was also on the *Iris II*, but this ferryboat was unable to make fast alongside the Mole and could not land her men. Admiral Keyes reported that the *Vindictive* "overran her station and was berthed some 400 yards further to westward than was intended," and this exposed the landing party on the Mole to gunfire, which prevented them from carrying the German guns on the Mole, and did not allow them to carry out their plans for demolition.

Two old submarines had been detailed, with exploding charges placed in them to blow up the viaduct of the Mole. They were fitted with gyro control, so that they could be headed at the viaduct, abandoned by their crews, and left to run between the piers and cause destructive explosions. These two submarines were towed to Zeebrugge by destroyers, but one was delayed by parting her towline until too late for the attack. The other submarine (C 3) ran in under fire, was headed at the right place in the viaduct, and her crew left in a motor skiff, after igniting the fuses. The explosion seriously damaged the viaduct, and caused so much confusion that the crew escaped to their attending picket boat.

Favored by these diversions, the three block-ships were sent in to obstruct the canal. They were under heavier fire than had been expected, owing to the failure of the landing party against the German guns on the Mole. The *Thetis*, leading, was hit heavily, her engines stopped, and she settled aground outside the channel. The other two block-ships, *Intrepid* and *Iphigenia*, reached their assigned positions and were actually sunk in the canal. The crews of all three were taken off by the attending motor launches in the most daring manner, and there were fewer casualties than would have been thought possible.

The landing party on the Mole was recalled to the *Vindictive*, after she had been in her perilous position for nearly an hour. The *Daffodil* had continued to hold her in place, and it was only by this aid that the British on the Mole were able to get on board again. Then the expedition withdrew from Zeebrugge. *Iris II* was heavily hit several times on her way out, and, as she had crowded on board the detachment which was to have been used as a landing party, there were many casualties.

At Ostend the simultaneous attempt to block the canal failed on the night of April 22–23. Admiral Keyes stated in his report: "The success of the Ostend enterprise was affected to some extent by two adverse factors: (1) at 12: 15 A.M. the wind (N. N. E.), which so far had been favorable for purposes of the smoke screen, shifted into an unfavorable quarter (S. S. W.), hereby exposing the attacking forces to the enemy: (2) the buoy which marks the channel to Ostend harbour had been moved very shortly before, unknown to us to a position some 2400 yards further east, so that when *Brilliant* and *Sirius* found it and put their helms to starboard they ran ashore." The two British block-ships were thus far aside from the canal entrance, and made no obstruction to free use of the canal. There was the same daring efficiency shown in the rescue of the crews of the block-ships that had been so notable a feature at Zeebrugge. Admiral Keyes reported of both operations: "The manner in which the survivors of the crews of the five blocking ships and of Submarine C 3 were rescued and brought away by volunteer crews in motor launches and a picket boat was beyond praise."

Admiral Keyes also stated in his report: "In the course of the St. George's Day our casualties to officers and men were as follows: — Killed, 176; wounded, 412; missing, 49; of the latter 35 are believed to have been killed."

As the enemy were left free to use the Ostend egress,

aside from any question of the block-ships sunk at Zee-brugge, Admiral Keyes urged upon the British Admiralty the necessity for a new attempt. "When I learnt on the 23rd April that the attempt to block Ostend had not succeeded, I represented to their Lordships the desirability of repeating the operation at once." [1] The *Vindictive* was thereupon prepared as a block-ship in time to take advantage of the last right coincidence of high tide and darkness on April 27. But unfavorable weather conditions caused postponement until this needed condition recurred.

This delay gave time to prepare another block-ship, the old cruiser *Sappho* of the same class as the cruisers which had been used in the previous attempt. The operation was undertaken on the night of May 9–10, 1918. The *Sappho* met with a boiler accident on the way, "which reduced her speed to such an extent that she was unable to reach her destination in time to take part. This halved the chances of success, and was a great misfortune." [2] The *Vindictive* kept on alone, but came under a heavy fire as she was attempting to get into position to obstruct the entrance of the canal. A shell wrecked her conning tower, killing her commander,[3] and this block-ship also grounded in a position too far to the east to obstruct the canal.

On his way back, Admiral Keyes' command was delayed by picking up a disabled motor boat with survivors from the *Vindictive*, and was forced by the fall of the tide into an unswept route, where Admiral Keyes' flag-

[1] Vice Admiral Keyes, Dispatch June 15, 1918.

[2] Vice Admiral Keyes, Report.

[3] Commander Godsal who had led the former attempt in *Brilliant* and gallantly volunteered for the second effort.

ship *Warwick* struck a mine. This broke her back "and destroyed the after part of the ship." The *Warwick* was taken in tow and brought into Dover at 4.50 P.M., May 10.

These gallant operations showed great initiative and ingenuity in planning. Their dangerous adventures were carried out with the utmost bravery and self-devotion, and they reflect the greatest credit upon the British Navy. This sudden change to a daring British offensive also had a stimulating moral effect which was of great benefit.

CHAPTER XXVII

THE GERMAN U-BOAT RAIDS OFF THE AMERICAN COAST

ON the American side of the Atlantic careful preparations had been made to guard against U-boat attacks, which were regarded as inevitable sooner or later. Of course the main task must be to safeguard the egress of the convoys. If the Germans had been able to interrupt these by operations of their U-boats in the Western Atlantic, it would have saved the whole situation for Germany. But it should be stated at once that the German attempts with their submarines off the American coasts never brought about the slightest delay in the rush of troops to France. Much less was there even the threat of an interruption.

Precautions for the safety of the convoys were unremitting. There was never any relaxation of vigilance throughout the many months in which there were no signs of the presence of U-boats. The channels of sailing were as carefully swept, and the convoys as vigilantly guarded by anti-submarine forces, as if there had been frequent U-boat attacks. The decision had been wisely made not to allow this escort duty on our side of the Atlantic to prevent any great number of destroyers from going overseas, and very few destroyers were retained for this service in the Western Atlantic. But the watch over the convoys was all the more painstaking from the very fact that it had to be carried on without them. It was here that the new submarine chasers were of value, and a large force of these craft was especially trained for this purpose. The energetic and adaptable young men who made up the personnel of this naval force performed a most arduous duty, as their activities extended from Halifax to Key West, and few realize what an experience of wind and weather this involved.

Upon our declaration of war, the Coast Guard had become a part of the Naval Establishment for war duty, in accordance with an act of Congress of 1915. Its cruising cutters had been given more powerful guns, and a number of them were sent overseas. The rest rendered most valuable service in this great undertaking of patrolling the Western Atlantic. They were well adapted to our waters and were an important part of the system of cruisers and mother ships which supported the anti-submarine small craft.

The first appearance of German U-boats in the Western Atlantic was heralded by sudden attacks on shipping off the Delaware Capes.[1] Two coastwise schooners were sunk on May 25, 1918, and there were sinkings in the first days of June, most of them on June 2 when seven vessels were sunk. These were coastwise craft, mainly schooners, with the steamship *Carolina* of 5000 tons the most important loss. There were renewed attacks in July, especially off Cape Cod, and again in August. On August 10 no less than nine coastwise schooners were sunk from 50 to 60 miles off Nantucket. "The appearance of enemy submarines in these waters necessitated the putting into effect of the convoy system

[1] Admiral Sims had forwarded to the Navy Department very exact information from the British Admiralty as to the time when these raiding U-boats would arrive.

for coastwise shipping and for the protection of individual ships engaged in the coastwise trade." [1] "To forestall enemy submarine operations in the Gulf and Caribbean, a force was established called the American Patrol Force, and its headquarters was in the vicinity of Key West. . . . As was foreseen, the protection of the oil supplies from the Gulf to our own coast and then abroad was quite vital to the success of the general campaign, and these supplies the patrol detachment was prepared to safeguard by adopting at once the convoy system the instant they were threatened." [2]

Consequently, the German U-boat attacks never won success beyond these depredations against coastwise and incoming individual vessels. The U-boats never came near threatening the regular convoys, which were thus protected by sweeping their channels clear of the mines which the Germans spread, and guarded by escorting patrols of anti-submarine craft. These last were constantly hunting the U-boats with listening devices and depth bombs.

"On the whole the operations of the German submarines against our coast can be spoken of as one of the minor incidents of the war. . . ." [3] That these futile U-boat attacks can be thus dismissed, is evident from the fact that transportation of troops instead of being diminished leapt to the great totals, which have been given, in the very months of these attacks. Only one American fighting ship was lost off our coast, the armored cruiser *San Diego* of the Cruiser and Transport Force. She was sunk by a mine off Fire Island on July 19, 1918, with the loss of six lives, three of these from the explosion.

[1] Report of Secretary of the Navy, December, 1918.   [2] Ibid.   [3] Ibid.

Not only did these German raids with the U-boats against the American coast fail to produce any impression that would make us retain naval forces on this side of the Atlantic, but the Germans thus failed absolutely in what must be considered their one necessary object in these U-boat attacks — to break the chain of communications which was bringing and sustaining the American reinforcement that meant ruin to the confident military plans of the Germans. The American Expeditionary Forces remained successfully "based on the American Continent." The full measure of German failure was the fact that not one American troopship was torpedoed. And this meant German failure, not only in American waters, but also in the other stages of transportation to the final destination at the ports of disbarkation overseas.

It would be well here to describe the losses in this service, in order to show beyond any question their small effect upon the great volume of American troops which at this stage of the World War poured into France without hindrance from the enemy. In addition to the *San Diego*, the only fighting ship of any size lost by the United States Navy, our Navy lost the destroyer *Jacob Jones*, the armed converted yacht *Alcedo*, the collier *Cyclops*, and the Coast Guard cutter *Tampa* taken over by the Navy.

The *Jacob Jones* was torpedoed December 6, 1917, when on her way alone from off Brest to Queenstown.[1] The *Alcedo* was one of the American armed yachts in French waters, and she was sunk by a U-boat while acting as convoy escort off the coast of France, November 5, 1917. The loss of the collier *Cyclops* was another of

---

[1] The American destroyer *Cassin* was also torpedoed, but reached port.

the many mysteries of the seas. She had reported at Barbadoes March 4, 1918, for coal, and left for Baltimore. She was never heard from again. The *Tampa* was one of the six Coast Guard cutters overseas, which performed valuable services in the force of the United States Navy based at Gibraltar for escort and protection of convoys. She was acting as escort for a convoy from Gibraltar when she was destroyed in the Bristol Channel on the night of September 26, 1918. "Vessels following heard an explosion, but when they reached the vicinity there were only bits of floating wreckage to show where the ship had gone down. Not one of the 111 officers and men of her crew was rescued. . . ." [1]

Of the transports carrying American troops overseas, the most notable loss from enemy attack was the *Tuscania* (14,348 tons), a chartered Cunard liner under the British convoy system. She was torpedoed off the Irish coast on February 5, 1918, with the loss of 166 missing. The British chartered transport *Moldavia* was also sunk, with the loss of 56 lives. The unbroken record of immunity of the American troopships on their voyages to Europe was not maintained on their homeward voyages. Three of these American transports, *Antilles*, *President Lincoln*, *Covington*, were sunk on their way back to American ports, with loss of life in each case. The *Mount Vernon* (late German liner *Kronprinzessen Cecile*) and the *Finland* were torpedoed on homeward voyages, but each reached port and was repaired for service. The British chartered steamship *Dvinsk* was torpedoed and sunk on a homeward voyage.

These losses, compared with the great numbers of troopships, which were plying between the United

---

[1] Report of Secretary of the Navy, December, 1918.

States and Europe to deliver the American reinforcement on the battlefield in France, show most strikingly
that the Germans were not accomplishing any appreciable results, so far as concerned preventing this reinforcement from being thrown against their armies on the
Western Front. In fact, the battle in France was actually being won on the seas.

CHAPTER XXVIII

THE NORTHERN BARRAGE

AS has been stated in a previous chapter, the American project for the Northern Barrage had been adopted after the antenna type of mine, developed in the United States as described, had so greatly decreased the number of mines required that the scheme was evidently practicable. In 1918 this project was being carried out by the British and Americans in concert. This undertaking was typical of the new order of material and operations in the World War. Before the vast scale of everything in this war had become a matter of fact, who would have conceived a barrier of mines in position 240 miles long, in rows one below the other to a depth of 250 feet? The diagrams on pages 230, 231 show the scheme of the barrier across the North Sea extending from Norwegian territorial waters to a channel 10 miles wide left free off the Orkney Islands.

The original plan was for the United States Navy to lay the mines in Area "A," and the British in Areas "B" and "C." But in actual operations the American also laid mines in Areas "B" and "C," on account of the greater capacity of the minelayers of the United States Navy. The share of the task performed by each was shown by the fact that 56,600 American and 16,300 British mines were laid. The Norwegians also mined their own territorial waters.

In February, 1918, Rear Admiral Joseph Strauss was given the command of the Mine Force of the Atlantic

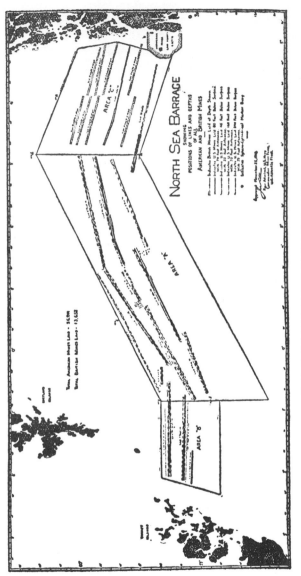

THE AREAS OF THE NORTH SEA BARRAGE

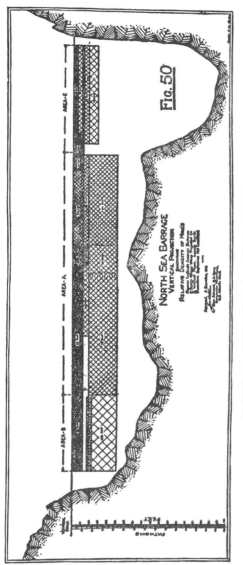

VERTICAL PROJECTION OF THE NORTH SEA BARRAGE

Showing depth of water and relative density of mines in the different areas.

Fleet, which was to carry out the American share of the operation. The material and parts for the American mines were manufactured in the United States, but the mines themselves were not to be assembled until they reached the bases overseas. A special fleet of 24 Lake cargo carriers was allotted for transporting this mine material. They were given Naval Reserve crews and were handled by the Naval Overseas Transportation Service of the Office of Operations. A special plant for the difficult task of receiving and loading the mine material was built at St. Juliens Creek, Va., near the Norfolk Navy Yard. A loading plant of this type and scale had hitherto been unknown, not only in this country, but abroad, and there was a great deal of anxiety as to its safe operation. But it worked out efficiently and most successfully, under the command of Commander W. L. Pryor, operated by a personnel of petty officers and enlisted men of the Naval Reserve Force, who cheerfully accepted the risk involved.

In Scotland, two bases [1] were established for assembling the mines and putting them on board the minelayers. Both were on the east coast, one at Invergordon on Cromarty Firth, the other at Inverness on the Firth of Inverness. On the west coast of Scotland two landing points were established, one at Kyle at the entrance of Loch Alsh, the other at the western end of the Caledonian Canal at Carpach. These were for unloading the mine material, and they were chosen on the west coast in order to avoid additional risk for the Lake steamers, which brought these dangerous cargoes from the United States. Taking these carriers of mine material around to the bases on the east coast would have meant

[1] "Bases 17 and 18."

increased chances for U-boat attacks. The wisdom of
this precaution was proved by the fact that, in their
many dangerous voyages, only one of these ships was
lost, the *Lake Moor* sunk by a U-boat off the coast of
Ireland April 11, 1918. Their sailings were about two
ships each week, half in Norfolk convoys, half in Halifax
convoys.

Inverness was the headquarters of Admiral Strauss.
At each of the two bases about 1,100 men were employed, all of whom belonged to the enlisted force of the
United States Navy. Commander Murfin was Commanding Officer of the two bases, and his organization
consisted of petty and commissioned officers, the latter
nearly all of the Naval Reserve Force. At these bases
the work of receiving, assembling, and loading the mines
on the minelayers, was carried on with great efficiency.
They were able to handle 2,000 mines a day, and, after a
two days minelaying trip in the North Sea, the minelayers could return and find their cargoes ready for
them.

The fleet of minelayers actually employed in planting
the mines in the designated Areas of the North Sea consisted of U. S. S. *San Francisco,* U. S. S. *Baltimore,* cruisers of the United States Navy which had been converted into minelayers, and eight purchased merchant
steamers, which had been altered for this new service.[1]
This made a very able fleet of minelayers, with a total
capacity of about 5,500 mines. The *San Francisco* was
the flagship of Captain R. R. Belknap, who commanded
the minelayers. Captain Belknap had previously per-

[1] U. S. S. *Roanoke* (late *El Dia*), U. S. S. *Housatonic* (late *El Rio*), U. S. S.
Canandaiga (late *El Siglo*), U. S. S. *Canonicus* (late *El Cid*), U. S. S. *Shaw-
mut* (late *Massachusetts*), U. S. S. *Aroostook* (late *Bunker Hill*), U. S. S.
Quinnebaug (late *Jefferson*), U. S. S. *Saranac* (late *Hamilton*).

formed valuable service in the Office of Operations in coördinating the different elements of this great project.

Minelaying operations were begun in March, 1918, by the British. But these mines in Area "B" were found unsatisfactory and were swept up, as a result of protests by Admiral Beatty of the Grand Fleet.[1] Minelaying was begun by the Americans in June, 1918.

"The new mine, instead of consisting of a sphere from thirty two to thirty six inches in diameter, actual contact with which was necessary to produce an explosion, was so devised as to carry an antenna supported by a small float, and the contact with the float or any part of the antenna would detonate the mine. . . . It was determined by experiment that the antennae for the two lower rows could be 70 feet, and the upper row half that length, or 35 feet. The mines carried 300 lbs. of T. N. T., and the explosion of such a mine would be quite effective at the several depths. It was decided to plant the upper row of mines at a depth of 45 feet, the middle row at a depth of 160 feet, and the lower row at 240 feet. A vessel drawing more than 10 feet would then come in contact with the upper floats and produce an explosion less than 35 feet distant. The upper row's danger space would extend from the surface to 60 feet below. The middle row's danger would extend from 75 feet below the surface 100 feet downward. The lower row from 155 feet from the surface down to 245 feet. It was found after experiment, that the mines should not be planted laterally closer than 300 feet. This distance was somewhat greater than that at which one mine would coun-

[1] British Admiralty to Commander-in-Chief, Grand Fleet, April 24, 1918: "It is not at present proposed to lay any more mines in Area 'B.'"

termine its neighbor, but allowing for errors in distance in planting 300 feet was fixed upon."

The foregoing is Admiral Strauss' own description of the Northern Barrage,[1] and nothing could give a clearer idea of its makeup. It will be evident that these successive rows of mines, as shown on page 230, must be a formidable barrier against the egress of U-boats. Admiral Strauss has also given [2] the following description of the methods of minelaying: "I had arranged with Admiral Beatty, commanding the Grand Fleet, to notify him four days ahead of time when we would probably be ready to proceed to sea, and two days beforehand we named an hour when we would be ready to meet his escorting force off the entrance to Cromarty Firth. The day before the finally appointed time, the commanding officer of the British Destroyer Squadron called upon me at my headquarters for consultation as to the procedure. All points having been agreed upon, at the appointed hour the minelayers would meet his squadron off Cromarty Firth and proceed under his escort to the minefields and lay the mines. The expedition was further guarded by a squadron of battleships or battle cruisers sent out from Scapa or the Firth of Forth to protect the expedition from possible attack by armored vessels of the enemy. No such attack ever took place nor did we encounter any evidence of the enemy save once when two submarines were sighted, both of which sought safety by diving as soon as the destroyer escort made for them."

These statements from Admiral Strauss give a vivid picture of this great undertaking. There were difficul-

---

[1] "A Guide to the Military History of the World War," pp. 328–330.
[2] Ibid., page 333.

ties, especially with premature explosions which gave much trouble. There were also delays from waiting for escort and coördination with the British, and the whole barrage was not completed at the time of the Armistice on November 11, 1918. But at that time a dangerous barrier had been stretched across the North Sea, as will be evident from the following summing up by the Historical Section, U. S. N.: "In all 70,263 mines had been laid, 56,611 being American mines laid by the United States Mining Squadron. Area 'A,' which was originally allotted as the United States portion of the barrage, was completed except for 6,400 mines more, which could have been laid in approximately 10 days. Besides mining Area 'A,' exclusively, the United States mining squadron had laid 10,440 mines in Area 'B,' and 5,080 mines in Area 'C'."

There had been other projects for mine barrages suggested by the United States, notably in the Mediterranean in consequence of the continued serious situation as to the U-boats. "The enemy had gradually increased the number of submarines in the Mediterranean by sending them from Germany around through the Straits of Gibraltar to be based on Mediterranean ports, and also by shipping the disassembled parts over land to be assembled there. In June, 1918, there were approximately 68 Austrian and German submarines based on the Adriatic, practically all of these operating from Cattaro; and 21 submarines, including 14 ex-Russian boats operating from the Dardanelles." [1]

It was proposed to deny exit to the Mediterranean by a barrage across the Straits of Otranto, to throw a simi-

[1] "The Northern Barrage and Other Mining Activities." Hist. Section, U. S. N.

lar barrage across the Aegean Sea, with other mining operations at the Dardanelles, off Tunis, and off Gibraltar. A mining base had been projected at Bizerta, but the collapse of the allies of Germany came before mines were laid. In the Adriatic the light forces of the United States Navy were of great assistance to the Italian Navy in its operations against the Austrian Navy. At the time of the Armistice, there were 36 submarine chasers and a tender at the base at Corfu, and the official thanks of the Italian Naval Staff were expressed for the services of the American submarine chasers "in protecting major vessels" at the taking of Durazzo (October 2–14, 1918).

CHAPTER XXIX

THE TURN OF THE TIDE

ALL the strenuous efforts, extending over the wide seas, to rush the necessary American reinforcement for the Allied armies on the Western Front, accomplished their result barely in time. In July, 1918, the military situation for the Entente Allies had become desperate. The first victorious onslaught of the Germans in March had at length taught the lesson that a united command was necessary, and the Allied armies on the Western Front had been coördinated under Marshal Foch. But, in spite of this benefit, the German successes continued. There had been another serious British reverse in April, and in May the Germans swept over the supposedly impregnable Chemin des Dames defenses of the French, capturing Soissons and winning another broad salient, of which the apex was Château-Thierry. In June the Germans made another gain south of Noyon, which straightened their line west of Soissons.

These defeats were staggering for the French. The German drive had broken through what were considered the strongest French defenses. The Germans were back on the Marne, and a long way on the road to Paris.[1] It was this deadly threat against Paris, always the aim of German strategy and at last apparently within their

[1] ". . . and the German advance was directed toward Paris. During the first days of June something akin to a panic seized the city, and it was said that 1,000,000 people left during the spring of 1918." — General Pershing, Report.

238

grasp, which was the measure of the emergency. The Germans were almost openly massing their troops for a final drive to the city. Events had proved beyond any question that the existing Allied armies would not be able to check them. And a desperate call was made upon the American troops.

There have been many crises in military history, but it would be hard to find one so unmistakably set forth by the written testimony of the highest authorities. The following clearly defined this crisis of the World War.

"General Foch has presented to us a statement of the utmost gravity . . . as there is no possibility of the British and French increasing the numbers of their divisions . . . there is great danger of the war being lost unless the numerical inferiority of the Allies can be remedied as rapidly as possible by the advent of American troops. . . . We are satisfied that General Foch . . . is not overestimating the needs of the case. . . .

D. LLOYD GEORGE
CLEMENCEAU
ORLANDO

VERSAILLES CONFERENCE, June 12, 1918."

"We recognize that the combatant troops to be dispatched in July may have to include troops which have had insufficient training, but we consider the present emergency such as to justify a temporary and exceptionable departure by the United States. . . .

FOCH
MILNER
PERSHING

AGREEMENT, June 5, 1918."

There is no need to add a word to this, and for all time there will never be any question of the necessity for the seaborne reinforcement which was about to be thrown into the battle. In response to this call, every effort was made to gather American troops against the anticipated German assault through the Château-Thierry salient to Paris.[1] Of the American troops in France, six divisions [2] were made available at this point of attack. This last culmination of the great German offensive of 1918 came on July 15, 1918, and the assault was delivered with all the strength of long preparation behind it. The Germans were confident that it would win the World War.[3] Never was there a greater disappointment. Not only was the German advance decisively arrested, but Marshal Foch was at last strong enough to undertake for the first time a counter attack against the Germans. This was launched towards Soissons on July 18, and pushed successfully until before the end of the month "the operation of reducing the salient was finished." [4]

The above is a bald account of the events of the turn of the tide of war, but these events do not express a fraction of the moral effect produced by the enforced retreat of the Germans, after four months of uninterrupted victorious advance. The rebound of the Allies from the

[1] "It was no longer a question as to which division had completed training according to any alleged schedule; it was a dire emergency, and a question as to what troops of any class were most available for Château-Thierry, . . . to help the French in a desperate attempt to save Paris." Colonel R. H. C. Kelton, General Staff, U. S. A.

[2] The equivalent of 12 Allied or German divisions, as has been explained.

[3] "The enemy had encouraged his soldiers to believe that the July 15 attack would conclude the war with a German peace." — General Pershing, Report.

[4] Ibid.

depths of depression to exultation was immediate, "for in those three days the morale of all the Allies had been born anew." [1] Equally marked was the effect upon the Germans of this startling overturn. The transition of the Germans from the elation of victory to the despondency of defeat followed at once. Nothing that could be written would express this great change as forcibly as the statement given out by the broken German Chancellor Hertling a few days before his death: "At the beginning of July, 1918, I was convinced, I confess it, that before the first of September our adversaries would send us peace proposals. . . . We expected grave events in Paris for the end of July. That was on the 15th. On the 18th even the most optimistic among us knew that all was lost. The history of the world was played out in three days."

This actually was the beginning of the end — but enormous military difficulties were still to be overcome. And, above all things, the reader must realize the immense importance of finishing the war in the year 1918. If the war had lasted into 1919 the effect of the strain upon the overwrought nations of the Entente Allies cannot be estimated. It is in this regard that the insistence of General Pershing and Secretary Baker for the use of our troops as an American Army was justified by the events — and the events moved rapidly. After the showing of the American troops in July, "from every point of view the immediate organization of an independent American force was indicated," [2] and in this Marshal Foch acquiesced on August 9. The first task of the First American Army was the successful St. Mihiel

[1] Colonel R. H. C. Kelton, General Staff, U. S. A.

[2] General Pershing, Report.

operation (September 12–13, 1918). To show the pace at which things were moving, it is enough to state that 430,000 American troops were used in this operation.

In conference (August 30), at which no hope was expressed by the Allied leaders that the war could be ended in 1918,[1] an offensive in the Meuse-Argonne sector was assigned as General Pershing's share of the operations against the Germans (begun September 26, 1918). "In fact, it was believed by the French high command that the Meuse-Argonne attack could not get much beyond Montfaucon before the arrival of winter would force a cessation of operations."[2] Instead of there being any check at Montfaucon, it is a matter of record that the Meuse-Argonne attack pushed through to Sedan, with 1,200,000 American troops actually engaged. In all 1,390,000 American troops saw active service at the front.

These astonishing figures, showing the rapid increase of effectives on the battle line of the Western Front, are in themselves the best tribute to the success of the vast naval transportation operation which was then being carried on over three thousand miles of ocean. And these numbers tell the story of the result of the full cooperation of British shipping, after the danger signal in March as has been described. The American troopships were able to bring the early reinforcement of troops, but the British troopships were the factors that turned our numbers into the "hordes" of Tirpitz's bitter complaint. Of all the American troops transported overseas, the British carried 49 per cent, the Americans 45 per cent,

[1] "It should be recorded that although this general offensive was fully outlined at the conference no one present expressed the opinion that the final victory could be won in 1918." — General Pershing, Report.

[2] Ibid.

other nations 6 per cent. In other words, the American reinforcement would only have been about half as large if it had not been for the British troopships. It was a great drain upon the available supply of British shipping, with so many other urgent needs, but, on the other hand, the achievement of delivering a reinforcement of 1,000,000 men at the crisis of the war went beyond anything that had been thought possible for British shipping as a contribution to the cause of the Entente Allies.

CHAPTER XXX

THE UNCHANGED GERMAN NAVAL STRATEGY

AT last the one thing had happened which was outside all the calculations of the Germans — and they could no longer be blind to the unexpected fact that the reinforcement of the American Army was actually present on the battlefield. The effect upon the Germans of this stunning revelation has been graphically described by General Pershing: [1] "An American Army was an accomplished fact. No form of propaganda could overcome the depressing effect on the morale of the enemy of this demonstration of our ability to organize a large American force and drive it successfully through his defenses." General Pershing has also emphasized the result of the American doctrines for training, which have been described: "It gave our troops implicit confidence in their superiority and raised their morale to the highest pitch. For the first time wire entanglements ceased to be regarded as impassible barriers and open warfare training, which had been so urgently insisted upon, proved to be the correct doctrine."

The Germans could no longer delude themselves, in view of the radical change in the military situation. The German armies were no longer on the offensive, but were being pushed back by their reinforced enemies. And behind these repulsed German armies a sense of defeat was spreading back through the German people. It was natural that the first effect of this was a reaction against the German Naval Staff, which had promised to win the

[1] General Pershing, Report.

war by means of the U-boats. The German Naval Staff thus stood convicted, in the eyes of the German people, not only of failure to win the war with the U-boats, but also of failure to prevent the arrival of the American reinforcement on the Western Front, which had turned the tide of battle.

So strong was this reaction, that there was an overturn in the German Navy, and Admiral Cappelle retired from his post as Secretary of State of the Imperial Ministry of Marine. Admiral Scheer was made Chief of the Admiralty Staff (August 11, 1918), and Admiral Hipper succeeded to the command of the High Sea Fleet.

In view of these changes in the German Navy, there was a very natural suspicion among the Allied and American authorities that there would be also a change in German naval tactics, and a use of the warships of the High Sea Fleet to attempt to upset the situation on the seas. Special precautions were taken by the United States Navy against any such change of tactics. The main danger was held to be the possibility of raids by German battle cruisers to attack the troop convoys.[1] To guard against this, a division of three American battleships,[2] under the command of Rear Admiral T. S. Rodgers, was sent overseas, and based on Berehaven, Ireland. "The enemy raiders never appeared. This division made two trips into the Channel, escorting convoys, when enemy submarines were reported in the vicinity." [3]

[1] "It was learned from Intelligence sources that for these reasons, if no other, the enemy contemplated an effort to send out battle cruisers to attack convoys, particularly troop convoys." — Office of Naval Intelligence.

[2] *Utah* (flag), arrived September 10, 1918; *Nevada*, arrived August 23, 1918; *Oklahoma*, arrived August 23, 1918.

[3] Office of Naval Intelligence.

The reason for the lack of any such attempt is now an established matter of fact, and all speculation on this subject can be ended by knowing that the Germans never had any such intention at this time. The attitude of the German Naval leaders was then characteristic of the German trend of mind in the World War. Their Naval leaders were all so imbued with the doctrine of the U-boat, and so carried away by their own calculations, that, at this stage in 1918, all their thoughts were concentrated on plans for more extensive U-boat warfare. It followed that the new German Naval Secretary of State was the former head of the U-boat Office, Vice Admiral Mann-Tiechler, "in view of the fact that the chief task of this office now lay in furthering the construction of U-boats; and the building of reinforcements for the surface warships, which could no longer exercise any influence on the success of the war, was either given up or postponed, so that our entire capacity in shipbuilding was devoted to this one task." [1]

Admiral Scheer, on his new duty as Naval Chief of Staff, took his staff to General Headquarters in order to be in coördination with the Army Command in carrying out these plans for an increase of the U-boats. He has stated that, as a result of his arguments placed before Hindenburg and Ludendorff, "They both admitted that the main hope of a favorable end to the war lay in a successful offensive of the U-boats, and General Ludendorff promised, in spite of the great lack of personnel in the Army to do his utmost to help to develop it further."

Admiral Scheer has also expressed beyond any mistaking the attitude of the whole German Navy as to the

[1] Admiral Scheer, "Germany's High Sea Fleet."

U-boats at this time: "We felt that we were responsible for the attainment of such an end to the war as had been promised to the German people, and that we could achieve it by these means alone. The Fleet was animated by one sole idea — we must and will succeed." Nothing can be more explicit than this, and we must look upon German naval strategy as still tied to the U-boat campaign, with the German Battle Fleet still allotted to its sole task of forwarding the U-boat campaign.

If we think in these terms, which are the only deductions in accord with the facts, there is no difficulty in understanding the naval situation in Germany at this stage, when the rapid dissolution of the whole German structure was approaching. All the efforts of the German leaders were being concentrated on securing a greater output of U-boats. In 1917 the production of U-boats had been "certainly strongly influenced by the opinion of the Chief of the Naval Staff that the boats would achieve their effect within a definite period of time, and that the existing U-boats would suffice." [1] This was an altogether amazing proof of the unbounded confidence of the German leaders in the quick success of the U-boat campaign of 1917.

Admiral Scheer has stated: "After the U-boat Office had been instituted on December 5, 1917, 120 boats were placed on order in the same month, and in January, 1918, a further 220 boats. During 1918 the monthly return of the boats supplied was still influenced by the earlier building policy: January, 3; February, 6; March, 8; April, 8; May, 10; June, 12; July, 9; August, 8; September, 10. With these numbers the losses were cov-

[1] "Germany's High Sea Fleet," Admiral Scheer.

ered, but no noticeable increase in the actual number of new boats was achieved."

Admiral Scheer's plan was to secure a greater output of U-boats by inducing the German Supreme Army Command to assign an increased number of workmen for building U-boats. In June, 1918, the Army Command had stated: "The Army cannot afford to be deprived of any more workmen; the people at home must supply the Army with more and more men, but cannot by a long way cover the demand caused by the losses. The most urgent need of the hour is the supply of more men for the Army." On the other hand, it was the conviction of the German Naval leaders that all depended upon the U-boats, and Admiral Scheer worked out his plan to this end. "But if we wanted to achieve great things with the U-boat campaign then the whole industrial power of Germany must be at our disposal for the accomplishment of our task. I had got into communication with the principal controllers of industry, and at a conference with them and the Imperial Ministry of Marine had drawn up the following figures for the indispensable minimum for the increase in U-boats:

In the last	quarter of 1918.....	per month 16
In the first	quarter of 1919.....	per month 20
In the second	quarter of 1919.....	per month 25
In the third	quarter of 1919.....	per month 30."

"Of course the Navy must first of all give up every man that could be spared for the construction and commissioning of U-boats. That could only be done if the Navy Command took ruthless action. Despite the menacing situation on our Western Front, the First Quartermaster General (Ludendorff) drew the necessary conclusions, as soon as it had been proved to him that it was within the range of possibility to carry out the new U-boat programme if we could depend on obtaining 40,000 to 60,000 workmen. For the next few months a considerably smaller number would suffice to ensure the more rapid delivery of the boats now under construction."

"In the course of September the discussions with employers of industry and the shipyards were continued, to ascertain whether it would be possible to carry out the extended programme of U-boat construction. On September 24th the Ministry of Marine informed the Naval Command that the possibility of carrying it out had, on the whole, been established. In view of the great importance that now attached to the U-boats, seeing that they were to give a favorable turn to the end of the war, I suggested to his Majesty that he should visit our U-boat School at Kiel. His Majesty accordingly left General Headquarters on September 23 for Kiel, and on the 24th he inspected first the torpedo workshops, and then the establishment of the Imperial shipyards, which had been very considerably enlarged for the purposes of the U-boat war." [1]

There can be no possibility of mistaking this state of mind. The Germans were again dealing in formulas of their own, with no conception of anything outside. It is strange to read that this program "for the next few months," with a grandiose increase in 1919, was being ratified by the visit of the German Emperor only two days before the enemy launched the great series of attacks, which were destined to break down all German resistance. Consequently, it is established that the German Naval leaders, although they knew that Germany

[1] "Germany's High Sea Fleet," Admiral Scheer.

was losing the war, yet could not believe that the end would come so soon, and they were absorbed in naval plans which could not produce any result before the downfall of Germany. Admiral Scheer has left no doubt of this by his own admission: "If I had foreseen the rapid development of events I would have preferred remaining with the Fleet rather than organizing the conduct of war at sea, for my plans never reached fulfillment." As a result of all this, there was no danger of a change to the offensive on the part of the warships of the German Battle Fleet before the total defeat of Germany put anything of the kind out of the question, as will be narrated. The convoys of troops and supplies remained free from the expected raids of German warships throughout the short remainder of the war.

CHAPTER XXXI

THE DISINTEGRATION OF THE CENTRAL POWERS

THE effect of German defeat in France was a shock that caused the whole edifice of the Central Powers to fall in ruins. As long as the Germans were winning, they held their allies together — but at the touch of defeat the coalition collapsed. Austria-Hungary, Turkey, and Bulgaria had suffered more severely from the war than had Germany. The war had come home more closely to their peoples. There had been more actual privations. In fact, throughout these countries there were almost famine conditions in the last year of the war. Their peoples were utterly tired of the war and longed for peace.

Another element that undermined the structure, which Germany had so carefully built, was the unsettling effect of the revolution in Russia upon the neighboring peoples, who had been demoralized by the hardships of the war, and were ready to welcome revolution as a way out. The Russian revolution had been deliberately fomented by Germany as a military means of putting an enemy out of action. Ludendorff has written: "How often had I not hoped for a revolution in order to lighten our military burden! . . . At that time I never contemplated the possibility that it might later on undermine our own strength also." Upon Austria-Hungary this disturbing influence was especially strong. The Dual Empire had always been loosely knit, with jarring factions of Slav and Teutonic races. These already existing enmities were quick to feel the spur of the successful social revolution near their borders, especially from the tendency of communities to break away and set up governments for themselves. As a result, the cleavage between the different parts of the empire grew into actual rifts, and the groups which afterwards became the states of the Czecho-Slovaks and Jugo-Slavs began to take form.

While Germany was still winning victories in the first half of 1918, these causes of demoralization were only working under the surface, and the prestige of a victorious Germany still remained a strong dominating power in every region. A proof of this was the surrender of Rumania to the Central Powers in May, 1918. Under the same stimulus of these German victories, the Austro-Hungarian armies had also been induced to take the offensive against the Italians in June, 1918. The Austro-Hungarians seemed on the point of winning a new success, as they had forced the crossing of the Piave River. But there were sudden floods, which swept away their bridges, leaving the Austro-Hungarians on the west bank of the river isolated and exposed to Italian counter attacks. This misfortune quickly changed success into disaster, and ended any danger for the Italian armies. These retained their positions from the Piave to the Asiago plateau, and there was no other operation on this front until October.

The beginning of the general collapse, due to German defeat, came in September, 1918, when Bulgaria was quickly put out of the war. The Salonica Army, which had been established and maintained by Sea Power as has been described, completed its successful guardianship of that region, and justified all efforts in maintaining it, by accomplishing the decisive result of striking down this ally of Germany. There was an advance on a front of 100 miles from Monastir to Lake Doiran, with the Greeks and Serbians coöperating. The Bulgarians were tired of the war, and they had no idea of prolonging the struggle. There was hardly any resistance, and the Allies advanced at will. On September 27, 1918, Bulgaria asked for an armistice, which was only granted on the terms of the Entente Allies. These included occupation of the Bulgarian railroads. The Italian army, which had been maintained in Albania, had also taken the offensive, and Albania was cleared of the enemy.

The Bulgarian surrender meant that communication between the Central Powers and Turkey had been broken, and the last vestige of Mittel Europa had been destroyed. The Turks were even more tired of the war than the Bulgarians. They were angry with Germany, and with the pro-German party in Turkey. They had been practically abandoned by Germany, after so well serving Germany at the Dardanelles, and their troops were no longer organized and equipped by the Germans. In September the British under General Allenby broke up the Turkish defense of the Holy Land. Damascus was taken on September 30, and the way was opened for cutting the line of the Constantinople-Bagdad Railroad at Aleppo. This meant that the Turkish troops in Mesopotamia were cut off from supplies and helpless — and immediate Turkish defeat was inevitable.

Consequently, when the reinforced enemies of Germany began the final great series of battles on the Western Front (September 26, 1918), all the rest of the structure of the Central Powers was ready to fall like a house of cards at the touch of defeat. And the truth, that the

German armies were being defeated in France, became too evident to be concealed from the allies of Germany. The great offensive launched by Foch was begun by a drive of the American Army in the Meuse-Argonne sector (September 26, 1918), with the French also attacking in the Champagne on the same day. This offensive was followed on the next day by a British attack toward Cambrai. On successive days there were strong assaults in Flanders by the British and Belgians, and an attack in force toward St. Quentin.

All of these offensives gained ground at once. It was shown beyond mistaking that the Germans were no longer strong enough to check the advance of their enemies — and a wave of the depression of defeat spread back throughout Germany. This absolute evidence of defeat was the blow which threw down the weakened structure of the Central Powers. The end followed quickly for Austria-Hungary. The people were hungry and desperate. There was disaffection and revolt everywhere. These conditions spread to the armies on the Italian front. These Austro-Hungarian armies were also hungry and disaffected. Their morale was gone, and they were ready to break at the first assault. On October 24 the Italians attacked. The result was never in doubt. The formidable Austro-Hungarian armies, which had penetrated far into Italy, had become disorganized mobs. They offered no resistance to the enemy, and great numbers of them were captured. Austria-Hungary was in revolution, and completely eliminated as a factor in the World War.[1] At the same

[1] Armistice requested October 27, 1918. This was signed November 3. It was followed by the abdication of the Emperor, and Austria-Hungary had become a number of separate States.

time the Turks were also eliminated, as, on October 30, 1918, an armistice was signed, which amounted to an unconditional surrender.

In the meantime, Germany was also going down to defeat, although there was no such military collapse of her armies as in the case of her allies. The German armies retained their organization, and resisted to the last, although, of course, their morale fell away in defeat. The demoralization brought about by military reverses was spreading through all Germany — and leading to revolution. But it is an error to state that revolution brought about this defeat of the German armies.[1] The revolution was a result, not a cause, of German defeat.

As has been stated, if Ludendorff had been able to gain the promised victory, the German people would have stood by the German Government. But the German people had held the Government to this test, and, upon the failure of the Supreme Command to win the war before the arrival of the American reinforcement, the German people repudiated the German Government. The race had been won by the Americans, and the German people had lost all respect for the loser. Ludendorff's complaint was: "By working on our democratic sentiments the enemy propaganda succeeded in bringing our Government into discredit in Germany." But all the propaganda in the world would not have accomplished this, if the German armies had kept on winning. It was the actual physical defeat of the German armies that brought about disaffection and revolution in Germany.

[1] "The stab in the back."

CHAPTER XXXII

THE IMPELLING FORCE OF SEA POWER

AS has been stated, the results achieved, by what Tirpitz called "those hordes of American troops on the continent which turned the balance against us on the Western Front in 1918," were as much brought about by Sea Power as if the warships of Germany's enemies had been actually present on the battlefield. It is a convincing and inspiring picture to look over the vast expanses of the World War and to realize that in the last stage Sea Power was the impelling force which was bringing final defeat to Germany.

In the wide areas of warfare, of course the outstanding feature was the great volume of American troops and their maintenance poured into the very heart of things in France. As to this fatal thrust against Germany, it must always be reiterated that British shipping made possible an American reinforcement of more than double the numbers we would have been able to deliver in France by means of our own transports. The fact that great numbers of British ships were thus being used must be kept in mind, in order to understand the broad movements of shipping in this final situation on the seas.

But, in addition, all-important as was this necessary reinforcement on the Western Front, where the decisive battle must be fought, the picture would be incomplete unless we realize that, in the other areas of the World War also, Sea Power was pressing home the defeats of the Central Powers which have been described in the preceding chapter. The Salonica Army, the British forces operating against the Turks, the Italian army in Albania, all were products of Sea Power. Through no other means could these forces have been brought into action against the Central Powers.

At this stage, over all the seas, the vast fleets of warships, transports, and cargo carriers, were successfully working in concert for the one object of winning this war, which had grown to such unexpected proportions. From all over the world the convoys were bringing support and maintenance. The guardianship and protection of these large numbers of ships, as has been described, had brought about an urgent call for armed ships of all kinds and sizes, to an extent undreamt before. It is true that the distant seas had been swept clear of hostile naval forces, but, on the other hand, naval tasks had been greatly multiplied in the Mediterranean area and in the waters of the Atlantic — and the reader must picture the momentous activity in these seas, which reached its culmination in the last months of the World War.

As to the Mediterranean area, the Italian Navy in the Adriatic had continued to dominate the inactive Austrian Battle Fleet. It had maintained the Italian army in Albania; had coöperated in winning Albania, especially at the capture of Durazzo (bombarded by the fleet October 2, 1918; captured October 14, 1918); and had struck a last blow by destroying the Austrian flagship, the dreadnought *Viribis Unitis*. This should be noted as one of the most daring feats of the war. Two Italian officers, Colonel Rosetti and Dr. Paolucci, in the night of October 31–November 1, by means of an ingenious small motor device invented by Colonel Rosetti, penetrated all obstructions and floated themselves and two powerful mines far into the harbor of Pola. They managed to attach their explosives under the Austrian flagship, timed to blow her up in two hours. They then cast loose their motor float, with a mine attached to destroy it. As they were swimming away, they were discovered and brought on board the *Viribis Unitis* as prisoners. They were on board when the explosion destroyed the ship, which listed and capsized about ten minutes afterwards. But the two brave Italian officers survived, and were released at the time of the armistice between Italy and Austria-Hungary.

Although the Italian Navy had thus controlled the surface of the Adriatic, the U-boats remained a constant danger there to the very end, and made necessary a continual anti-submarine warfare in that sea. The same was also true of the rest of the Mediterranean area throughout which the U-boat attacks continued to be so grave a menace that it never was safe to relax the efforts against them. In fact, the Mediterranean shared with the North Sea the record of destruction of shipping which was overcome with so much difficulty. The plans under way at the time of the Armistice to hem in the U-boats in this area, by means of mine barrages, have been explained in the chapter on the great barrage.

In regard to the Atlantic, this work has described the development on a great scale of a naval warfare new to history — but devoid to the end of the set actions of former wars. And yet, from Gibraltar to Iceland, these last months of the war saw a constant harassing naval activity that made the old days appear like a calm — in comparison with this modern storm. In these waterways of the Atlantic, the necessities of the World War demanded that large numbers of ships should be concentrated, on their voyages to and from the central area adjacent to the field of the gigantic struggle which was then deciding the fate of the war. And these crowding ships were obliged to play their parts in a drama of attack and defense created by the two most dangerous weapons of naval warfare, the submarine and the mine. The development of these weapons, as has been explained, had called into being a multiplicity of naval forces, and the final act presented scenes of feverish activity on the seas, which have not been generally realized. Yet they must be understood, in order to appreciate new adventures on the seas utterly outside of all former experiences in naval warfare.

As has been told, the two opposing battle fleets remained inactive, in the old sense of the word so far as concerned set naval actions. The British Grand Fleet, which had been the main factor in the Allied command of the seas was held aloof, with its auxiliaries, to meet any sortie of the German Battle Fleet, which continued to be dedicated solely to forwarding the U-boat campaign. Consequently, it is a true statement to say that these new naval activities were brought about by the use of the submarine and mine.

But what an extraordinary variety of conditions must be depicted to show the situation on the seas in the last months of the World War. On land, this war, carried on by means of all the resources of nations, had called into unexpected services hosts of men from civil life that dwarfed all the regular armies of the world. On the seas, it was even a stranger story. The numbers of men, outside the regular navies, who were called into the war on the seas were enormous — and these men were suddenly confronted with novel and exacting tasks, far beyond even the developments of the military tactics of the World War. It is strange reading to compare former ideas of European warfare with the actualities of the World War. As has been said in regard to other phases of the World War, the only comparison might be with the American Civil War, in which great numbers of men outside the regular Navy faced novel tasks on the seas.

This final situation of the World War, on the seas, should here be passed in review. Consider first the tasks that had come into being from the use of mines. The tentative experiments at the beginning of the war, in scattering a few mines on the waters, had grown into the vast systems of minefields, with the constant use by both sides of great quantities of mines, in defense and in offensives against the enemy. Both sides were constantly occupied in minelaying and minesweeping. Day and night, in all sorts of craft, these mine forces, recruited for the most part outside of the regular navies, were at work on their dangerous service. These mine forces grew to proportions that were navies in themselves. And they deserve their own epics of daring adventure to describe the hazards of their service in the World War. The peaceful British trawlers had become bustling little warships, and they, and all other craft employed in mine-warfare, should be given a high place in any naval history of the war.

But it is safe to say that the submarines, directly and indirectly, brought more men into hazardous service on the seas than any other factor in naval warfare. The fearful risks for those who served in the submarines have not been generally understood. The proportion of U-boats lost was very great [1] — and the horrible fate of the crew of a sunken submarine needs no description.

Of the men whose service on the seas called them to contend with the submarines, the numbers had gone still farther beyond the former ideas of navies. From the preceding narratives of this work, the reader must have realized the large totals of craft of all kinds which were engaged in anti-submarine operations. It even came to submarine against submarine. The British were thus using their submarines, and, for use against the U-boats, in 1918 the United States Navy was maintaining Division 4 (5 submarines) at the Azores, and Division 5 (7 submarines) at Berehaven.

There was also a wide use of aircraft in anti-submarine warfare. In order to coöperate with the Entente Allies in this, the United States Navy developed an aviation service, of which the main object was anti-submarine warfare. On September 16, 1917, the Navy Department had "authorized the establishment of 15 naval air stations abroad." [2] Of these, four were to be in Ireland, and early in 1918 headquarters for these Irish stations had been fixed at Queenstown. In England a station was established at Killingholme. On July 1, 1918, six stations were operating in France. The most important functions of this service were anti-submarine bombing and patrolling operations, in the North Sea, off the Belgian coast, and in the Channel, especially the Northern Bombing Group in close coöperation with the British air forces in that area against the U-boat bases, under the orders of Admiral Keyes. This service was also extended to Italy. At the time of the Armistice our

---

[1] The Germans have stated the losses of U-boats as over 45%.

[2] Office of Naval Intelligence.

aviation service was operating: in France, 16 stations; in Ireland, 5 stations; in England, 3 stations; in Italy, 2 stations.

Admiral Sims has thus summed up this American naval effort: "At the cessation of hostilities we had a total of more than 500 planes of various descriptions actually in commission, a large number of which were in actual operation over the North Sea, the Irish Sea, the Bay of Biscay, and the Adriatic; our bombing planes were making frequent flights over enemy submarine bases and 2500 officers and 22,000 enlisted men were making raids, doing patrols, bombing submarines, bombing enemy bases, taking photographs, making reconnaissance over enemy waters, and engaging enemy aircraft. There can be no doubt but that this great force was a factor in persuading the enemy to acknowledge defeat when he did."

In addition to the various naval forces engaged in anti-submarine warfare, we must include the great numbers of ships which were obliged to face the dangers of U-boat attacks, in their services as transports and cargo carriers. These ships were perforce participants in submarine warfare. It was not alone the ships protecting the convoys that must contend with the U-boats. Every ship must be prepared to fight or manoeuvre. Many of them, as has been stated, were armed. Of American ships alone, about 500 carried guns for protection against U-boats. This meant some 1000 guns and 10,000 young Americans as gun crews. But not only the gun crews but all the crews must be counted as taking part in submarine warfare. It will at once be apparent that the numbers of men involved in this new and hazardous naval warfare had grown to totals that were amazing.

It was altogether a tremendous picture spread over the seas, and made bizarre by the camouflage coloring, which had been widely adopted by the last months of the war. What would a deep water sailor of the old type have thought, if he had been dropped into the midst of the parti-colored ships of 1918? Concealment camouflage had been practically given up, and the British had led the way in daring designs of stripes and blocks of color to deceive as to sizes and courses of ships. An immense amount of ingenuity was shown in the use of designs and "dazzle" coloring on all kinds of ships — and this was typical of the startling changes of warfare on the seas. If the reader will think in terms of this vast and varied panorama, the last scenes of the World War on the seas will take their true form.

As has been explained, the careful protection afforded by the convoy system had preserved the transports carrying American troops overseas from losses inflicted by the enemy that would bring about any appreciable percentage of interruption or delay. The one danger that actually threatened the success of this undertaking was from an unexpected source. It came from the sudden outbreak of influenza in America in September and October of 1918. "Thirty-eight troopships carried nearly 130,000 men across the ocean during the epidemic. . . . It is conservative to estimate that the influenza at sea cost, altogether, 2000 lives. Many of the victims were buried at sea. . . . Judging by the statistics of the epidemic at the established camps, it is probable that if the troops had been held in quarantine more of them would have died than actually did die on the way across the ocean." [1] Both at the camps and on the

[1] "The Road to France," Crowell and Wilson.

transports heroic efforts were made to stem the disease. On the transports, the War Department decreased the number of troops loaded on each ship by 10 per cent. Consequently this epidemic had a much greater effect upon the transportation of American troops than all the efforts of the enemy.

Early in September, 1918, the Cardiff Naval Base was established, which was organized by Rear Admiral Philip Andrews and under his command. This greatly increased the efficiency of the American Cross-Channel Fleet, a most necessary element in the situation, as in the last months of the war there was an urgent demand from General Pershing for increased shipments of coal.

In regard to the cargo carriers, theirs was a service which cannot be rated too highly — and, in all this far flung picture of the naval warfare of the World War, their place should be kept before the reader's eye. As has been stated, the ships of any speed were being used as transports, and the defense of speed was denied to the cargo carriers. There was no romance in their service, and the general public has hardly ever heard of them. But their crews were "heroes unsung" [1] in very truth. Their adventures, their dangers, and their fights — for they fought like heroes indeed — should be recorded. "No branch of naval service lived in greater danger or called for hardihood, resolution, and judgment in a higher degree. . . . The men knew that, as things went, the odds were against them; that they could expect no quarter. Yet they stood at their posts and faced the foe gallantly on unequal terms; and sometimes they emerged from the encounters in triumph." [2]

[1] "The Road to France," Crowell and Wilson.
[2] Ibid.

The United States cargo carriers had many fights with U-boats, and often were successful in saving their ships by their own gunfire. The American tanker *Sea Shell*, in the Mediterranean, must be given the credit of putting out an attacking U-boat by gunfire. The *J. L. Luckenbach* stood off a U-boat for four hours, until rescued in a badly battered condition by the destroyer *Nicholson*. The *Navajo* and *Nyanza* won commendation for successfully resisting U-boats, and the *Chincha* and *Paulsboro* beat off attacking U-boats. In the cases of the *Norlena* and *Borrinquin*, the crews had started to abandon ship after hits by torpedoes, but returned and drove off the U-boats by gunfire.

The crews of the cargo carriers showed equal courage in defeat. The *Campana* fought for four hours, and the *Moreni* for two hours, before being sunk by U-boat attacks. The most serious loss of life for the N. O. T. S. came from the loss of the *Ticonderoga* (late German steamer *Camilla Rickners*). She had fallen behind her convoy, from lack of speed owing to poor coal, and was attacked by a U-boat in the early morning of September 30, 1918. After the *Ticonderoga* had been badly cut up by gunfire with many killed and wounded, she was sunk by a torpedo. Of 240 on board only 25 were saved, most of them wounded, and only "after four days of incredible hardship." [1] These are but examples of the hazardous adventures of those who manned the American cargo carriers, and it will be evident that these men had accepted the call to a service that implied great sacrifice of life.

With these dangers common to all, not only must all the American elements on the seas be considered one

---

[1] "A History of the Transport Force," Admiral Gleaves.

great American naval force working for the one great object, but we must also realize how intimately bound together were the American naval and military forces in this vast joint operation. The preceding narrative has shown how closely interlocked were the Army and Navy in the administration and control of operations. This close association ramified through all ranks. Soldiers and sailors grew to know one another, as they were working together to forward the great joint offensive, "based on the American Continent" and striking at the very vitals of Germany. Perhaps there has never been so close an association of an Army and a Navy — certainly never on anything approaching the scale of this decisive joint operation of the World War.

It was typical of this close union of American forces that two regiments of the United States Marine Corps were included in the Second Division of the American Expeditionary Forces. These performed distinguished service in some of the hottest engagements of the war,[1] and added to the high reputation of the corps.

There was another contribution of the United States Navy on the firing line which should be mentioned, the long range mobile batteries of naval guns. The Germans had attained some extraordinary long ranges of guns, notably in the bombardment of Dunkirk and the long range firing upon Paris. But these were guns in fixed positions on solidly laid concrete foundations. Consequently, these German guns were at a disadvantage, and they never developed into any serious factor in the War. The United States Navy designed a mobile railway mount for the type of 50 caliber 14 inch gun which had been allotted to the battle cruisers of the 1916 pro-

---

[1] Especially at Belleau Wood in the first week of June, 1918.

gram. As has been stated the construction of these ships had been suspended, and a supply of these fine guns was available. Each gun was to be a complete self-sustaining unit with its own railway train, comprising the mobile mount for the gun, cars to carry ammunition, all berthing and maintenance accommodations for the naval personnel which was to man the guns, and its own locomotives.

All of this material was manufactured in the United States, and five complete units were shipped to France, and placed under the command of Rear Admiral C. P. Plunkett. All were operated entirely by a naval personnel.[1] "The first gun was mounted August 5, 1918." [2] "On August 13, 1918, a telegram was received from the Commanding General, American Expeditionary Forces, to dispatch two of the guns at the earliest possible date for an important special mission. This mission was to fire on the German long range gun which was bombarding Paris. Nos. 1 and 2 guns left St. Nazaire on August 17 and 18, respectively, but the long range gun was moved before the naval guns could get into position." [3] All five units were used in bombardments on the Western Front. "The extreme range of these guns is 42,500 yards or 24 sea miles, and it is particularly noteworthy that the shooting done was remarkably accurate for such a long range." [4] Unquestionably these guns marked a stride in the development of long range mobile guns.[5]

An ingenious contribution of the United States Navy to the ordnance of the World War was the Y-gun. As

---

[1] Officers, 30; men, 486.

[2] Office of Naval Intelligence U. S. N.

[3] Ibid.   [4] Ibid.

[5] Both the French and the British had used mobile mounts, but these were the most powerful of the mobile guns.

has been stated, depth bombs had proved very effective against the U-boats. These depth charges had been dropped over the supposed position of the U-boat by a destroyer or other anti-submarine craft. The Y-gun derived its name from its two tubes, at an angle like the letter. By use of this gun two depth charges could be thrown out, at angles, some distance from the attacking craft. The use of these guns thus widened the area of danger for the U-boat attacked by depth charges, and the Y-guns were successfully used on American destroyers and submarine chasers. As the destroyer was the most dangerous enemy of the U-boat, this device, which increased the danger, was of definite value.

Of course, these activities of the Americans must only be considered in due proportion, as being parts of the whole aggregate of the many forces which were working to defeat Germany. Their adventures, and their records of resourcefulness, were typical of the achievements of all those who were engaged in this great united effort against the enemy. On land, the military operation was coördinated under a united command. On the sea, all the united forces of Sea Power were being devoted to pushing home this military operation.

And it is to be hoped that the foregoing has given some idea of the stirring scenes on the sea, which were being enacted in order to make possible the final drive against the Germans on the Western Front.

CHAPTER XXXIII

THE COLLAPSE OF GERMANY

AS a result of the combined assaults of the Allied and American armies, which began in the last days of September, 1918, the whole military defense of the Germans on the Western Front crumbled and was swept back in defeat. From this time, it became evident that the battered German armies were being compelled to retreat by the reinforced enemies of Germany. The extent of the reverses of the German armies was plainly defined for all to see by the milestones of terrain abandoned by them. These included areas where the Germans were supposed to be established for good, and consequently a revelation of utter defeat spread back through Germany. With this evidence before the eyes of the Germans, it was no longer possible for the German Government to conceal the extent of the disaster from the German people.

As has been explained, the hold of the German Government upon the German people, at this stage, derived its strength solely from the promise of military victory. When victory changed to an ebbing tide of defeat, the German Government soon began to lose its only hold upon the German people. Discontent became open revolt, and social revolution spread throughout Germany. This inevitable factor in the situation was bringing the end much sooner than was realized, either by the German leaders or by the leaders of the Entente Allies.

Of this last, there was unmistakable proof given by each side. As has been explained, the French high command had not believed that the offensive could win the war before winter would force a cessation of operations. It is also a fact that on October 4, 1918, Marshal Foch had called the American Secretary of War to a conference as to the share of the United States in the campaign of 1919. "This was one day before the first German peace note and 38 days before the end of the war, but Marshal Foch was then calling upon America to make her great shipments of munitions and her supreme contribution of manpower for the campaign of the following year." [1]

As stated above, it had become evident, even to the most obsessed of the German militarists, that it was impossible to withstand the new strength of the Allied and American armies, and a note had been sent in the first week of October asking for an armistice. Yet it is also indisputable that the German leaders still continued to pin their naval strategy to the U-boat campaign — and were busy even then on a program which could only bring results in 1919! Admiral Scheer has stated: "None of us had the vaguest notion that the situation of the war on land was such that the cessation of all hostilities would soon be urged, and that in a few weeks the U-boat campaign would be abandoned." At a meeting on October 1, attended by representatives of both the Army and Navy, "everyone agreed that it would be possible to carry out the extended U-boat programme, so long as the requisite number of workmen, amounting to 69,000 altogether, was forthcoming; these men were chiefly wanted in the shipyards. For the year 1918 only 15,000

[1] "The War with Germany," Statistics Branch, General Staff, U. S. A.

to 20,000 men were asked for. The representative of the Supreme Army Command declared that the Army was ready to further the undertaking with all the means at its disposal. I did not feel myself called upon to make any statement on the changed situation on the Army front, but I pointed out that all those in charge of the conduct of the war were unanimous in their desire for us to adhere to this plan, whatever events might occur on the Army front, for the collapse in the South-East might well have serious consequences for us." [1]

In this same spirit the German leaders still clung to their U-boat strategy after the evacuation of the Bruges bases, and even through the negotiations which followed the first German request for an armistice. These negotiations were accompanied by further outbreaks of revolutionary discontent, and by the downfall of the German Government founded upon militarism. President Wilson, who was the spokesman for the Entente Allies, had answered the first German note on October 8 by taking the firm stand: "No armistice negotiations so long as the German armies remain upon enemy soil." This was followed by his note of October 14, containing the demand: "Cessation of U-boat hostilities against passenger ships and change of the form of Government in Germany." To this the German Government replied on October 21: "U-boats have received orders which exclude the torpedoing of passenger ships, and with regard to the form of Government: The responsibility of the Imperial Chancellor to the representatives of the people is being legally developed and made secure."

Throughout these exchanges, the German Naval leaders had been only concerned in regard to the U-boat

---

[1] Admiral Scheer, "Germany's High Sea Fleet."

campaign — whether it was to be suspended or not. It was not until after this German note of October 21, with its practical surrender of unrestricted U-boat warfare, that the German Naval leaders turned to a change of naval strategy. Admiral Scheer has stated this as follows: "This decision as to the limitation of the U-boat campaign was very important because the further operative measures of the Navy Command depended upon it; the High Sea Fleet must again now obtain complete freedom of action." Here there can be no mistaking the record of German naval strategy at this stage. There was no thought of a change to the offensive use of the German Battle Fleet until the Germans were on the point of surrender — and then it was too late from any practical point of view.

This very important element in the naval situation of the last months of the war has thus been established by the Germans themselves beyond any recall. The Germans have shown that they clung to their U-boat strategy to the last, and any danger of interruption of the vast movement of troops and supplies to France by means of the battle cruisers or battleships of the German High Sea Fleet can be now dismissed as out of the question. It is no wonder that there was much anxiety on this account, while the great movement was in operation, as it can be readily imagined that a raid of German capital ships against the convoys might have done in a few hours incalculable harm. But it is not even worth while to speculate as to this, because it was outside the trend of the German mind — and consequently something that was not to be undertaken by the Germans.

It is almost equally useless to discuss the projected change of German naval strategy, undertaken at the

last stage. Admiral Scheer, himself, has described this
as an attempt to call upon the German Battle Fleet "to
exert its full powers at the eleventh hour." He should
have called it the twelfth hour. For at that time the final
hour had struck for Germany. Sea Power had already
delivered the decisive blow which had ruined Germany
— beyond any repair!

This last minute effort of the German Navy was to be
"a plan directed against the English Channel." [1] Admiral Scheer has stated: "The Fleet was finally assembled for this enterprise in the outer roads of Wilhelmshaven on October 28." By this time there was no
chance for any naval move that would avert the onrushing course of events. The whole militaristic structure
of Germany had already fallen. After a stormy session
in Berlin, Ludendorff, who had been the incarnation of
the last phase of German militarism had been forced to
resign (October 26). This meant the final fall of the
régime that had staked its existence upon German victory in 1918.

The reaction against this discredited régime had
spread through the German nation. Disorders broke
out all over the country, and red flags began to appear in
the German cities. How complete had been the overturn
in Germany was best shown by the answer to the Wilson
note of October 23, in which was repeated the demand
for abolition of the Imperial Government: "The German
Government has duly noted the reply of the President
of the United States. The President is aware of the fundamental changes that have taken place and are still
taking place in the German Constitution. The peace
negotiations will be carried on by a Government of the

[1] "Germany's High Sea Fleet," Admiral Scheer.

people, in whose hands the decisive power actually and constitutionally lies. The military forces are also subject to it." Nothing more opposite to the former truculent Imperial Government could be imagined.

As the German naval policy had been to build up and organize a Battle Fleet especially adapted for service in the areas of the North Sea about the German naval bases, this in itself implied the condition that the High Sea Fleet was much in port. Consequently, its crews were in touch with the German people. Naturally, when the realization of defeat came home to the German people, the naval personnel shared this knowledge, and became infected by the prevailing spirit of revolt against the Imperial Government, which had promised German victory and then led Germany to defeat. As was the case with the German people, this disaffection of the naval crews was a direct result of the overwhelming German defeat.

In each instance, it is blurring the issue to call this a cause of German defeat. Particularly in the case of the German Navy, this excuse for defeat cannot stand the test of truth. The German leaders have shown unmistakably their own record of persisting in their naval strategy, of concentrating their efforts wholly on their U-boat campaign until all was lost. Why should it be any surprise that they met mutiny at the sudden change to a last minute plan for a desperate sortie of the Battle Fleet?

"Insubordination broke out when, on October 29, the Commander in Chief of the Fleet was making preparations to weigh anchor for the planned attack. . . . Since October 29, when the first signs of dissatisfaction had become manifest, the movement had continued to spread, so that he did not think it possible to undertake an offensive with the Fleet."[1] That was all there was to the matter. The artificial militaristic German Government had lost its hold, for the one reason that it had met final defeat on the battlefield — and all German resistance was at an end.

Under these circumstances any last minute naval plan for the German Battle Fleet is not worth consideration, for it could never have been carried out. But, even if there had been the possibility of a sortie that would do great damage, it is only commonsense to see that it would have been too late to change the great result, which was already an accomplished fact. Events had moved too rapidly, and there was nothing that could turn back the torrent which had overwhelmed Germany. The phrase "a Government of the people" in the German note meant that the Imperial Government had acknowledged its downfall.

The war party had attempted to delay the departure of a German delegation to treat for an armistice, but Hindenburg himself declared there was no other course, and that any delay in obtaining peace would only do harm. This ended the last hope of prolonging resistance and the final negotiations for an armistice were carried on by a new German Government, as the revolt had spread to Berlin, and on November 9, 1918, the German Emperor abdicated, taking refuge in Holland. The Armistice was signed, and became effective at 11 A.M., November 11, 1918 — and the hostilities of the World War were at an end.

With the Armistice, ended the naval history of the World War. The demobilization of the forces and many

---

[1] "Germany's High Sea Fleet," Admiral Scheer.

discussions of the aftermath of the war are outside the province of this book. But we must never forget that the final curtain had been rung down by the decisive victory, on a military field of battle, gained by a military force which had obtained its military superiority by means of Sea Power. This, in itself, is the whole sermon on the World War. Its military history and its naval history are closely interwoven. No naval history of the World War can be a true history, if it is only a log of naval events. More than has been the case in other wars, did the military events of the World War depend upon naval strategy. Its military strategy and its naval strategy must never be thought of as things apart. Only by looking at the doubly braided strands can the true fabric be seen, and throughout the whole pattern the record of Sea Power is written indelibly. Here is the lesson of this far written sermon, for us never to let slip from our minds — the proof of the might and compelling force of Sea Power.

APPENDICES

APPENDIX A

MEMORANDUM OF ADMIRAL VON HOLTZENDORFF, CHIEF OF THE GERMAN ADMIRALTY

THE CHIEF OF THE GERMAN ADMIRALTY

To B 35840 I

BERLIN, *Dec. 22, 1916.*

(Strictly secret)

I HAVE the honor to transmit to Your Excellency in the annex a note on the necessity of a speedy commencement of the unrestricted U-boat war.

Based on the detailed explanations of the annex, I may beg Your Excellency to consider the following ideas, and I hope to gain a complete agreement in our opinions that it is absolutely necessary to intensify to the utmost possibility our measures against England's sea traffic in order to take advantage of the favorable situation and to secure for us a speedy victory.

The war requires a decision before Autumn, 1917, if it is not to end in a general exhaustion of all parties, which would be fatal for us too. Among our adversaries, the economical conditions of Italy and France have been so seriously shaken that they can only be maintained by the energy and strength of England. If we succeed in overcoming England the war will be decided at once in our favor. But the resource of England is her tonnage, which supplies the islands of Great Britain with the necessities for life and the war industry and at the same time secures her solvency abroad.

The present state of the tonnage question is in short as follows:

The freight for a great number of important goods has risen enormously, in certain places to tenfold amount and more. We also know for certain from numerous other proofs that the lack of tonnage is universal.

The English tonnage at present still existing may be reckoned to be about 20 million gross register tons. At least 8.6 million tons of these are requisitioned for military purposes and one-half million tons is employed in coastal traffic; approximately one million tons is under repair or temporarily out of use; about two million tons are used in the interest of the Allies; so that, at the highest, eight million tons of British tonnage are at the disposal of England's supplies.

A perusal of the statistics of the sea traffic in English harbors would return even a lower figure. Thus in the months of July–September, 1916, there were only $6\frac{3}{4}$ million gross register tons of British tonnage available for England. Apart from this, the other tonnage bound for England may be calculated at 900,000 tons of enemy tonnage, none English, and quite three million tons of neutral tonnage. All in all, England is therefore supplied by only just $10\frac{3}{4}$ million gross register tons.

Besides the fact that, based on the achievements hitherto performed in the struggle against the tonnage, it seems to be very promising for us to proceed on the way once taken. The unusually bad result of this year's world harvest in cereals and cattle food has given us a unique opportunity, which cannot be neglected by any one with a sense of responsibility. Already after February the United States and Canada will probably be unable to provide England with corn, therefore England must procure her supply from over long distances, Argentina, and as Argentina can supply only a little on account of its bad harvest, she will be compelled to import from India and chiefly from Australia.

Under such favorable conditions an energetic powerful blow against the English tonnage promises to have an absolutely certain success. I do not hesitate to declare that, under the prevailing conditions, we may force England into peace within five months through the unrestricted U-boat war.

However, this can only be achieved by the unrestricted U-boat war, not by the U-boat cruising as practiced at present, and not even if all armed vessels were free to be sunk.

Based on the formerly mentioned monthly rate of destruction of 600,000 tons of tonnage by the unrestricted U-boat war, and on the expectation that by it at least two-fifths of the neutral traffic will be frightened to undertake the voyage to England, it may be reckoned that the English sea traffic after five months will be reduced by about 39 per cent of the traffic.

England would not be able to bear this, neither in view of the conditions after the war nor as regards the possibility of continuing the war. She is now already facing a scarcity of food, which forces her to try measures of economy which we, as a blockaded country, had to adopt during the war. The conditions for such an organization are totally different in England and comparatively much more unfavorable than with ourselves. There are lacking authorities as well as the sense of the people to submit to such force.

Also from another cause the general reduction of the bread ration for the whole population cannot now be enforced in England. This measure was possible in Germany at a time when temporarily other foodstuffs could make good the sudden reduction of the bread ration.

This opportunity has been allowed to pass and cannot possibly be brought back. But the maintenance of the war industry, and at the same time that of the food supply, cannot be kept up with about three-fifths of the sea traffic, without universal severe rationing of the consumption of cereals. The argument that England might have sufficient grain and raw materials in the country in order to overcome the danger until the next harvest is refuted exhaustively in the annex.

In addition, the unrestricted U-boat war with the subsequent cessation of supply by Denmark and Holland would mean for England at once the scarcity of fat, as one-third of the whole British import of butter originates from Denmark, and the entire supply of margarine comes from Holland.

Furthermore, it would mean the severity of the lack of raw materials and wood by endangering the supply of these products from Scandinavia and at the same time increasing the attenuation of the Spanish supply of metal.

Finally we shall have the long wished for opportunity to deal with the neutral supply of ammunition and thus relieve somewhat the army. (These ammunition supplies came chiefly from America.)

In the face of such facts the U-boat war, as practiced hitherto, would even after general permission to sink all armed vessels result in five months' time in the diminution of all the tonnage bound for England by only 5,400,000 tons — viz., about 18 per cent of the present monthly sea traffic, therefore less than one-half what could be obtained by the unrestricted U-boat war.

In addition, the lack of psychological effects of panic and terror is to be considered. I regard these effects, expected only by the unrestricted U-boat war, as an essential preconception of success. The experiences gained at the beginning of the U-boat war after the Spring of 1915, when the English still believed its bitter seriousness, and even in the short U-boat war of March and April, 1916, proved how weighty these effects are.

A further condition is that the declaration and commencement of the unrestricted U-boat war should be simultaneous, so that there is no time for negotiations, especially between England and the neutrals. Only on these conditions will the enemy and the neutrals be inspired with "holy" terror.

The declaration of the unrestricted U-boat war will place before the Government of the United States of North America afresh the question whether or not she will take the consequences of her hitherto adopted attitude toward the use of U-boats. I am quite of the opinion that the war against America is so serious an affair that all must be done to avert it. However, the dread of a break must not, in my opinion, go so far as to make us shrink in the decisive moment from the use of the weapon which will bring us victory.

At any rate it will be expedient to consider what influence the entrance of America into the war on the side of our adversaries would have upon the trend of the war.

As regards tonnage, this influence would be very negligible. It is not to be expected that more than a small fraction of the tonnage of the Central Powers lying in America and many other neutral harbors could then be enlisted for the traffic to England.

For the far greatest part of this shipping can be damaged in such a way that it cannot sail in the decisive time of the first months. Preparations to this effect have been made. There would also be no crews to be found for them. Just as little decisive effect can be ascribed to any considerable extent to American troops, which, in the first place, cannot be brought over, through lack of tonnage.

There remains only the question, what attitude would America take in the face of a conclusion of peace into which England would be coerced? It is not to be supposed that she would then decide to continue the war, as she would have no means at her disposal to take any decisive action against us, while her sea traffic will be liable to be damaged by us. On the contrary, it is to be expected that she will participate in the English conclusion of peace in order to obtain as quickly as possible again sound economic conditions.

I therefore draw the conclusion that an unrestricted U-boat war, which must be recommended as early as possible in order to bring about peace before the world's harvest of Summer, 1917, that is, before August 1st, should even take the consequences of a break with America, because we have no other alternative. A quickly launched, unrestricted U-boat war is therefore the only correct means to end the war victoriously, in spite of the risk of a break with America. It is also the only way to this goal.

In order to obtain in due time the necessary effect, the unrestricted U-boat war must commence at the latest on February 1st. I beg Your Excellency to inform me whether the military situation on the Continent, especially in the face of the still remaining neutrals, will permit of this date. I require a period of three weeks in order to make the necessary preparations.

V. HOLTZENDORFF.

APPENDIX B

AMERICAN NAVAL VESSELS ACTUALLY PRESENT IN EUROPEAN WATERS UPON THE CESSATION OF HOSTILITIES, GROUPED BY BASES

	TOTAL
Queenstown (2 tenders, 24 destroyers, 30 chasers, 3 tugs)	59
Berehaven (3 battleships, 1 tender, 7 submarines, 1 tug, 1 oiler)	13
Brest (1 gunboat, 16 yachts, 3 tenders, 38 destroyers, 9 tugs, 1 station ship, 4 steam barges, 4 barges, 9 minesweepers)	85
Cardiff (1 tender, 1 refrigerator hulk, 55 colliers)	57
Gibraltar (2 cruisers, 4 gunboats, 5 coast guard cutters, 9 yachts, 1 tender, 6 destroyers, 18 chasers)	45
Genoa (2 tugs)	2
Azores (2 yachts, 1 tender, 1 oiler, 2 minesweepers, 5 submarines, 1 tug)	12
Grand fleet (5 battleships)	5
Murmansk (1 cruiser, also 3 Russian destroyers)	1
Mine force (1 tender, 10 minelayers, 2 minesweepers)	13
Southampton (4 transports)	4
Plymouth (1 tender, 2 destroyers, 36 chasers)	39
Corfu (1 tender, 36 chasers)	37
Liverpool (1 oiler)	1
	—
Grand total naval vessels in European waters	373

OFFICE OF NAVAL INTELLIGENCE, U. S. N.

APPENDIX C

TABLE OF DATES OF THE WORLD WAR

JANUARY, 1917

9. Decision by the German Emperor, against the Imperial Chancellor, for unrestricted U-boat warfare, on the strength of assurance by German Admiralty Staff that this would bring a quick victory.
10. Entente Allies stated specific terms of peace at the request of President Wilson.
11. British predreadnought *Cornwallis* sunk by U-boat off Malta.
24. German surrender in East Africa.

FEBRUARY, 1917

1. Unrestricted U-boat warfare begun by Germany.
3. The United States broke off relations with Germany.
10. Replies from various capitals showed neutrals declined President Wilson's invitation to break with Germany.
16. British war loan of over £1,000,000,000 closed.
25. Liner *Laconia* torpedoed with American casualties.
26. President Wilson asked Congress for authority to arm American merchantmen.

MARCH, 1917

1. The Administration published the Zimmermann Note, which invited Japan and Mexico to make war upon the United States, with promises of the cession of American territory.
3. German Foreign Secretary Zimmermann admitted genuineness of the note as to Japan and Mexico.

5. Austria-Hungary announced agreement with the German U-boat policy.
7. President Wilson made decision to arm merchantmen, in spite of refusal of Congress.
11. Outbreak of revolution in Russia.
   British captured Bagdad.
13. British advanced in their spring offensive on Western Front.
15. Czar of Russia abdicated.
19. French dreadnought *Danton* torpedoed in Mediterranean.
20–31. German retirement to new Hindenburg Line carried out, and the British offensive checked.

April, 1917

2. President Wilson asked Congress to declare that a state of war existed with Germany.
4. Senate passed war resolution.
6. House of Representatives passed war resolution. President Wilson signed declaration of war.
   Seizure of German ships in American ports begun.
8. Austria-Hungary broke off relations with the United States.
9. British began Battle of Arras–Canadians took Vimy Ridge.
   Admiral Sims in Great Britain.
14. First American destroyers ordered overseas.
16. General Nivelle's great offensive begun (Second Battle of the Aisne).
21. Special Commission from the Entente Allies arrived in America.
24. President Wilson signed $7,000,000,000 War Bond Bill.
   First American destroyers sailed overseas.
28. British renewed the attempted Arras offensive.
   Failure of General Nivelle's offensive.

MAY, 1917

3. British attempted new attacks in Battle of Arras.
4. Changes in British Admiralty.
   Arrival of first American destroyers overseas.
6. Allied War Council in Paris — Abandonment of the Nivelle offensive.
11. American Commission to Russia named by the President with Elihu Root as chairman.
14. Sir Eric Geddes Controller in British Admiralty.
15. General Nivelle superseded by General Petain in command of French armies — General Foch chief of General Staff.
18. President Wilson signed Selective Service Act, calling on all men between 21 and 30, inclusive.
23. Italians on the offensive.
24. First Atlantic convoy to Great Britain started.
26. General Pershing made Commander-in-Chief of American Expeditionary Forces.
28. General Pershing sailed from New York.
29. Rear Admiral Gleaves designated Commander of Convoy Operations in the Atlantic.

JUNE, 1917

5. First registration under Selective Service of more than 9,500,000.
6. British captured Messines-Wytschaete salient — Greatest mining operation in history (1,000,000 lbs.).
8. General Pershing arrived in London.
12. King Constantine of Greece abdicated.
13. General Pershing in France.
14. Liberty Loan of $2,000,000,000 oversubscribed.
    First transports with United States troops sailed from New York.
26. First United States troops in France.

JULY 1, 1917

1. Russian troops, urged on by Kerensky, in temporary offensive.

   Initial successes in Galicia.
7. Great German daylight airplane raid on London.
10. American National Guard called into Federal service.
13. Administration issued first Selective Service call for 687,000 men.

   German Emperor made decision to dismiss Bethmann-Hollweg — Michaelis appointed Chancellor.
16. Russians in retreat in Galicia.
19. Resolution in German Reichstag for peace without annexations or indemnities, as a result of Austro-Hungarian representations following the entrance of the United States.
23-30. Collapse of the Kerensky Russian offensive.

   Stanislau and Tarnopol recaptured by Austro-Hungarians, and Russians in demoralized retreat.
31. Battle of Flanders began — British offensive in attempt to win Belgian Coast (Third Battle of Ypres).

AUGUST, 1917

3. Government requisitioned all steel vessels, of 2500 tons or over, building in the United States.
6. Changes in German cabinet — Kuehlmann succeeded Zimmermann as Foreign Secretary.
10. President Wilson signed Food Control bill.
14. The Pope made proposals for peace.
21. Great fire at Salonica.
29. President Wilson replied to peace note of the Pope, stating that no terms could be made with the existing German Government.
29-31. Battle of Flanders continued without any decisive British success.

   The Russian armies disintegrated, and the Germans moved against Riga.

September, 1917

2. Germans captured Riga.
6. Sir Eric Geddes First Lord of British Admiralty — Admiral Wemyss Deputy First Sea Lord.
8. Disclosure that Luxburg, German Minister at Buenos Aires, had transmitted lists of sailings to Berlin, with suggestion "to be sunk without trace."
12. Argentine Government handed passports to Luxburg.
20. Battle of Flanders renewed.

October, 1917

1. Second successful Liberty Loan of $3,000,000,000.
4–10. Attacks in Battle of Flanders.
13–15. Germans captured islands of Gulf of Riga.
15. United States Government requisitioned all American shipping suitable for foreign service (over 2,500,000 tons).
24. Battle of Caporetto begun — Surprise offensive of Austro-Hungarians against the Italians — Italian lines broken.
30. Udine, Cadorna's headquarters, taken — Italian armies in general retreat.

November, 1917

1. Hertling German Chancellor, succeeding Michaelis.
2– 7. Continued retreat of the Italians on Trentino and Tagliamento fronts.
7. Reds in control in Russia–Kerensky deposed.
9. Rapallo Conference created the Supreme Allied Council for Western Front.
16. Clemenceau formed French Ministry.
20. Battle of Cambrai. Successful British attack, using tanks.
    Soviet peace negotiations with Central Powers begun.
29. Allied Conference at Paris opened.
30. German counter attack at Cambrai — Serious British reverse.

December, 1917

1. United States war estimates for 1917–1918 were over $11,000,000,000.
4. Supreme Allied Naval Council formed.
6. Explosion of munition ship at Halifax — Great destruction of lives and property.
9. British captured Jerusalem.
17. Russo-German armistice.

January, 1918

8. President Wilson stated the "Fourteen Points" for basis of peace. Conference at Brest-Litovsk for peace between Russian Bolshevists and Central Powers.
28. President Wilson appealed to the American people for voluntary rationing.

February, 1918

9. Ukraine signed separate peace with Central Powers.
10. Soviet Russia out of the war — Order given to demobilize army.
15. President Wilson placed embargo on cargo space to insure movement of troops and supplies to Europe.
19. Germans resumed hostilities, to force peace on Russia.

March, 1918

3. Peace of Brest-Litovsk between Soviet Russia and Central Powers.
11. Turks recaptured Erzerum.
20. President Wilson authorized seizure of Dutch ships in American ports.
21. Great German offensive began with drive against British front (Battle of Picadie).
    300,000 American troops in France.

23. British defense broken west of St. Quentin — Enforced retreat on a wide front.

Paris bombarded by long range gun.

Arrangement for French troops to take over Noyon sector.

25–31. Continued British retreat. Péronne, Bapaume, Albert, Roye, Noyon, and Montdidier were occupied by the Germans. General Foch was given control to "coördinate" the Allied armies. All available American forces offered by General Pershing.

April, 1918

9. Second assault of great German offensive (Battle of the Lys).

10–13. British reverses — Armentières captured.

14. General Foch's appointment as Commander-in-Chief announced — Allied and American armies under a united command.

15. British reverses continued — Messines heights and Bailleul captured.

Count Czernin resigned.

23. British naval attacks at Zeebrugge and Ostend.

23–24. Last sortie of German High Sea Fleet into North Sea.

25. Germans captured Kemmel Hill from British.

118,642 American troops transported overseas in April.

May, 1918

7. Surrender of Rumania — Peace treaty signed at Bucharest.

10. Second British attempt to block Ostend.

19. Last German air raid on London.

25. First appearance of U-boats off American coast.

27. Third assault of great German offensive — French line broken and Chemin des Dames carried (Third Battle of the Aisne).

28. First American Division engaged at Cantigny.

  British shipping, assigned in the emergency, and rush of American troops overseas. 245,945 American troops were transported in May.

JUNE, 1918

2. U-boats off American coast.

4-7. Germans won Château-Thierry salient, and were again on the Marne.

9. Fourth attack of great German offensive, with gains in region of Noyon and Montdidier (Battle of Noyon).

15. Austro-Hungarians drove the Italians back from the Piave.

19-23. Disaster to the Austro-Hungarians across the Piave, and defeat of their offensive.

27. Second registration under the Selective Service.

  278,864 American troops transported overseas in June.

JULY, 1918

2. Berlin claimed 2,476 guns and 15,024 machine guns captured since March 21, 1917.

4. 95 ships launched in the United States.

15. Fifth Assault of the great German offensive on front from Château-Thierry to the edge of the Argonne (Second Battle of the Marne).

17. The Germans attempting the decisive drive on Paris were checked by the Franco-American defense.

18. French and American counter attack between the Aisne and the Marne, which drove into the German flank toward Soissons (Battle of Tardenois).

22-29. Château-Thierry salient won from the Germans.

  306,350 American troops transported overseas in July.

AUGUST, 1918

2. Soissons was retaken by the French.

2-5. Germans retreating in Aisne-Ourc region.

8. French and British launched an offensive between Amiens and Montdidier.
11. Admiral Scheer Chief of German Admiralty Staff. German naval leaders still adhered to U-boat strategy.
10–29. Foch's offensives continued — Germans were giving way on wide fronts — Montdidier, Péronne, Bapaume, Albert, and Noyon evacuated.
29–31. Germans were retreating in Flanders.

286,974 American troops transported overseas in August.

SEPTEMBER, 1918

1–10. Germans in retreat from Soissons to the North Sea.
12–13. St. Mihiel salient won by the Americans.
22. Nazareth captured by the British.
23–27. Salonica Army began operations against the Bulgarians, with Serbians and Greeks coöperating.
24. German Ministry of Marine reported that the extended program of U-boat construction was to be carried through — German Emperor visited U-boat School at Kiel.
26. Foch's final great offensive opened by the Americans in the Meuse-Argonne and by the French in the Champagne.
27. Bulgarians asked for an armistice, following defeats in Macedonia.
27–29. Foch's offensive developed in successive attacks — British advanced toward Cambrai — British and Belgian attacks in Flanders — Attacks toward St. Quentin.
30. Bulgaria surrendered on Allied terms, including railway occupation, thus breaking direct communication between Central Powers and Turkey.

257,557 American troops transported overseas in September.

OCTOBER, 1918

1. British captured Damascus.

   German Army and Navy conference still adhered to U-boat program.

1–5. Progress of Allied offensives — St. Quentin, Lens, and Armentières evacuated by the Germans.

   Americans advanced in Meuse-Argonne offensive.

5. German note proposing an armistice.

8. President Wilson refused to negotiate for an armistice while Germans remained in Allied territory.

9. Allies captured Cambrai.

11–18. German defense crumbled — Chemin des Dames, Lille, Laon, La Fère, and Channel ports evacuated by the Germans.

14. President Wilson demanded cessation of U-boat attacks against passenger ships and change of the form of government in Germany.

21. German note stated that U-boats had received orders which excluded torpedoing passenger ships, and representative government was being "legally developed."

24. Franco-American and British armies advanced in France and Flanders.

   Italian armies took the offensive against the Austro-Hungarians on the Piave.

26. Ludendorff forced to resign.

28. German Battle Fleet assembled at Wilhelmshaven for "eleventh hour" attempt.

   Austro-Hungarian armies broken and in retreat — Austria-Hungary asked for an armistice.

30. Turkey surrendered — Armistice signed on Allied terms.

30–31. Disorders in Germany — Mutiny broke out in German Battle Fleet.

   180,326 American troops transported overseas in October.

NOVEMBER, 1918

1–11. Uninterrupted advance of Allied and American armies — Sedan and Mézières railway communications of the Germans untenable.

4. Austria-Hungary signed armistice.

6. German delegates left for the front to obtain an armistice.

Germany in revolt.

8. German delegates taken behind the Allied lines to receive terms from Foch.

9. German Emperor abdicated and fled into Holland.

11. Armistice signed, and effective at 11 A.M.

Revolution in Germany, with German Republic in control.

INDEX

INDEX